THE PREVENTIVE TURN IN CRIMINAL LAW

OXFORD MONOGRAPHS ON CRIMINAL LAW AND JUSTICE

Series Editor: Andrew Ashworth CBE QC, Emeritus Vinerian Professor of English Law, All Souls College, Oxford

This series aims to cover all aspects of criminal law and procedure including criminal evidence. The scope of this series is wide, encompassing both practical and theoretical works.

OTHER TITLES IN THIS SERIES

The Preventive Turn
in Criminal Law

HENRIQUE CARVALHO

OXFORD
UNIVERSITY PRESS

OXFORD
UNIVERSITY PRESS

Great Clarendon Street, Oxford, OX2 6DP,
United Kingdom

Oxford University Press is a department of the University of Oxford.
It furthers the University's objective of excellence in research, scholarship,
and education by publishing worldwide. Oxford is a registered trade mark of
Oxford University Press in the UK and in certain other countries

© Henrique Carvalho 2017

The moral rights of the author have been asserted

First Edition published in 2017

Impression: 1

Crown copyright material is reproduced under Class Licence
Number C01P0000148 with the permission of OPSI
and the Queen's Printer for Scotland

Published in the United States of America by Oxford University Press
198 Madison Avenue, New York, NY 10016, United States of America

British Library Cataloguing in Publication Data
Data available

Library of Congress Control Number: 2017931337

ISBN 978-0-19-873785-8

Printed and bound by
CPI Group (UK) Ltd, Croydon, CR0 4YY

Para minha família, com amor.

General Editor's Preface

This volume throws down a challenge to traditional methods of thought about the criminal law. At a time when the principles of criminalization are much analysed and when features of the 'preventive turn' in criminal law are strongly opposed, this monograph examines the values that allegedly underlie the criminal law (notably, autonomy and liberty) and shows how in practice they tend to operate in tension with concerns about how that liberty is exercised by others, concerns which result in an emphasis on risk, security, and prevention. It is argued that the subject of criminal law is characterized both as an autonomous agent and as potentially dangerous, one of several dichotomies that represent a challenge to liberal criminal law theory. The flow of Henrique Carvalho's argument draws the reader towards the case for re-engineering established concepts such as subjectivity and responsibility so as better to reflect the human condition and its political locus. Indeed, a substantial part of the reasoning derives from detailed discussion of the political philosophies of Hobbes, Locke, Hegel, and Bentham, while keeping the reader in touch with examples that demonstrate the difficulties that traditional criminal law theory encounters in supplying justifications for swathes of our current criminal laws. This is a timely and important book, marking a significant step in debates about the philosophy of criminal law.

Andrew Ashworth

Foreword

In *The Preventive Turn in Criminal Law*, Henrique Carvalho takes a critical and dialectical view of how criminal law contributes to its own unravelling, acting, as he puts it, as a 'gateway to its own insecurity'.[1] In an analysis that is both historical and contemporary, he reviews the deep structures of the law to show how these undermine the normative claims of modern criminal justice and lead it in directions it thought itself against.

If the criminal law is a central element in the modern Western conception of a civil society,[2] it is in significant part because of the legitimative claim that its abstract legal subject delivers justice as it achieves security.[3] Delivering justice is itself a means of providing security, but security is a value in its own right.[4] Criminal law is thus founded on, and must negotiate the relationship between, these terms. The law's aim is at once to punish the responsible subject and to render society safe by controlling dangerous behaviour. The responsible subject is seen both as rational and responsible, and as capable of dangerous irresponsibility. Hence the law's plural approach to criminal liability in terms of character, risk and outcomes as well as capacity and opportunity.[5] Welcome to the contradictory problematic of the criminal law, in which criminal justice assumes different shapes and balances in different historical settings. The complex of criminal law and justice terms, its architectonic,[6] will shift its shape as the context changes. Yet, what emerges in one period or another is just as much a variant on the basic structure of the law.

Consider the difference between mid- and late nineteenth century arrangements, or the transition from a criminal justice system located in a post-war welfare state-based settlement to today's neo-liberal state of insecurity and fracturing community. Carvalho's argument, developed through telling and acute analysis of writing in the field,[7] is that these are all recognizable possibilities within the structural logic of criminal justice. The shift from one

---

[1] See p. 187 below.

[2] L. Farmer, *Making the Modern Criminal Law* (Oxford: Oxford University Press, 2016).

[3] A. Norrie, *Crime, Reason and History* third edition (Cambridge: Cambridge University Press, 2014).

[4] P. Ramsay, *The Insecurity State* (Oxford: Oxford University Press, 2007).

[5] N. Lacey, *In Search of the Responsible Subject* (Oxford: Oxford University Press, 2016).

[6] A. Norrie, *Justice and the Slaughter Bench* (Abingdon: Routledge GlassHouse, 2017).

[7] See for example the reading of arguments by Jeremy Horder in Chapter 1, or Antony Duff in Chapter 6, as well as the modern classical writers in Chapters 3–5.

to another is enabled by the nature of the criminal law, so that seemingly opposed positions betray underlying commonalities. Thus if we take debates today in which a 'neo-classical' liberal approach[8] seeks to mount a critique of the security state's preventive practices, we should recognize the ways in which that approach concedes the ground for new 'anti-liberal' forms at the same time as it seeks to criticize them. There is no pleasure in the sense of a 'form of life that is now grown old', for people get badly hurt in the process. Carvalho wants to think creatively about what would be needed for a more progressive direction in law and politics; but he also wishes to be clear about the state we are in.

In what sense is this a critical and dialectical account? Briefly, there are three different elements. The first is the claim that criminal law works with conflicts *intrinsic to it*, that it never resolves. The responsible subject is one who has nonetheless acted irresponsibly; it involves an agent who is in control, yet needs controlling. This is a dialectical tension in the legal subject which stems from its abstract universal form. Responsibility and control are asserted in abstraction from the real world settings in which the subject acts. Yet these are crucial to understanding how responsible agency is exercised and might be controlled. The resulting process of abstraction and reinsertion is at the core of the law's deep structure.

The second element might be expressed by seeing dialectics as 'the art of thinking the coincidence of distinctions and connections'.[9] This is particularly helpful in terms of thinking about the legal subject and the changing shape of the criminal law. In the setting of the post-war, welfare-based criminal law, the choosing subject with capacity and fair opportunity to do otherwise[10] played the important role of *distinguishing* the remit of the criminal law from a variety of alternative means of control, including ideas of psychological causation, criminogenic social relations, character and individual dangerousness, extended moral affect, and potentials for future risk. The distinction was solid enough in that social, political and economic context to keep at bay the connections to other aspects of crime. Now, in the time of the neo-liberal, authoritarian, security and prevention-based state, the ways in which criminal justice discourse distinguishes and connects its different aspects must be reassessed. In the current feverish political climate, it is tempting to wonder where it will go next.

Finally, this brings us to a third element, the idea of a phenomenology of criminal justice forms. By this, Carvalho means a method of 'examining a

---

[8] Lindsay Farmer's term (note 2).
[9] R. Bhaskar, *Dialectic: the Pulse of Freedom* (London: Verso, 1993).
[10] H.L.A. Hart, *Punishment and Responsibility* (Oxford: Clarendon, 1968).

concept through the relation between the ways it is idealized and imagined on the one hand, and ways it is actualized and concretely developed on the other'.[11] Literally, the term denotes a study of appearances, and in the way he uses it, I think Carvalho wants especially to express how forms have their own (phenomenal) reality in the world, but also reflect and express an underlying structure as it emerges, moves and shifts shape in different historical periods. He is influenced by Hegel, who appears in various parts of the book as both a source of support and an object of critique. The stress on history and the deep structure of law, which underlie the twists and turns in criminal justice, is central to Carvalho's phenomenology. Together with the lack of a higher level resolution of the problems of justice, these aspects at once point to the debt to Hegel and the critical distance from him (in the direction of modern critical dialectics).[12] Ultimately, Carvalho's commitment to a broad politics of recognition affirms the possibility of an ethics, and attendant social and legal forms, which could unify humanity. Yet his understanding of history, the structural violence of modernity, and the relation of both to modern criminal justice indicates the ethically broken nature of the present.

This fine book is the latest in a number of recent critical works on criminal law. Carvalho has been able to draw on these to pull together themes from this phase of critical legal thinking. It is fitting that this should be done by a member of the new generation of scholars, and it will be interesting to see how things develop further. With its solid base in modern classical political philosophy and its acute intelligence for critical engagement, this is a well-grounded and important work at an important time. In a world in which authors ask if the criminal law is a 'lost cause',[13] or predict its end,[14] Carvalho's argument needs to be heard.

Alan Norrie

---

[11] See p. 19 below.
[12] For example, Roy Bhaskar, Charles Taylor, and Alexandre Kojeve all feature in the text.
[13] A. Ashworth, 'Is the Criminal Law a Lost Cause?' (2000) 116 *Law Quarterly Review* 225.
[14] R. Erickson, *Crime in an Insecure World* (Cambridge: Polity Press, 2007), 213.

Preface

This is not a legal book. It is certainly a book about the law; but the aim of this work is precisely to conceive the law as a socio-political phenomenon, as something inextricably linked to the ways in which our societies are imagined, and in which we experience social relations, norms, and institutions. In this sense, *The Preventive Turn in Criminal Law* is the theoretical pursuit of a phenomenology of law. More specifically, what I mainly strive to do in this book is to make a case for the need for such phenomenological work, by examining how concepts and ideas within criminal law conceal problems and complexities which can only be adequately investigated if coupled with an awareness of their intrinsic social and political dimensions. The criminal law can only be understood through its relation with the function it performs in society and the place it has in the political constitution of that society. And in this relation, what I found is that the main aspect of the criminal law is also phenomenological, in that its main purpose is to shape and condition, to regulate and control, our socio-political experience.

The argument of the book, in a nutshell, is that what came to be known as the preventive turn is a direct consequence of a tension which lies at the core of liberal society and which is expressed through its law. This is a tension between the intrinsic value given to individual freedom and to the worth of human beings, and the perceived need to curtail and limit that very same freedom in the name of security. Ultimately, then, the idea of individual autonomy and liberty which is seen to be the cornerstone of liberal societies is intrinsically ambivalent, in that it espouses two contradictory normative positions in the way these societies are imagined: individual freedom is the primary purpose of society, and it is also the primary threat to it. I theorize and examine the ambivalence of individual freedom in three different levels throughout the book.

The first level is that of legal theory. Especially in Chapters 1, 2, and 7, I look at the ways in which the criminal law has been conceptualized and interpreted, in order to show how it both conceals and espouses a fundamental ambivalence with regards to its subject. I define this ambivalence as preserving a dialectic relation between two contradictory notions, that of responsibility and that of dangerousness. The subject of criminal law is thus composed of two dimensions, one in which s/he possesses a semblance of responsibility, and is approximated to the image of a law-abiding citizen of the community, and one in which s/he resonates with an idea of danger, of a potential threat to society. And since the criminal law is both about express-ing the responsibility and repressing the dangerousness of its subjects, its jus-tificatory framework is torn between the need to respect autonomy and the need to promote security, so that the same normative structure is found to be able to legitimate the so-called liberal model of criminal law as well as the excessive authoritarianism of the preventive turn.

The second level of analysis is that of political theory. Here, the ambiva-lence of the subject of criminal law is revealed as a political condition. It is essentially born out of a model of society which is meant to both promote socio-political equality and to preserve structural and ideological conditions of pervasive and often intense inequality. The main function of the criminal law in this political project is to maintain civil order, a specific form of social order which encapsulates the emancipatory promise and the structural vio-lence of modernity together, repressing this political conflict through notions such as civilization and civility. The criminal law maintains civil order by means of a dialectic relation between individual autonomy and political authority. In this relation, individuals whose autonomy is in league with the public interest expressed by the state find themselves deemed trustworthy and reassured by the security provided by criminalization and punishment, while those whose autonomy is found at odds with the interests of the com-munity are conceptualized as dangerous others, and forcibly restrained or removed from the community altogether. Chapters 3, 4, and 5 are dedicated to tracking the conceptual foundations of this dynamic relation in the history of political thought, through a deep engagement with the political theories of Thomas Hobbes, John Locke, and G.W.F. Hegel. In critically analysing these classic works, I elaborate a theoretical perspective which I deploy in order to expose reproductions of the same problematic logics, both in liberal thought in general—illustrated primarily through the work of Jeremy Bentham and his disciple, John Stuart Mill—and in liberal criminal law in particular.

The third level of investigation is based on social theory. Throughout the book, and particularly in Chapters 2, 6, and 7, I scrutinize the meaning and consequences of this political conflict expressed through criminal law to the ways in which we experience and imagine society. I therefore conceptualize the ambivalence of the subject of criminal law as having an intrinsic relation to social inequality, and the political and legal repression of this ambivalence as deeply connected to conditions of insecurity and anxiety in contemporary social life. In this level of analysis, the preventive turn represents the radical-ization of the political conflict at the heart of liberal society, and the exposure of the limits of the liberal project in criminal law. Especially in Chapter 6, I rely on a critical theory of recognition in order to examine the limits of this emancipatory ideal in liberal law, and look for a possible pathway to move beyond such limits.

In the end, this book constitutes an attempt to pursue, through criminal law theory, a serious engagement with the contemporary challenges and perplexities surrounding the human condition in liberal societies. I can only hope that, in talking about the law from the perspective of political and social thought, I may have contributed to making legal thought a more social, political, and critical affair.

Acknowledgements

This monograph started its life as a PhD thesis, which was generously funded by the School of Law at King's College London. I would like to thank Alan Norrie and Penny Green for the encouragement and guidance which they offered me throughout my doctoral research as supervisors. Alan, in particular, has been a mentor, a source of inspiration, and an invaluable colleague ever since, who taught me to trust my own instincts and to value my ideas. For that I am incommensurably grateful. I would also like to extend my gratitude to Andrew Ashworth for taking this book into the Oxford Monographs on Criminal Law and Justice series, and to Alex Flach, Natasha Flemming, Elinor Shields, Eve Ryle-Hodges, and everyone else at Oxford University Press, who helped make this book a reality.

I am greatly indebted to Nicola Lacey and Lindsay Farmer, who took the time to read and examine this work when it was a thesis, and who since then continued to offer their advice and support, without which this book would probably not have been written. Furthermore, I am obliged to Peter Ramsay and Craig Reeves for the valuable feedback on several chapters of this book, and for the lively discussions in our research group. Their eagerness to engage with this project, as well as their thoughtful and friendly advice, contributed to making this a much more enjoyable and enriching experience. I would also like to offer my sincerest gratitude to John Charney, Sabrina Gilani, Thomas Goldup, and Stefan Mandelbaum for our intellectual exchanges, which maintained the perfect harmony between rigorous criticism, honest encouragement, and warm friendship. In addition, I would like to thank Stephen Anderson, Isra Black, Melanie Collard, Lisa Forsberg, Lacrson Guilherme, Emmanuel Melissaris, Harry Nikolaidis, Can Öztaş, Federico Picinali, Thiago Sales, and Josué Santiago for their friendship and support.

Draft versions of parts of this monograph were discussed at a number of seminars and read by several people, and I am grateful for all the comments and criticisms I received, as well as for the patience offered to me. I am especially thankful for the feedback I received from colleagues at the Institute of Global Law and Policy workshops at Harvard Law School, at the Criminal Law and Criminal Justice Theory seminar at the LSE, at the Birkbeck Law School seminar, at the Readings and Reflections seminar at the University of Warwick, at the PUC Valparaiso criminal law and legal theory seminar, and at the Congreso sobre Derecho y Cambio Social at the Universidad Austral de Chile.

The text of this book borrows material from work that I previously published. Chapter 3 draws extensively on the article 'Liberty and Insecurity in the Criminal Law: Lessons from Thomas Hobbes' (2015) *Criminal Law and Philosophy* (Online First), 1–23, while Chapter 6 draws on the discussion first published in 'Terrorism, Punishment, and Recognition' (2012) 15(3) *New Criminal Law Review*, 345–74. I am obliged to the editors and anonymous reviewers involved in the publication of these pieces, as well as to those who anonymously reviewed the proposal for this book.

Finally, I would like to thank Alexandre da Costa Carvalho, Erika Carmen Randau, Marcela Randau Carvalho-Burgess, and Cleide Venâncio Lopes for their love, unending support, and unflinching reassurance, and Anastasia Chamberlen for sharing with me the best years of my life, opening my world to a deeper truth about emotions and teaching me the real meaning of happiness. Reflecting at the end of this journey, I have only a lot to be thankful for, and nothing to regret.

Contents

1

Setting the Problem

Liberal Criminal Law and the Preventive Turn

We are witnessing the end of criminal law.[1]

The world in the beginning of the twenty-first century appears to be full of risks and violent threats. The notion of terrorism has changed from a localized and exceptional danger to an almost quotidian event, something against which we must be constantly guarding ourselves. In addition, at the present moment we are still dealing with the consequences of an ongoing economic crisis, which is itself intermeshed with one of the most significant geopolitical crises in recent times, in which a multitude of wars, socio-economic challenges, and political uprisings clash with the largest displacement of populations since the Second World War. The other side of this condition of living in an environment of constant flux and uncertainty is the experience of accentuated feelings of insecurity and anxiety.[2] This state of insecurity has had significant implications for the framework of criminal law. On the one hand, this general atmosphere often translates into a heightened sense of vulnerability with regards to crime.[3] On the other, and because of this, the criminal law is seen as one of the main instruments which the state possesses in order to address these many concerns. As a result, for the last couple of decades, a predominant focus on security and public protection has been identified in the legal and political spheres of many liberal democratic countries, and especially in the United Kingdom and the United States.[4] In England and

---

[1] R. Ericson, *Crime in an Insecure World* (Cambridge: Polity Press, 2007), 213.

[2] See A. Giddens, *Modernity and Self-Identity: Self and Society in the Late Modern Age* (Cambridge: Polity Press, 1991); U. Beck, *Risk Society: Towards a New Modernity* (London: Sage, 1992); N. Rose, *Powers of Freedom: Reframing Political Thought* (Cambridge: Cambridge University Press, 1999).

[3] See Ericson, *Crime in an Insecure World*; P. Ramsay, *The Insecurity State: Vulnerable Autonomy and the Right to Security in the Criminal Law* (Oxford: Oxford University Press, 2012).

[4] See D. Husak, *Overcriminalization* (Oxford: Oxford University Press, 2008); B. McSherry, A. Norrie, S. Bronitt (eds), *Regulating Deviance* (Portland: Hart, 2009); R.A. Duff, L. Farmer, S.E. Marshall, M. Renzo, V. Tadros (eds), *The Boundaries of the Criminal Law* (Oxford: Oxford University

The Preventive Turn in Criminal Law. First Edition. Henrique Carvalho. © Henrique Carvalho 2017. Published 2017 by Oxford University Press.

Wales, the outcome of these efforts has been an unprecedented expansion of the boundaries of the criminal law and its framework of criminal liability, manifested through the proliferation of criminal offences and of far-reaching powers of surveillance and crime control. From terrorism and serious violence, through cybercrime and pornography, to anti-social behaviour and immigration, the liberal state has left virtually no stone unturned in its efforts to secure what is increasingly being seen as an anxious public and a fragile social order.

These developments are particularly problematic to the liberal project in criminal law and justice. The criminal law, as far as legal theory is concerned, is at a turning point. Recent changes to the framework of criminal justice and criminalization have brought forward significant challenges, not necessarily to the importance of criminal law per se—in many respects, it is increasingly seen, and used,[5] as an essential element of law and governance in contemporary society—but mainly with respect to its legitimacy as a modern, liberal institution.[6] Underlying this preoccupation is the idea that what is most distinctive about modern criminal law and punishment, what sets them apart from pre-modern and pre-liberal exercises of penal power, is their concern with individual justice; that is, with providing for a system of criminal justice that treats individuals with respect.[7] The cornerstone for this conception is the image of individuals as responsible subjects who are not only able but also entitled to live their lives according to their own plans and reasons, and thus that it is necessary for the law to respect them as such. This 'alignment of law and morality around the model of individual choice and responsibility'[8] is a core tenet of liberal criminal law thinking, and seen as the corollary for the justification of the state's power to punish.

What is particularly challenging about the present moment in liberal societies, and particularly in England and Wales, is that the contemporary concern

---

Press, 2010), *The Structures of the Criminal Law* (Oxford: Oxford University Press, 2011), *The Constitution of the Criminal Law* (Oxford: Oxford University Press, 2013), and *Criminalization: The Political Morality of the Criminal Law* (Oxford: Oxford University Press, 2014); A. Ashworth, L. Zedner, P. Tomlin (eds), *Prevention and the Limits of the Criminal Law* (Oxford: Oxford University Press, 2013); A. Ashworth, L. Zedner, *Preventive Justice* (Oxford: Oxford University Press, 2014).

[5] A. Ashworth, L. Zedner, 'Defending the Criminal Law: Reflections on the Changing Character of Crime, Procedure, and Sanctions' (2008) 2 *Criminal Law and Philosophy*, 21–51, 38.

[6] See A. Ashworth, 'Is the Criminal Law a Lost Cause?' (2000) 116 *Law Quarterly Review*, 225–56; Husak, *Overcriminalization*; L. Farmer, *Making the Modern Criminal Law: Criminalization and Civil Order* (Oxford: Oxford University Press, 2016).

[7] See D. Garland, *Punishment and Welfare: A History of Penal Strategies* (Aldershot: Gower, 1985).

[8] A. Norrie, *Punishment, Responsibility, and Justice* (Oxford: Oxford University Press, 2000), 2. See also L. Farmer, *Criminal Law, Tradition and Legal Order* (Cambridge: Cambridge University Press, 1997), chapter 1.

with security appears to have given so much importance to the need for criminal law to effectively prevent crime, that this preventive function has been prioritized over the promotion and protection of individual justice upheld by liberal legal theory.[9] From this perspective, then, this preventive turn[10] stands against the main justificatory framework available to criminal law and justice in these societies, bringing either the legitimacy of contemporary criminal law or, perhaps, the validity of the justificatory framework itself, into question. But although there is little doubt that the contemporary condition of criminal law and justice is problematic, there is a risk that the novelty and specificity of the preventive turn might be overstressed. In other words, paying too much attention to what is deemed to be new or different about the contemporary emphasis on prevention might distract us from the extent to which the issues currently faced by liberal criminal legal systems might also be related to enduring aspects of these systems themselves. Perhaps the problem of prevention is not only a challenge to liberal law, but mainly a problem that liberal law has brought upon itself.

This book presents an effort to bridge this gap between a theoretical understanding of the preventive turn and a critical analysis of the liberal project in criminal law. For this purpose, I examine the issues around the rise of preventive criminal offences through an engagement with the conceptual foundations of liberal criminal law, tracing the theoretical development of specific ideas which lie at the core of the liberal legal project, while contrasting this development with the legal and socio-political context in which they were embedded and actualized. The main postulate I advance in this analysis is that the idea of individual autonomy and liberty—together with its main manifestation in the framework of criminal law, the notion of criminal responsibility—can be used as the main lens through which to understand not only the problems surrounding the liberal project in criminal law, but also the challenges presented to this project by the preventive turn. The main question I explore considers how to conceptualize individual liberty and autonomy, as well as the liberal idea of society grounded upon these concepts, and how to trace the conceptual genealogy of these notions. In order to address this

---

[9] See A. Ashworth, L. Zedner, 'Just Prevention: Preventive Rationales and the Limits of the Criminal Law' in R.A. Duff, S.P. Green (eds), *Philosophical Foundations of Criminal Law* (Oxford: Oxford University Press, 2011), 279–303.

[10] See G. Hughes, *Understanding Crime Prevention: Social Control, Risk and Late Modernity* (Maidenhead: Open University Press, 2000); A. Crawford (ed), *Crime Prevention Policies in Comparative Perspective* (Cullompton: Willan Publishing, 2009); L. Zedner, 'Fixing the Future? The Pre-emptive Turn in Criminal Justice' in B. McSherry, A. Norrie, S. Bronitt (eds), *Regulating Deviance* (Portland: Hart Publishing, 2009), 35–58; N. Lacey, *In Search of Criminal Responsibility: Ideas, Interests and Institutions* (Oxford: Oxford University Press, 2016).

question, I pursue throughout the book a methodological perspective which intentionally distances itself from legal doctrine, seeking the aforementioned genealogy of ideas which ground the framework of criminal law outside of its institutional confines, focusing on works of social and political theory. In doing so, however, I hope to uncover aspects of the law that a purely or a mainly legal perspective would otherwise tend to neglect.

This initial chapter introduces the context of the preventive turn, looking at how it is represented in terms of doctrine and criminalization, and paying particular attention to how recent changes and transformations to the framework of criminal law and liability have been interpreted by criminal law scholars. I focus specifically on the comprehensive work on prevention undertaken by Andrew Ashworth and Lucia Zedner, which I take to be a paradigmatic example of liberal criminal law scholarship. Then, by engaging with this literature, I identify a certain tension around dichotomies found in criminal law theory, such as that between punishment and prevention, which suggests a paradoxical relationship between liberal law and arguably the central notion in its normative framework, that of individual autonomy and liberty. This tension leads to an ambivalent conception of the subject which lies at the core of criminal liability, which is not fully recognized by the liberal model but which is exposed by the preventive turn. The last part of the chapter lays out the methodological framework for the rest of the book, its main assumptions, and its overall structure.

THE PROBLEM
OF PREVENTIVE CRIMINAL LAW

One of the main concerns of legal theorists examining the current moment in criminal law relates to understanding and defining the appropriate contours of the framework of criminal law.[11] The definition that arguably best encapsulates what appears to be the predominant interpretation of these boundaries is what Andrew Ashworth and Lucia Zedner have called the 'liberal model of criminal law'.[12] This model is grounded on 'a liberal conception of criminal justice that emphasises both the purpose of the criminal law in providing for censure and punishment and the need to respect the autonomy and dignity

[11] See for instance Duff et al, *The Boundaries of the Criminal Law*.
[12] Many references to what constitutes the liberal model of criminal law rely on the scholarship of Andrew Ashworth, either on his own work or on his rich collaboration with Lucia Zedner. This is in great part because Ashworth's work has managed to eloquently express a theoretical image of the criminal law that has become paradigmatic among contemporary criminal law scholars. For details on this perspective, see Farmer, *Making the Modern Criminal Law*.

of individuals in the criminal process'.[13] This normative demand of respect for the individual stems from the position of individual autonomy as 'one of the fundamental concepts in the justification of criminal laws', which maintains 'that each individual should be treated as responsible for his or her own behaviour'.[14] The subjective principle of responsibility which arises from this postulate legitimates the penal power of the state, by according 'individuals the status of autonomous moral agents who ... can fairly be held accountable and punishable' for their wrongdoing.[15] At the same time, however, it also limits this power, by holding the retributive understanding that 'only those who have in some sense willed their own violation of the law should be punished, and ... the punishment should be proportionate to the wrong'.[16] Thus although it recognizes that criminal law has a role in the maintenance of social order, the liberal model gives primacy to individual justice; so that the former aim should not be achieved at the latter's expense.

In addition, according to the liberal model, the primary focus of the criminal law should be on punishment, so that criminalization should concentrate on 'the censure ... for past wrongdoing'.[17] One of the main reasons for limiting criminalization generally to instances of harm done is to allow space for individuals to exercise their agency, giving them the opportunity to act responsibly and only punishing them if they fail to do so. This perspective is thus also intrinsically linked to notions of responsible subjectivity, as to anticipate the harmful consequences of an individual's conduct through criminalization 'is to fail to treat the law's subjects as rational moral agents who are able to adjust their conduct to the law'.[18] This respect for autonomy is crystallized above all in the presumption of innocence, which is seen within liberal theory as 'the bedrock of the individual subject's, and more especially citizen's, independence of the state'.[19] This series of concerns, expressive of an emphasis on the

[13] Ashworth, Zedner, 'Defending the Criminal Law', 22.
[14] A. Ashworth, J. Horder, *Principles of Criminal Law* (Oxford: Oxford University Press, 2013), 23.
[15] I. Dennis, 'The Critical Condition of Criminal Law' (1997) 50 *Current Legal Problems*, 213–49, 237.
[16] P. Ramsay, 'The Responsible Subject as Citizen: Criminal Law, Democracy and the Welfare State' (2006) 69(1) *Modern Law Review*, 29–58, 31.
[17] Ashworth, Zedner, *Preventive Justice*, 96.
[18] P. Ramsay, 'Preparation Offences, Security Interests, Political Freedom' in R.A. Duff, L. Farmer, S.E. Marshall, M. Renzo, V. Tadros (eds), *The Structures of the Criminal Law* (New York: Oxford University Press, 2011), 203–28, 217. For a criminological critique of preventive criminalization, see M. Hildebrand, 'Proactive Forensic Profiling: Proactive Criminalization?' in R.A. Duff, L. Farmer, S.E. Marshall, M. Renzo, V. Tadros (eds), *The Boundaries of the Criminal Law* (New York: Oxford University Press, 2010), 113–37.
[19] Ramsay, ibid.

moral significance of the individual, aligns the liberal model of criminal law with a perspective which 'purport[s] to take a restrictive, "minimalist" view of the justifiability of criminalisation'.[20] The bedrock of this view on criminalization is the idea that the 'paradigm form of substantive criminal offences' should be that of the ' "harm plus culpability" model',[21] which requires proof of both harm done and culpable wrongdoing, represented in offences such as murder and criminal damage. Although this model of offences also possesses the aim of preventing future harm, especially through the idea of deterrence through the communication of censure and the threat of punishment, its primary rationale is said to be punitive, not preventive.

In contrast with the liberal model, the justificatory framework embedded in the preventive turn, with its focus on the management of risk and insecurity,[22] seems to be grounded on a critique of, and disenchantment with, the minimalism and restraint championed by the liberal model, aligned with the sentiment that the aspirations upheld by this model are unrealistic and unrealizable and that, by placing too much emphasis on the redressing of harms, it hinders their actual prevention.[23] Reflecting this concern, many of the currently proliferating criminal offences have a predominantly preventive rationale. While some preventive criminal offences can be somewhat reconciled with a liberal conception of criminal law,[24] many of the offences enacted in the last couple of decades tend to criminalize conduct or circumstances that are so distant from the targeted harm that their connection to it can only be characterized as remote, established more on the basis of the risk or danger assumed to be inherent to these activities than on an actual link with the proscribed harm.[25] These offences have been termed 'pre-inchoate',[26] since they expand the scope of liability well beyond the traditional spectrum of inchoacy deemed acceptable by the liberal model.

Such offences include, among others, preparatory or mere preparation offences, possession offences, and offences linked to the breach of a preventive

---

[20] J. Horder, 'Harmless Wrongdoing and the Anticipatory Perspective on Criminalisation' in R. Sullivan, I. Dennis (eds), *Seeking Security* (Oxford: Hart, 2012), 79–102, 79.

[21] Ashworth, Zedner, *Preventive Justice*, 96.

[22] See Ericson, *Crime in an Insecure World*.   [23] See Horder, 'Harmless Wrongdoing'.

[24] For instance, it is commonly accepted that the traditional inchoate offences of attempt, conspiracy, and incitement (now replaced by the offences of assisting or encouraging crime in the Serious Crime Act 2007, ss. 44–50), as well as some crimes of 'endangerment' (see R.A. Duff, 'Criminalising Endangerment' in R.A. Duff, S.P. Green (eds), *Defining Crimes: Essays on the Special Part of the Criminal Law* (Oxford: Oxford University Press, 2005), 43–64), have their place in a liberal polity.

[25] See P. Ramsay, 'Democratic Limits to Preventive Criminal Law' in A. Ashworth, L. Zedner, P. Tomlin (eds), *Prevention and the Limits of the Criminal Law* (Oxford: Oxford University Press, 2013), 214–34.

[26] See Ramsay, ibid.

order, such as a Terrorism Prevention and Investigation Measure (TPIM),[27] an injunction,[28] or a Criminal Behaviour Order.[29] Preparatory offences are those deemed to criminalize conduct before it would amount to a traditional inchoate offence; for instance, before the act could be considered a 'more than merely preparatory' act, thus still constituting an act of 'mere preparation'.[30] Examples include 'engag[ing] in any conduct in preparation for giving effect' to an intention to commit or assist acts of terrorism,[31] and facilitating child sex offences.[32] Possession offences, by their turn, essentially 'criminalize a state of affairs',[33] not requiring any specific act, and often no specific intent, on the part of the defendant, such as possession of an article for use in connection with any fraud[34] and, most notoriously, the offences covering possession of information likely to be useful to a person preparing an act of terrorism, and possession of any article giving rise to a reasonable suspicion that the possession is for a purpose connected with terrorism.[35] The last two offences, in particular, criminalize states of affairs so broadly conceived that they are potentially capable of encompassing entirely common and ordinary activities, distinguished only by the suspicion that they might lead to an act of terrorism.[36]

The rise of pre-inchoate offences, worrisome as it is in itself, is but one manifestation of the preventive turn and the challenges it presents to the centrality of the liberal model. The preventive endeavour has affected virtually all facets of the criminal justice system, including that which is the bastion of the procedural guarantees which lie at the heart of criminal law: the criminal trial. In their paper 'Defending the Criminal Law', Ashworth and Zedner note that there are strong indications that the criminal trial is losing its primacy in the criminal justice system, on the grounds that it is not cost-effective, not preventive, not necessary, not appropriate, and not effective in most circumstances.[37] They identify at least seven trends supporting their claim. These include: a greater use of diversion from prosecution, such as the conditional caution introduced for adults by the Criminal Justice Act

---

[27] Terrorism Prevention and Investigation Measures Act 2011.
[28] Anti-social Behaviour, Crime and Policing Act 2014, Part 1.
[29] Ibid, Part 2. The Injunction and the Criminal Behaviour Order have replaced the old Anti-social Behaviour Order (ASBO), originally enacted in the Crime and Disorder Act 1998, s. 1. For a comprehensive discussion of the links between the ASBO and the preventive turn, see Ramsay, *The Insecurity State*.
[30] Criminal Attempts Act 1981, s. 1(1).   [31] Terrorism Act 2006, s. 5.
[32] Sexual Offences Act 2003, s. 14.   [33] Ashworth, Zedner, *Preventive Justice*, 99.
[34] Fraud Act 2006, s. 6(1).   [35] Terrorism Act 2000, ss. 57–8.
[36] See J. Hodgson, V. Tadros, 'How to Make a Terrorist Out of Nothing' (2009) 72(6) *Modern Law Review*, 984–98. See also Chapter 6 of this book.
[37] Ashworth, Zedner, 'Defending the Criminal Law', 23.

2003 and the youth conditional caution inaugurated by the Criminal Justice and Immigration Act 2008; a greater use of fixed penalties—such as fines for various traffic offences and the more general Penalty Notice for Disorder—issuable by a police officer on the spot, contestable only in court, and where failure to comply can incur imprisonment; a greater use of summary trials; a greater use of hybrid civil–criminal processes, where a civil order restraining the subject's behaviour is imposed and where breaking the order constitutes a criminal offence; a greater use of strict liability elements, not only in regulatory offences but also in serious offences, such as rape;[38] a greater use of incentives for defendants to avoid trial by pleading guilty, thus receiving a discount on custodial sentences which is greater the sooner the plea is made, thus giving rise to an effective culture of plea bargaining;[39] and a greater use of the preventive orders mentioned above, which can be imposed in the name of public protection independently of a criminal conviction.[40]

It is thus not surprising that liberal theorists view these developments with great preoccupation, as in their view these changes represent not only a shift in paradigm but a tendency towards an 'unprincipled and chaotic construction of the criminal law' which 'prompts the question whether the criminal law is a lost cause'.[41] Among undesirable consequences which may be brought about by this 'chaotic' construction, diversion from prosecution and fixed penalties may produce a 'net-widening'[42] effect, extending the reach of criminal justice to offenders who would otherwise not have been prosecuted. Greater reliance on summary trials is likely to weaken the procedural safeguards of defendants; a similar effect can be expected from the use of hybrid orders, since they also avoid the need to rely on trial convictions. The increased use of strict liability and of incentives to plead guilty may indicate a growing distrust towards the criminal law's traditional modes of assigning blame, deeming them exaggerated, burdensome, or unnecessary. Within these examples it is possible to identify that the criticisms directed at the criminal trial involve a rather robust, if tacit, challenge to the conception of responsible subjectivity embedded within the liberal model: the image of the subject of criminal law as an autonomous and responsible individual who can generally be trusted to follow the law,[43] and who should thus be presumed innocent until appropriately proven guilty.

---

[38] For instance, rape of a child under 13 (Sexual Offences Act 2003, s. 5). See *R v G* [2008] UKHL 37.

[39] See Lacey, *In Search of Criminal Responsibility*, 148.

[40] Ashworth, Zedner, 'Defending the Criminal Law', 24–36.

[41] Ashworth, 'Is the Criminal Law a Lost Cause?', 225.

[42] Ashworth, Zedner, 'Defending the Criminal Law', 26. See also S. Cohen, *Visions of Social Control* (Cambridge: Polity Press, 1985).

[43] The link between individual autonomy, responsibility, and trust is discussed in detail in Chapter 2.

It should be noted, as mentioned above, that the dilution of the safeguards of the liberal model does not reflect an overall rejection of the criminal law as a system of punishment and social control, quite the contrary. Besides the enactment of new criminal offences, which has been prolific in every legislature at least since the second half of the 1990s, these challenges to the centrality of the trial have been coupled with a steady growth of criminal convictions, as well as an increase in the severity of sentences[44] and the proliferation of other penal measures such as preventive detention and Imprisonment for Public Protection, now replaced with Extended Determinate Sentences[45] and Mandatory Life Sentences for dangerous offenders.[46] Indeed, the preventive turn appears to have been developed alongside a 'punitive turn'[47] in criminal justice, linked to a politicization and a 're-emotionalisation of the law'.[48] This rise in punitiveness is reflected in a culture of increased reliance on institutions of control and an expansion of the penal state,[49] and seems to be inseparable from the observed increased focus on security, surveillance, and prevention. Preventive criminal offences in themselves seem to rely on 'an increasing emphasis on the retributive understanding of behaviour',[50] at the same time as they compromise the logic of individual justice usually linked with the traditional idea of retribution in criminal law.

In this sense, it must be kept in mind that the idea of a preventive turn in criminal law emphasizes one aspect of what is in reality a complex and multifaceted moment in the legal and socio-political environment of certain liberal democratic societies. For instance, Ashworth and Zedner highlight that the over-development of the preventive function of the state is only one of the forces behind the contemporary 'volatility in the English criminal law'.[51] Besides the preventive function, which they identify as being guided by a precautionary logic grounded on risk and harm prevention,[52] they also mention

[44] Ashworth, Zedner, 'Defending the Criminal Law', 38.

[45] Legal Aid, Sentencing and Punishment of Offenders Act 2012, s. 124.

[46] Ibid, s. 122.

[47] S. Hallsworth, 'Rethinking the Punitive Turn: Economies of Excess and the Criminology of the Other' (2000) 2(2) *Punishment & Society*, 145–60; J. Pratt, D. Brown, M. Brown, S. Hallsworth (eds), *The New Punitiveness* (Abingdon: Routledge, 2011).

[48] S. Karstedt, 'Handle with Care: Emotions, Crime and Justice' in S. Karstedt, I. Loader, H. Strang (eds), *Emotions, Crime and Justice* (Oxford: Hart Publishing, 2011), 1–22. See also H. Carvalho, A. Chamberlen, 'Punishment, Justice, and Emotions' (2016) *Oxford Handbooks Online* (criminology and criminal justice; punishment theory).

[49] D. Garland, *The Culture of Control* (Oxford: Oxford University Press, 2002); L. Wacquant, *Punishing the Poor: The Neoliberal Government of Social Insecurity* (London: Duke University Press, 2009).

[50] A. Norrie, 'Citizenship, Authoritarianism and the Changing Shape of the Criminal Law' in B. McSherry, A. Norrie, S. Bronitt (eds), *Regulating Deviance* (Portland: Hart, 2009), 13–34, 15.

[51] Ashworth, Zedner, 'Defending the Criminal Law', 38.

[52] See Ericson, *Crime in an Insecure World*.

an expansion of the regulatory function, which supports a normalization of the criminal law by turning many of its elements into a matter of economic analysis, privileging the manipulation of costs and disincentives over the censure of punishment.[53] Finally, they also stress the manifestation of an authoritarian vein in the contemporary state, linked to the punitive turn mentioned above, geared by penal populism and a demand for public protection. A focus on prevention should be careful not to neglect this complexity; rather, it is necessary to understand the preventive turn as the result of the intermeshing of these different tendencies, and as conditioned by the socio-political environment in which it occurs. In order to preserve this nuanced understanding, the distinctiveness of prevention should not be overstressed; the preventive turn is as much a consequence of the development of a regulatory impulse within criminal law, as well as of a rising authoritarianism in criminal justice and penal policy. In fact, what can be said to be most problematic about the contemporary emphasis on prevention is that this notion manages to encapsulate all these different tendencies in a way that appears to address an urgent and legitimate need. In other words, although different measures may be impelled by distinct logics, they may all seek justification on the grounds that they provide security by preventing crime and harm.

What thus seems to be most problematic about preventive criminal law is that it upholds a justificatory framework which seemingly defies the logic and the principles of the liberal model. And since this model is what is taken to preserve the legitimacy of the criminal law as a modern, civilized institution, the preventive turn does present criminal law theory with a significant challenge. Furthermore, it can be said that, in dealing with this challenge, criminal law theory finds itself at a sort of impasse. For, at the same time as there is a broad consensus that the preventive turn compromises the liberal model, and with it the foundations for a legitimate, democratic criminal law,[54] there is also strong support for the proposition that the liberal model is the solution to its own problems. For instance, the solution proposed for the erosion of procedural guarantees and of the appropriate balance between individual liberty and security brought forth by preventive measures is often to advocate for these guarantees, and the appropriate balance which they provide, to be reinstated.[55] From this perspective, the preventive turn is often interpreted as a series of interventions that have invaded the framework of criminal law, so

---

[53] Ashworth, Zedner, 'Defending the Criminal Law', 39.

[54] See Ramsay, *The Insecurity State*.

[55] See L. Zedner, 'Security, the State, and the Citizen: the Changing Architecture of Crime Control' (2010) 13(2) *New Criminal Law Review*, 379–403; D. Husak, 'The Criminal Law as a Last Resort' (2004) 24(2) *Oxford Journal of Legal Studies*, 207–35.

to speak, so that the liberal model has mainly to be rescued from it, to be reaffirmed. The problem with this view is that it poses the liberal model and the preventive turn as isolated phenomena, thus neglecting a substantive engagement with the possibility that these two forms of framing criminal law and criminalization might be interrelated, and that what is currently being experienced in the preventive turn might have its roots within liberal law itself.

THE PARADOXES OF LIBERAL LAW

The traditional way of thinking about the relation between liberty and security is to see them as conflicting interests which must be balanced against each other.[56] The same logic is often reproduced in debates surrounding the place of prevention in criminal law. This conflictive view can be traced back to the beginning of modern political thought, and most definitely to the start of the liberal philosophical tradition. It is reflected, for instance, in John Stuart Mill's work on liberty. According to Mill's authoritative harm principle, still considered one of the main principles of criminalization, 'the sole end for which mankind are warranted, individually or collectively, in interfering with the liberty of action of any of their number, is self-protection', and 'the only purpose for which power can be rightfully exercised over any member of a civilized community, against his will, is to prevent harm to others'.[57] Although individual liberty is the main corollary of Mill's postulate, it can be legitimately curtailed by the state, as long as the purpose of such curtailment is to prevent harm to—and thus the interference with the liberty of—others. Mill is rather suspicious of the preventive power of the state, particularly with regards to the prevention of crime. This is because, although it is 'one of the undisputed functions of government', this preventive function 'is far more liable to be abused, to the prejudice of liberty, than the punitory function; for there is hardly any part of the legitimate freedom of action of a human being which would not admit of being represented, and fairly too, as increasing the facilities for some form or other of delinquency'.[58] In other words, Mill is suggesting that there is a danger in the idea of prevention, in that it can justify the restraint of nearly any form of human action, and all in the name of the protection of individual freedom. If not properly controlled, there is the risk that prevention itself becomes harmful to individual liberty.

---

[56] See C. Gearty, *Liberty and Security* (Cambridge: Polity Press, 2013); L. Zedner, *Security* (London: Routledge, 2009), chapter 2.

[57] J.S. Mill, *On Liberty and Other Writings* (Cambridge: Cambridge University Press, 1989), 13.

[58] Ibid, 96.

Interestingly, Mill's critique of prevention is essentially the same critique that is mostly made against the harm principle as a principle for criminalization: that the principle in itself does not provide any boundaries for the criminal law, as almost any offence could be grounded on the basis that it prevents harm or the risk of harm.[59] Ultimately, what these problems seem to indicate is that there is an uncomfortable relationship between liberty and prevention, which complicates the liberal critique of the preventive turn. This is well illustrated by what Ashworth and Zedner called the 'paradox of liberty: that a major justification for taking preventive powers is to secure or enhance the liberty of individuals, but that one possible effect of such powers is to deprive some individuals of their liberty'.[60] For this reason, the relationship between liberty and prevention is arguably best conceptualized not as one of conflict but as one of *tension* within the modern liberal context: at the same time as the two concepts condition and potentially undermine one another, they also necessitate each other. The maintained need for balancing individual liberty and autonomy against security and prevention reveals at the same time as it obscures the interdependence between these notions.

Individual liberty and prevention, or security, are therefore ideas which cannot be truly separated from each other within the context of liberal society. Security and prevention have been considered a fundamental aspect of the modern state, as essential conditions for the lawful and peaceful exercise of individual liberty. By the same token, individual autonomy has also been considered a condition for the exercise of prevention and the maintenance of security in society. What this interdependence also highlights, furthermore, is probably the most problematic aspect of the challenge posed by the preventive turn: that it is grounded on an essential ambivalence[61] regarding individual autonomy and liberty in liberal law. The relationship between autonomy and crime makes this ambivalence clear: individual liberty, it seems, is at the same time the main premise of the liberal social project, and the main threat to it. The paradox of liberty in the idea of prevention is in this sense a reflection of this ambivalent attitude towards liberty, as liberty needs to be protected *by* prevention at the same time as it needs to be protected *from* it.[62]

---

[59] See Duff et al, *The Boundaries of the Criminal Law*, Introduction; H. Stewart, 'The Limits of the Harm Principle' (2010) 4(1) *Criminal Law and Philosophy*, 17–35.

[60] Ashworth, Zedner, *Preventive Justice*, 257.

[61] See Z. Bauman, *Modernity and Ambivalence* (Cambridge: Polity Press, 1991).

[62] See I. Loader, N. Walker, *Civilizing Security* (Cambridge: Cambridge University Press, 2007); L. Zedner, 'Securing Liberty in the Face of Terror: Reflections from Criminal Justice' (2005) 32(4) *Journal of Law and Society*, 507–33.

The ambivalence of individual liberty can be examined through another dichotomy, often sustained by liberal legal theory, which arises from Mill's critique of prevention: that between prevention and punishment, or between the preventive and the 'punitory' function of criminal law. Following Mill, as mentioned above, Ashworth and other liberal—or 'neo-classical'[63]—thinkers consider the main function of criminal liability to be to address liability for past wrongdoing so that, in terms of harm, the criminal law should primarily focus on providing censure for harm already done. Ashworth's 'harm plus culpability' model of liability reflects the liberal model's focus on punishment and retributivism as its main corollaries. Although the criminal law is seen to have a preventive role, it is posited as secondary and, in normative terms, exceptional. The idea that punishment adheres to liberal law's concern with individual autonomy better than prevention, while illuminating in many respects, to a large extent also neglects how these two concepts are themselves deeply interrelated, in liberal thought as well as in the broader history of the modern state. Criminal laws and punishment have, at least since the work of the Enlightenment reformers of the eighteenth century—such as Beccaria[64] and Bentham,[65] derived their justification predominantly from the idea of prevention. Most importantly, however, punishment (understood as a concern with individual justice) and prevention are not that easily distinguishable. Although criminal law theory often attempts to differentiate these values, for instance, by stating that autonomy and responsibility are the province of criminal liability (which determines who should be liable for punishment), while the prevention of harm is the focus of criminalization,[66] in practice these two notions cannot avoid being intermeshed within both the institutional and the normative frameworks of criminal law.[67]

The interrelation between liberty and prevention, together with the ambivalence of individual autonomy and liberty within liberal legal thinking, defies the assumption that the liberal model and the preventive turn can be analysed as fundamentally opposite approaches to criminal law, suggesting instead that they share similar conceptual and normative foundations. This common ground can also potentially compromise the main approach to the contemporary problem of prevention put forward by liberal criminal law theorists, which is to promote a balanced and principled approach to the preventive

[63] Farmer, *Making the Modern Criminal Law*, 109.

[64] C. Beccaria, *On Crimes and Punishments and Other Writings* (Cambridge: Cambridge University Press, 1995).

[65] J. Bentham, *The Principles of Morals and Legislation* (Amherst: Prometheus Books, 1988).

[66] See Ashworth, Horder, *Principles of Criminal Law*.

[67] For a detailed analysis of this intermeshing from the perspective of criminal responsibility, See Lacey, *In Search of Criminal Responsibility*.

power of the state on the grounds that, if the ultimate goal of prevention is to protect and promote individual autonomy and liberty, then unless prevention is principled and limited, it becomes self-defeating.[68] The main problem, however, is that the same frame of reference can be used to justify the preventive turn itself, by claiming that criminal law needs to become more preventive if it is to effectively promote its stated values and achieve its goals. The paradox of liberty, it seems, works both ways. This is partly because the distinction made between punishment (as an expression of the redressing of past wrongs) and prevention (as directed at future harms) is itself unstable, and very difficult to maintain at any practical level. The punishment of offenders is often justified on preventive terms, either in terms of deterrence, rehabilitation, or incapacitation,[69] and as mentioned above, preventive measures and criminal offences are often also justified on punitive terms. In addition, the idea that the criminal law should focus on punishment and retribution instead of on prevention is fairly recent; rather, the main rationale for criminalization and punishment has been predominantly preventive in the modern history of the criminal law.[70] As it will be seen in subsequent chapters, the coexistence of punishment and prevention as rationales for the criminal law is inevitable, and the relation between these two tendencies lies at the heart of the tensions between liberal law and the preventive turn.

One illustration of this ambivalence in the justificatory framework of criminal law can be seen in Jeremy Horder's critique of the liberal model—which he dubs the 'harm-done' perspective—through his defence of the preventive turn—which he characterizes as the 'anticipatory perspective' on criminalization.[71] For Horder, inconsistencies found in the liberal model give rise to an 'implicit recognition ... that there are sound arguments for giving at least equal status to the anticipatory perspective in any theory of the justification for criminalisation'.[72] The main grounds for his critique lie in that both the harm done and the anticipatory perspective have a common moral background based on a 'shared interest in deterring people from engaging in wrongful harm-doing'.[73] This shared interest, moreover, is primarily concerned with the exercise of individual autonomy, for only 'if (amongst other things) enough is done to deter such activity, can the conditions be secured in which people can reliably be expected to participate in important kinds of collective commitment, such as the commitment to live by the rule of

---

[68] See Ashworth, Zedner, *Preventive Justice*.
[69] See for instance the aims of sentencing in English law found in the Criminal Justice Act 2003, s. 142, and more generally T. Mathiesen, *Prison on Trial* (Winchester: Waterside, 2003).
[70] See Ashworth, Zedner, *Preventive Justice*, chapter 2.
[71] Horder, 'Harmless Wrongdoing'.   [72] Ibid, 79.   [73] Ibid.

law and participate in a culture respectful of human rights'.[74] This results in a shared concern, held by both perspectives, with the need for the law to achieve an appropriate balance between liberty and security, in order to respect the values constitutive of those collective commitments.

The distinctions between the two perspectives therefore do not derive from the particular values which each of them endorses, but from how common values are balanced and prioritized. For instance, there is a clear shift, in the anticipatory perspective, from wrongfulness to harmfulness as the priority for criminalization. This shift, however, is not intended to eschew the importance of individual autonomy to criminal law; on the contrary, it depends to a large extent on this importance. Horder's defence of the anticipatory perspective relies precisely on the notion that criminal law necessitates a stronger focus on harm prevention in order to stay true to its principles. In order to make his case for how criminal law depends on its preventive function, he dedicates a significant portion of his paper to arguing that Ashworth cannot avoid allowing space in his framework for offences which do not fit into his own approach to criminalization, such as inchoate offences and possession offences, which Ashworth himself justifies on the grounds of 'preventable victimisation'.[75] Rather than representing an erosion of the core values in criminal law, then, the preventive turn can appear as the only way to preserve them. This is why, for Horder, the anticipatory perspective may constitute a 'civilizing move' in criminal law, since '[t]oo narrow a concern only with harm done might, ironically, undermine respect amongst the law-abiding for the very values ... that motivate some theorists to work within a predominantly harm-done perspective'.[76] Understood in this way, the preventive turn may be seen as grounded on 'a moral argument, sensitive to the idea that a focus only on harm done will lead, ... to nothing but Pyrrhic victories that may threaten people's trust and confidence in the rule of law'.[77]

The moral basis for the argument in favour of the preventive turn suggested by Horder points to yet another tension found within the normative framework of criminal law, related to the issue of trust. As mentioned above, the idea of individual autonomy suggests that, in order to respect it, it is necessary for a degree of trust to be conferred to individuals, with regards to their ability to make good decisions. However, the idea of trust in individuals cannot be fully dissociated from a degree of trust in the order and laws of the society in which these individuals interact. In other words, trust, just like liberty, can be said to have an individual as well as a socio-political dimension.

---

[74] Ibid.   [75] Ashworth cited in Horder, ibid, 89.
[76] Horder, ibid, 100, 85.   [77] Ibid, 94.

The concepts on which the criminal law tends to focus, such as autonomy and responsibility, seem to put too much emphasis on the former, and to neglect the importance and inevitability of dealing with the latter. The result of this neglect, however, is that the criminal law preserves an ambiguity with regards to its main concepts and values, and it is precisely this ambiguity that allows the preventive turn to engender a shift from liberty to security, from wrongfulness to harmfulness, and from responsibility to dangerousness. Horder's effort to reflect on a possible moral justification for preventive measures aptly exposes the interconnectedness between the normative grounds of the preventive turn and that of the liberal model, so that the problematic character of prevention reveals the existence of issues and tensions in liberal law.

Thus the main challenge posed to the liberal model by the preventive turn is that, in order to fully engage with the perplexities of preventive criminal offences and the broader preventive measures that surround them, criminal law theory needs to critically examine its own assumptions, conditions, and limitations. The aim of this book is to offer a pathway through which to pursue such an examination.

METHODOLOGICAL FRAMEWORK: CRIMINAL LAW AND AMBIVALENCE

In this book, I explore the conceptual foundations for the justificatory basis of the preventive turn in criminal law, by looking at how the recent transformations in criminal law and justice are intrinsically related to and embedded in the way liberal society and criminal law have been imagined, developed, and conditioned by their social, political, cultural, and historical context. At the core of this relation lies the ambivalence within the modern conception of individual autonomy and liberty, which is both repressed and preserved by the liberal framework of criminal law and punishment. The main source of this ambivalence is the abstract character of normative conceptions of individual autonomy and liberty promoted by liberal law, which are often in tension with the socio-political dimension of these conceptions—that is, with the concrete forms they take when they are actualized by the criminal law.

Individualism and Criminal Subjectivity

The paradigmatic form of subjectivity within the liberal framework, which strives to give expression to the normative idea of individual liberty within the context of criminal law, is that of the responsible legal subject, embedded within notions of individual responsibility and autonomy. As Nicola Lacey has suggested, ideas of criminal responsibility can be seen to encapsulate the 'very conception of what it is to be a subject of criminal law'.[78] The conceptual roots of this specific form of imagining criminal subjectivity can be traced back to the tendency towards individualism in modern and liberal thinking. This tendency finds its foundations at the very start of modern political thinking, most prominently illustrated by the works of Thomas Hobbes[79] and John Locke,[80] which placed the individual as the constitutive element of political society.[81] The most comprehensive expression of this conceptual development, moreover, is found in the tradition initiated by the ideals of human agency and rationality put forward by the Enlightenment thinkers of the eighteenth and nineteenth centuries, which promoted the corollary 'that at the heart of moral, political, social, economic—*and legal*—discourse there should be placed the idea of the free individual'.[82] The result of this tendency is a normative primacy given to questions of individual autonomy and freedom, which constitute 'the primary focus of concern in the moral assessment of any particular set of political arrangements'.[83] Due to its inherent individualism, then, the liberal framework posits individual autonomy as the start and end point from which all the elements of a legitimate legal system ought to be developed, from the existence of rights and the basis of contracts to the importance of welfare and security, and the justification for criminal law and punishment.

The responsible legal subject which the liberal model posits at the core of criminal liability is the primary expression of the individualism which predominates within the framework of liberal law. In criminal law, this dominant conception of individual responsibility focuses on the subjective aspects of the fault element of liability, expressed through cognitive notions such as intention and recklessness, as the main basis for individual justice,[84] and is derived from a school of thought known as 'orthodox subjectivism', a position 'founded on the political values of individualism, liberty, and

---

[78] N. Lacey, 'In Search of the Responsible Subject: History, Philosophy and Social Sciences in Criminal Law Theory' (2001) 64(3) *Modern Law Review*, 350–71, 351.

[79] T. Hobbes, *Leviathan* (Oxford: Oxford University Press, 1996).

[80] J. Locke, *Two Treatises of Government* (Cambridge: Cambridge University Press, 2010).

[81] See C.B. MacPherson, *The Political Theory of Possessive Individualism: Hobbes to Locke* (Ontario: Oxford University Press, 2011). The importance of these theories to the argument pursued in this book is fully discussed in Chapters 3 and 4.

[82] A. Norrie, *Crime, Reason and History* (Cambridge: Cambridge University Press, 2014), 21 (emphasis in original).

[83] N. Lacey, *State Punishment* (New York: Routledge, 1988), 144.

[84] See Ashworth, Horder, *Principles of Criminal Law*; R.A. Duff, *Answering for Crime: Responsibility and Liability in Criminal Law* (Portland: Hart Publishing, 2007).

self-determination'.[85] This perspective is grounded on a Kantian standpoint that emphasizes the capacity for individual self-government, and is seen to ground the legitimacy of criminal liability on the need for the state to prove that the crime was committed voluntarily. For instance, in the most illustrious elaboration of subjective responsibility, proposed by H.L.A. Hart, an individual cannot be deemed responsible and punished for a crime, unless it can be established that s/he had the capacity and a fair opportunity to do otherwise.[86]

The idea of the free individual which underpins the subjective conception of responsibility can thus be seen to delineate a specific notion of subjectivity in the framework of criminal law, one which 'accords individuals the status of autonomous moral agents who, because they have axiomatic freedom of choice, can fairly be held accountable and punishable for the rational choices of wrongdoing that they make'.[87] From this perspective, those who are exposed to the criminal law are considered to be, and should thus be treated as, responsible subjects who are capable of understanding and responding to the normative demands set by the law—and who can consequently be held liable for their wrongdoing. While this form of subjectivity provides a strong justification for criminal liability and punishment, in that crime appears to be a direct consequence of the individual's rational agency, it is mainly associated with a minimalist approach to criminalization. This is in great part because it promotes the idea that individuals can be trusted to behave responsibly, and to only exceptionally commit crimes, which assume the primary image of moral mistakes.

This idea, however, finds itself at odds with the pervasiveness of criminal law and justice systems in contemporary liberal societies, and of the preoccupation within these societies with security and with the maintenance of social order. The preventive function of the criminal law shifts the focus from the expression of individual autonomy to the need for it to be restrained, so that individuals and society can be properly protected. Prevention is also linked to the very idea that crime is constituted by wrongful conduct and harmful outcomes, so that crime, by its very nature, always presents a potential threat to others. This notion of danger related to crime sits rather uneasily with responsible subjectivity, so that the more the criminal law focuses on the dangerousness of crime, the more it drifts away from the image of individuals as responsible subjects.

---

[85] Dennis, 'The Critical Condition of Criminal Law', 237. See also R.A. Duff, *Intention, Agency and Criminal Liability* (London: Blackwell, 1990).

[86] See H.L.A. Hart, *Punishment and Responsibility* (Oxford: Oxford University Press, 2008). A more detailed discussion of criminal responsibility can be found in Chapter 2.

[87] Dennis, 'The Critical Condition of Criminal Law', 237.

Although the problematic character of conceptions of responsibility and individuality arising from the normative structure of the criminal law has received substantial attention from some criminal law scholars,[88] it still remains a largely marginal preoccupation in criminal law theory more broadly. But if I am right that both the challenges brought forth by the preventive turn and the shortcomings of liberal criminal law in attempting to deal with these challenges can be traced back to the problem of criminal subjectivity, then it is necessary for us to try and develop a critical theoretical perspective which properly acknowledges and engages with this problem. Such a perspective must look beyond legal doctrine and scholarship, being sensitive to the intellectual, historical, and socio-political context from which forms of criminal subjectivity originate and in which they develop. The aforementioned critical literature on criminal law provides a solid foundation for this purpose, on which an understanding of the interaction between criminal law, criminal responsibility, and their context can be built.

In a nutshell, this book pursues a phenomenological[89] account of the subject of criminal law, looking at the conceptual history and context of ideas of individual liberty, autonomy, and responsibility in the modern liberal tradition, in order to produce a detailed and comprehensive picture of what criminal subjectivity entails within the contemporary environment of criminal law in England and Wales. In doing so, I hope to assist in better understanding the problems encountered in this environment.

The Dynamics between Criminal Subjectivity and Socio-Political Context: Book Structure

I start the substantive part of my account by discussing how, concealed within the liberal framework of criminal law, there is an inseparable link between what are essentially contradictory notions of human nature and subjectivity, as well as what the role of criminal law and punishment is or is imagined to be in the preservation of particular conceptions of autonomy

---

[88] See Lacey, *State Punishment*; *In Search of Criminal Responsibility*; A. Norrie, *Law, Ideology and Punishment* (Dordrecht: Kluwer Academic Publishers, 1990); Norrie, *Crime, Reason and History*; Farmer, *Criminal Law, Tradition and Legal Order*; Farmer, *Making the Modern Criminal Law*; Ramsay, *The Insecurity State*.

[89] The term 'phenomenology' is used here in Hegelian fashion, referring to the method of examining a concept through the relation between the ways in which it is idealized and imagined on the one hand, and ways in which it is actualized and concretely developed on the other. See G.W.F. Hegel, *Phenomenology of Spirit* (Oxford: Oxford Universtiy Press, 1977); G.W.F. Hegel, *Hegel's Philosophy of Right* (Oxford: Oxford University Press, 1967).

and social order. I discuss how the ambiguous and ambivalent aspect of the normative dimension of criminal law is the result of the need for the law to reflect and regulate a complex socio-political environment, and to cope with demands which are themselves contradictory or in tension with each other—such as the demand for respect for individual autonomy and the demand for security through crime control. The forms of subjectivity within criminal law are thus inherently related to images of the kind of society in which these subjects exercise their agency, and of the ways in which this society is politically organized. These images, by their turn, are dynamically related to the context in which they are actualized, so that they are conditioned by their environment at the same time as they strive to influence it. This dialectical[90] and relational perspective implies that an examination of subjectivity cannot be dissociated from an examination of the specific context in which this subjectivity is actualized; this context, however, is the result of specificities as well as of commonalities within a broader history. This is particularly the case when the focus is on normative concepts, which tend to have their sense of legitimacy grounded at least partly on their long philosophical and ideological tradition.

Chapter 2 explores how the conceptions of subjectivity at the core of contemporary criminal law are connected not only to notions of individual freedom and responsibility, but also to images of society and political community, as well as to conceptions such as citizenship and civilization. This exploration uncovers how the individualism in the law, more than having a moral undertone, mainly fulfils a socio-political purpose, which is to preserve and promote a specific model of society connected to a particular social imaginary. This model of society, just like the conception of individual liberty at its core, promotes an ambivalent conception of social and legal order, one which can both promote and undermine the strong normative values which lie at the core of the liberal model of criminal law. The main reason behind this ambivalence, and the main argument advanced in the chapter, is that the notion of criminal subjectivity which lies at the core of the framework of criminal law is driven by two normative conceptions instead of one. Besides the idea of responsible subjectivity, the criminal law also conceives of its subject as inherently dangerous. Since this ambivalence between responsibility and dangerousness is intrinsic to the framework of criminal subjectivity, this framework is predominantly affected by the dynamic interaction between these two notions, which are by their turn conditioned by structural and

---

[90] See A. Norrie, *Law and the Beautiful Soul* (London: GlassHouse Press, 2005); A. Norrie, *Dialectic and Difference* (Abingdon: Routledge, 2010).

socio-political contingency. From this perspective, changes and transformations in the criminal law can be understood as reflections of the need for the criminal law to manage and contain this ambivalence, by upholding a specific notion of civil order.

Having laid down the core assumptions and issues in my theoretical framework, I turn in the following chapters to an investigation of what I consider the conceptual foundations of these tensions within criminal subjectivity and criminalization, by pursuing a critical analysis of accounts of crime and punishment within seminal works in political theory which have deeply influenced the liberal social imaginary. In Chapter 3, I trace the conceptual foundations of insecurity through an engagement with the work of Thomas Hobbes. I look at how, from the moment the individual was placed at the centre of political society in modern thought, individual liberty was conceptualized in an inherently paradoxical and ambivalent way, as both the foundation for society and as the main threat to it. As a result of this ambivalence, which is linked to the model of society which lies at the core of modern conceptions of the state and of the law, the respect for individual liberty is effectively subsumed under the need to secure the conditions for its exercise. Individual liberty thus requires the reassurance of the law if it is to lead to mutual cooperation, and the main function of the criminal law in civil society is to provide such reassurance.

Chapter 4 then turns to an analysis of the conceptual foundations for the trust embedded within the liberal model of criminal law, by contrasting the interplay between individual liberty and political authority in Hobbes's work with that in John Locke's political theory. Locke represses the insecurity Hobbes found in the human condition under a naturalized conception of human sociability, in order to limit the dependence of individual liberty upon the security provided by political authority. This provides the groundwork for a differentiated conception of the role of punishment and criminal law in society, which effectively conceives of the dangerousness of crime as exceptional. However, paradoxes in the Lockean framework reveal that this reassured conception of human nature relies on specific structural conditions linked to the elements of civil society, with the result that the maintenance of these conditions ends up prevailing over individual liberty and its trustworthiness, and the criminal law ends up retaining its function as an instrument of social control.

After examining the conceptual foundations of both reassurance and trust in the liberal imaginary, I turn in Chapter 5 to a discussion of how the ambivalences and paradoxes found within the liberal imaginary are systematized in modern liberal political and legal thought and how, in doing so, they inform and legitimize a particular notion of civil order. I explore

the normative grounds for the dynamics between responsibility and dangerousness in the contemporary framework of criminal law through an analysis
of the work of two Enlightenment theorists, G. W. F. Hegel and Jeremy
Bentham. I do so by looking at how these two complex accounts of the
role of criminal law in society manage to actualize the primacy of individual responsibility only by recognizing the embeddedness of dangerousness
within criminal subjectivity. By promoting an ideal conception of social
order and human agency which is conceptualized as an embedded and persistent aspect of modern civil society, the conceptual logics laid down by
these two scholars manage to allow for the legitimacy of the authoritarian
and preventive power of the state at the same time as they uphold the primacy of individual autonomy and freedom.

With the notion that the core problem of the liberal imaginary is the normative presumption of an ideal social order underpinning civil society in
mind, Chapter 6 hosts a critical discussion of the ethical limits of the project
of pursuing emancipatory aspirations through criminal law and punishment.
I engage primarily with Antony Duff's communicative theory of punishment
in order to uncover the importance of the notion of recognition to a liberal
democratic conception of individual autonomy, and then move to elaborate
on a critical theory of recognition grounded on Hegelian dialectics. I conclude the chapter with a theoretical discussion of the problems surrounding the criminalization of terrorism, in which I suggest that these problems
are directly related to the intrinsically unequal and exclusionary character of
punishment.

The seventh and concluding chapter traces the dynamics of criminal subjectivity in the modern history of criminal law, by means of a theoretical
engagement with the political sociology of citizenship. It does so in order
to both identify the real character and origins of the preventive turn, and
discuss the difficulties faced by liberal law in its attempts to counteract
and overcome the radical ambivalence of the preventive turn. The main
argument in this chapter, which is a reflection of the main argument in the
book, is that the current state of the criminal law is mainly the manifestation of problems which are inherent to the liberal project of criminal law,
so that a critical engagement with preventive criminal offences can offer
broader insights and lessons with regards to the problematic condition of
law within liberal societies.

2

Criminal Subjectivity
and Socio-Political Imagination

[T]he image of the liberal state as one resting on 'right' as opposed to 'might' is from the beginning a false one. The liberal state—and its law—work *through* oppositions they embody, between law and force, freedom and sovereignty, *ratio* (the articulation of freedoms) and *voluntas* (the expression of power) .... Intrinsic opposition is reflected from the very beginning of liberalism .... Modern liberal law *combines* in its form individualist right and political necessity.[1]

It is undeniable that the modern history of criminal law has been significantly influenced by ideas of individual freedom and responsibility. However, it is much less frequently recognized that, alongside the development of categories of fault, general defences, and other rules associated with what some scholars came to call the 'general part' of the criminal law,[2] there can be identified another, equally predominant impulse in modern criminal law, which highlights its instrumental function as a system of social control.[3] For instance, at least since the nineteenth century, a significant proportion of the enactment of new criminal laws related to statutory offences preoccupied with the regulation of everyday social behaviour such as social and economic activities, which were 'prosecuted under summary procedure and often [contained] no fault element at all'.[4] This regulatory aspect of the criminal law has only become more pervasive as the years went by, so that today there is virtually no area of social life that has not been the target of criminalization. This other

---

[1] A. Norrie, *Justice and the Slaughter-Bench: Essays on Law's Broken Dialectic* (Oxon: Routledge, 2017), 35.

[2] See L. Farmer, *Criminal Law, Tradition and Legal Order* (Cambridge: Cambridge University Press, 1997), chapter 1; G. Williams, *Criminal Law. The General Part* (London: Stevens and Sons, 1961).

[3] See Farmer, *Criminal Law, Tradition and Legal Order*; L. Farmer, *Making the Modern Criminal Law: Criminalization and Civil Order* (Oxford: Oxford University Press, 2016); M.D. Dubber, *The Police Power: Patriarchy and the Foundations of American Government* (New York: Columbia University Press, 2005).

[4] Farmer, *Criminal Law, Tradition and Legal Order*, 182.

The Preventive Turn in Criminal Law. First Edition. Henrique Carvalho. © Henrique Carvalho 2017. Published 2017 by Oxford University Press.

side—so to speak—of the criminal law, which is an inherent aspect of its historical development, detracts from the emphasis on individual justice and the adjudication of right and wrong given by criminal law doctrine, and focuses instead on the notion that the criminal law has an important role to play in the preservation of the conditions for social order.

Lindsay Farmer has persuasively argued that the primacy given to individual liberty in criminal law theory is to a large extent a consequence of the influence that moral and political philosophy exerts on criminal law scholarship. Furthermore, he also stresses that this perspective is inadequate for a concrete understanding of the criminal law as a modern institution.[5] Attention to this institutional dimension reveals that the modern criminal law is largely shaped by 'the broad aim of securing civil order', so that it can only 'be made "fully intelligible" by looking at it from the perspective of the aim of securing the civility of civil society'.[6] Farmer's notion of civil order is something broader than simply maintaining the minimal conditions of social life; rather, it comprises 'the co-ordination of complex modern societies composed of a range of entities or legal persons that are responsible, in a range of different ways, for their own conduct, for the wellbeing of others, and for the maintenance of social institutions'.[7] In other words, criminal law not only has a specific social function, but this function is tied to a particular notion of society, one that is inextricably linked with the history and the idea of modernity and its conception of civility and civilization.

In shifting our attention from the importance of individual freedom to the need to pay attention to the institutional role of the criminal law, Farmer invites us to see the responsible subject coming out of ideas of individual autonomy as to a large extent a product of its socio-historical conditions, engendered by the criminal law in pursuit of its aim to preserve a specific notion of civil order. If this is correct, then the responsible subject of the criminal law cannot be understood through a universal conception of human agency, but rather has to be seen as inseparable from the model of society which s/he inhabits. In this chapter, I intend to follow this intuition by conceptualizing the subject of criminal law as indissociably related to specific notions of social order, which arise from the liberal socio-political imaginary[8] surrounding criminal law. However, in doing so, I want to resist the idea that notions of subjectivity linked to individual liberty are merely incidental to the modern project of civil order, as a product of a process of subjectification.[9] Rather, I see what I conceptualized as the socio-political dimension of individual liberty as the locus

[5] See ibid.   [6] Farmer, *Making the Modern Criminal Law*, 299.   [7] Ibid.
[8] See C. Taylor, *Modern Social Imaginaries* (Durham: Duke University Press, 2004).
[9] See M. Foucault, 'The Subject and Power' (1982) 8(4) *Critical Inquiry*, 777–95.

of a dynamic relationship between individuals' lived experiences of their social environment, the way they imagine the society in which they live, and how these images are given socio-political meaning and institutional form. Once individuals are expected to behave as responsible subjects, their own sense of identity is conditioned by this expectation, and this process in its turn influences and conditions how society and its institutions are imagined, as well as what is expected of them. As Michel Foucault pointed out, at the same time as the project of security in modern society engenders specific forms of subjectivity, the very modern idea of security only has meaning if understood within the context of a society of free individuals.[10]

The focus on subjectivity is therefore meant to highlight how the subject of criminal law and the image of civil order which requires it are dynamically related. It is the interaction between the two levels of this intersubjective process which generates the ambivalence identified around conceptions of individual autonomy and liberty, and which leads to the subject of criminal law being itself an ambivalent subject. Criminal subjectivity, I will argue, is caught between the need for the criminal law to preserve a normative framework geared at addressing individuals as responsible subjects, and the role of criminal law in preserving a specific notion of order that is seen to provide the conditions for individual autonomy in society.

THE SUBJECT OF CRIMINAL LAW: BETWEEN RESPONSIBILITY AND DANGEROUSNESS

The problem of crime[11] is challenging to the minimalist project of liberal law, because it shifts the focus of the criminal law from a matter of individual agency and morality to a broader social problem. This shift in perspective is intrinsically linked to the potential harmfulness of crime, but mainly because this harmfulness has an inherently social character. That is, the problem of crime largely derives from the notion that crime presents a potential threat to society as a whole. Possibly the main quality attributed to crime that links it with the notion of social harm is that of danger. Jeremy Bentham has long discussed that a crime can always be dangerous, in that it can generate harms and other undesired outcomes that go beyond its primary consequences or purpose; most importantly, a crime has the potential to increase the possibility

[10] M. Foucault, *Security, Territory, Population* (Basingstoke: Palgrave Macmillan, 2007).
[11] See J. Muncie, E. McLaughlin (eds), *The Problem of Crime* (London: Sage, 2001).

of more crimes being committed, either by making the idea of crime attractive or by 'weakening the resolve of the tutelary motives' that keep individuals in general from committing crimes.[12]

The danger in crime is therefore more far-reaching than any direct harm that may result from it, generating a much broader sense of insecurity.[13] The link between crime and dangerousness poses a significant obstacle to the idea of individual responsibility within the liberal model, mainly for two reasons. First, the more dangerous a crime is considered, the more society appears to be vulnerable against it, so the more that crime assumes the character of a social problem which must be prevented or controlled, instead of a matter of individual justice. And second, the idea that crimes are dangerous to society places individuals who commit them at odds with the social order. As a result, individuals who commit dangerous crimes might themselves be considered a danger to society, making it harder for them to be treated or seen as responsible subjects. Nowadays, the terrorist arguably represents the paradigmatic image of the dangerous offender, but it is only one of a number of examples where the notion of dangerousness, when related to specific crimes, compromises the possibility of acknowledging the responsible subjectivity of those who commit them. Examples range from violent and sexual offences to gang-related crime and anti-social behaviour more broadly.

The subjectivist perspective on individual responsibility resulting from the expressivist approach to individual autonomy cannot fully account for the social character of crime. The way liberal legal theory tends to deal with this limitation is by attempting to qualify the idea of individual autonomy in light of considerations of public interest. For instance, Ashworth concedes that the principle of individual autonomy cannot fully account for the complexity of the criminal law, so that it has to be balanced against the idea of welfare, 'which emphasizes the State's obligation to create the social conditions necessary for the exercise of full autonomy by individual citizens'.[14] From this perspective, then, the framework of criminal law is not shaped only by the need to treat individuals as responsible subjects, but also by the concern with maintaining the social conditions for their autonomy to be exercised. However, especially in light of the danger inherent to crime, the need to preserve the conditions for social welfare will often imply that the criminal law will not be able to respect individuals as responsible subjects. Furthermore, if

---

[12] J. Bentham, *The Principles of Morals and Legislation* (London: Penguin Random House, 1988), 154–5.

[13] Ibid, 158.

[14] A. Ashworth, J. Horder, *Principles of Criminal Law*, 7th ed. (Oxford: Oxford University Press, 2013), 26.

it is acknowledged that the exercise of autonomy requires social conditions, then the notion of autonomy in itself becomes conditional—and so does the notion of responsible subjectivity which it supports. This is because it becomes clear that the idea of individual autonomy is essentially linked with specific public interests, so that the flourishing of autonomy is not universal, but rather depends upon, and reflects, a particular form of social life.

It therefore seems that although the liberal model of criminal law aspires to universality, it does not in reality possess universal validity. This much appears to be recognized, as many scholars today posit that criminal law is only properly conceptualized if understood as belonging to a specific socio-political environment. According to Antony Duff, the appropriate environment of criminal law is that of a 'polity that aspires to be a liberal democracy'.[15] Although apparently subtle, if taken seriously, this qualification can fundamentally alter the way individual liberty and its limitations are conceived. This is because, from the moment we move from looking into individuality in the abstract to examining it within a particular context, our analysis of subjectivity becomes necessarily *intersubjective*, as we start thinking of the subjects of criminal law as existing among other subjects, whose agency and autonomy are intrinsically interrelated.

Within a liberal democratic context, it has been suggested that responsible subjectivity is best conceptualized when linked to the 'key moral role … of citizen'.[16] The environment of citizenship highlights the relationality of responsibility, as it relates responsibility to 'membership of the community in which one lives one's life', which in turn embodies 'a reciprocity of rights against, and duties towards' the community and its members.[17] One of the main duties in a polity that aspires to be a liberal democracy involves 'a certain kind of civic trust', which implies that we should 'recognise each other as fellows', and not 'assume in advance that others are enemies who might attack us, and against whom we need to guard ourselves'.[18] The idea of civic trust can in this sense be understood as the direct reflection of a liberal democratic society's commitment to individual autonomy and its conception of responsible subjectivity. This duty is primarily manifested in the structure of criminal

---

[15] R.A. Duff, 'Pre-Trial Detention and the Presumption of Innocence' in A. Ashworth, L. Zedner, P. Tomlin (eds), *Prevention and the Limits of the Criminal Law* (Oxford: Oxford University Press, 2012), 115–32, 122 at footnote 22.

[16] Ibid. See also R.A. Duff, 'Responsibility, Citizenship and Criminal Law' in R.A. Duff, S.P. Green (eds), *Philosophical Foundations of Criminal Law* (Oxford: Oxford University Press, 2011), 125–49.

[17] D. Held, 'Between State and Civil Society: Citizenship' in G. Andrews (ed), *Citizenship* (London: Lawrence & Wishart, 1991), 19–25, 20.

[18] Duff, 'Pre-Trial Detention and the Presumption of Innocence', 123.

law in the form of the presumption of innocence and the burden of proof, in that they effectively impose a 'formal burden of trust among citizens', which requires 'that *we act as if* we trust accused fellow citizens not to do wrong until it is proved otherwise'.[19]

The commitment to individual autonomy expressed through the burden of trust can only be maintained if, to some extent at least, it is grounded on the expectation that individuals in society can generally be trusted to behave responsibly. Therefore, embedded in this burden, there is a normative expectation that the law can 'presume that all have moral agency and that failure to adapt to the law's norms will be exceptional'.[20] But just as individual autonomy has to be qualified by considerations of public welfare, the burden of trust cannot be sustained indefinitely or unconditionally. At the same time as we carry a duty of trust in liberal democratic societies, Duff says that 'we also owe certain kinds of (re)assurance to each other, to make clear to them that we can be trusted'.[21] There is thus a reciprocal element to the duty of trust, not just in the sense that individuals have a duty to trust each other, but also that they have a duty to make sure others can trust them. 'Trust and assurance are clearly interdependent; lack of assurance undermines trust; lack of trust generates a felt need to seek assurance.'[22] However, at the same time as trust and reassurance appear to be interdependent, there appears to be a certain aspect of fragility attributed to trust. It seems that the less we trust, the more we need to be reassured, but the opposite is not true. Rather than being purely reciprocal, there is a sense in which trust is the main value to be sought, and reassurance is there to provide the conditions in which the burden of trust can be exercised. Just like the relationship between autonomy and welfare, then, trust is given a primary role in this conceptual coupling, but this ultimately means that trust is dependent upon reassurance. In order to be able to discharge their duty of trust, individuals must be reassured that the trust given to them is not unwarranted; likewise, when individuals act in a non-reassuring way, their capacity to be trusted is undermined.

If responsible subjectivity is linked with trust, then it seems that an individual's capacity to be treated as a responsible subject is dependent upon her/his capacity to reassure others of her/his trustworthiness. Within the context of criminal law, the dangerousness inherent to crime implies that an individual who commits crime acts in a non-reassuring way. Even if the criminal

---

[19] P. Ramsay, 'Democratic Limits to Preventive Criminal Law' in A. Ashworth, L. Zedner, P. Tomlin (eds), *Prevention and the Limits of the Criminal Law* (Oxford: Oxford University Press, 2013), 214–34, 228 (emphasis in original).

[20] Ibid.   [21] Duff, 'Pre-Trial Detention and the Presumption of Innocence', 123.

[22] Ibid.

law wants to uphold the burden of trust by treating its subjects as responsible until proven otherwise, the conditionality of trust means that the law's capacity to address its subjects in a trusting way will itself be conditioned by their apparent trustworthiness. The idea of dangerousness inherently suggests a lack of trust, and thus a need for reassurance. Furthermore, criminal subjectivity always potentially carries a dimension of dangerousness. This is because even the liberal notion of responsible subjectivity, once inserted into the framework of criminal law, cannot be fully dissociated from the notion of crime, as to be responsible in criminal law is to be responsible *for a crime*. Once individual responsibility becomes *criminal* responsibility, a tension is inevitably generated between the idea of responsibility and that of dangerousness. This 'contagion'[23] from the danger attributed to the act to a dangerousness inherent to the actor is also due to the very notion of agency implied in subjective responsibility. If it is presumed that individuals should be capable of understanding the consequences of their actions, then those who engage in dangerous activities either demonstrate a lack of such capacity to behave responsibly, or—perhaps worse—have voluntarily decided to pursue a dangerous course of action. In either case, dangerousness not only disrupts the presumption of trust predicated by individual responsibility, but it also suggests a dimension of criminal subjectivity that is shaped around untrustworthiness, and the need for reassurance that it implies.

There is much that criminal law theory can gain from an engagement with the concept of dangerousness. Although virtually absent until very recently from the criminal law vocabulary, dangerousness has long been common currency in many areas of criminology and criminal justice scholarship, particularly in policing, sentencing, and punishment.[24] The notion of a dangerous offender usually appears in literature referring to those whose relationship with offending appears persistent or exceptionally violent or threatening, for instance due to the nature of the crime perpetrated. Within this field of scholarship, the idea of dangerousness has long symbolized a limit to the expectation of responsible subjectivity, as dangerous offenders are represented as precisely those individuals who cannot be trusted to behave responsibly, who have broken or otherwise proved themselves unworthy of the burden of trust promoted by autonomy. From this perspective, it is understandable that scholarship on criminal responsibility and liability has traditionally paid little attention to discussions of dangerousness, as the very way in which this idea has figured in criminological debates functioned as a kind of limit to

[23] M. Douglas, *Purity and Danger* (London: Routledge, 1966), 28.
[24] See J. Pratt, *Governing the Dangerous* (Sydney: The Federation Press, 1997); M. Brown, J. Pratt (eds), *Dangerous Offenders: Punishment and Social Order* (London: Routledge, 2000).

considerations of responsibility. However, although seemingly conceptually incompatible, ideas of responsibility and dangerousness cannot be fully dissociated within the framework of criminal law.

If the social dimension of crime is always potentially related to danger, then conceptually speaking, criminal responsibility necessarily possesses an intrinsic link with dangerousness. This is not to say that every crime and every criminal is seen as dangerous, but rather that dangerousness always insinuates itself within the notion of crime. If this is correct, then the idea of responsibility in criminal law is always constellated—even if through an inherently tense relationship—with dangerousness. Dangerousness is the other side of responsibility, with regards to criminal subjectivity. From this perspective, the danger in crime limits and conditions the capacity of the framework of criminal law to uphold the burden of trust—and, by the same token, it also undermines criminal law's capacity to treat its subjects as responsible agents. Because of the relationship between crime and danger, the concept of criminal responsibility is inherently ambivalent, torn between a presumption of responsibility and the potential for dangerousness. The more an individual's agency is associated with crime, the more their capacity to be trusted becomes fragile, and dependent on reassurance.

The Multifaceted Condition of Responsibility

This conceptual framework grounded on the connection between responsibility and dangerousness within criminal subjectivity finds resonance with, and can be explored through perplexities found within the contemporary environment of criminal responsibility. Due to the specific way in which individual autonomy is understood within the liberal model, and its inability to engage with the problem of crime, the normative conception of responsible subjectivity which it espouses is incapable of grasping and fully explaining the nuances of liability in criminal law. As a result, the subjective conception of individual responsibility has been decried by critical legal scholars to be insensitive to the complexities of criminalization and punishment, as it is not only abstract and ideological, and thus tied to specific interests,[25] but also historically and empirically incorrect.[26] Instead, the positing of subjective responsibility as the core concept of criminal liability is mainly the result of attempts by liberal legal theory to construct criminal responsibility as a unitary and

[25] See A. Norrie, *Law, Ideology and Punishment* (Dordrecht: Kluwer Academic Publishers, 1990); A. Norrie, *Crime, Reason and History* (Cambridge: Cambridge University Press, 2014).

[26] See N. Lacey, 'In Search of the Responsible Subject: History, Philosophy and Social Sciences in Criminal Law Theory' (2001) 64(3) *Modern Law Review*, 350–71; N. Lacey, 'Space, Time and Function: Intersecting Principles of Responsibility Across the Terrain of Criminal Justice' (2007) 1

universalistic concept, which betray the fact that competing conceptions of responsibility can be identified in criminal law at different times and in different contexts, so that criminal responsibility should rather be understood as a complex and hybrid environment, where different conceptions coexist and dynamically interact.[27]

In her work on criminal responsibility, Nicola Lacey has identified four distinct patterns of responsibility attribution in the modern criminal law. She argues that three of these patterns or conceptions of responsibility, those of character, capacity, and outcome, have a longer history, while more recently, concomitantly with the preventive turn, the criminal law has developed a fourth pattern related to assessments of risk.[28] Capacity responsibility possesses a natural association with Kantian ethics and orthodox subjectivism, along with the notion of responsible subjectivity which they inform. This pattern operates at two different levels. First, it upholds the conceptualization of individuals as responsible subjects by assigning to them specific capacities which ground their responsible agency, and which are only exceptionally negated by special circumstances (such as age, insanity, etc.). Second, it establishes that responsible agency is only properly engaged when such capacities are unhindered, so that responsibility is only attributable when an individual's capacity has been exercised, such as in circumstances of advertent conduct. Hart's work on responsibility[29] is deemed to represent the most sophisticated account of capacity, due to its focus on fair opportunity, which allows it to reach beyond the subjective categories of *mens rea* and to tentatively rationalize liability for negligence.[30] Although capacity responsibility is 'the dominant way of thinking about responsibility in contemporary British and American criminal law doctrine',[31] Lacey stresses that, just as the other patterns, it only relates to part of the complex tapestry and history of criminal liability. For instance, her historical investigation points out that this conception of responsibility did not become established into criminal law doctrine until the mid-twentieth century, even if the normative ideas that inform it

---

Criminal Law and Philosophy, 233–50; Farmer, *Criminal Law, Tradition and Legal Order*, P. Ramsay, 'The Responsible Subject as Citizen: Criminal Law, Democracy and the Welfare State' (2006) 69(1) *Modern Law Review*, 31.

[27] See N. Lacey, 'Character, Capacity, Outcome: Toward a Framework for Assessing the Shifting Pattern of Criminal Responsibility in Modern English Law' in M.D. Dubber, L. Farmer (eds), *Modern Histories of Crime and Punishment* (Stanford: Stanford University Press, 2007); J. Horder, 'Criminal Culpability: The Possibility of a General Theory' (1993) 12 *Law and Philosophy*, 193–215.

[28] N. Lacey, *In Search of Criminal Responsibility: Ideas, Interests and Institutions* (Oxford: Oxford University Press, 2016), 26.

[29] H.L.A. Hart, *Punishment and Responsibility* (Oxford: Oxford University Press, 2008).

[30] Lacey, 'Character, Capacity, Outcome', 28.

[31] Lacey, 'Space, Time and Function', 236.

have been influential to criminal law thinking at least since the work of the Enlightenment reformers.[32]

In contrast, the character conception of responsibility appears to have a much longer history, being the prevalent form of responsibility attribution throughout the eighteenth and nineteenth centuries. Conceptually speaking, character responsibility can be traced back to the work of philosophers such as Aristotle and David Hume. This conception of responsibility focuses on an evaluation of the individual's conduct, in terms of how it expresses a specific kind of character or disposition. Lacey argues that the character conception can be manifested either in the form of a more radical 'overall-character principle' which 'holds that the attribution of criminal responsibility is founded in a judgment that the defendant's conduct is evidence of a wrongful, bad, disapproved character trait',[33] or in the form of a more 'cautious' principle, which 'restricts itself to an evaluation of the specific conduct that forms the basis for the present allegation'.[34] The more extreme overall-character principle seems to go as far as rejecting the individual's potential for responsible subjectivity, as its evaluation of 'bad character' is taken to reflect a persistent aspect of the individual's identity. The cautious principle is more nuanced, as it 'preserves the specific allegation of criminal conduct as central to the rationale for conviction and punishment and is founded on a particular understanding of D's status as a moral agent: a reasoning being responsible for his or her beliefs, desires, emotions, and values'.[35] This cautious principle is able to provide a rationale for many elements of criminal liability, such as defences like duress and loss of control, and particularly the many standards of reasonableness abounding in contemporary criminal law, in which responsibility is linked to the notion that the defendant's conduct has proven unsatisfactory when compared to that 'of an idealised conception of an agent of good character'.[36] On the other hand, Lacey argues that several contemporary offences display an affinity with the overall-character principle, such as many of the preventive criminal offences, and status offences more generally.[37]

The dynamics between capacity and character closely resemble the relation between responsibility and dangerousness in my conceptual framework of criminal subjectivity. For instance, while capacity responsibility highlights the conditions grounding responsible subjectivity, character responsibility emphasizes the extent to which the defendant's conduct *fell short* of the standard expected of responsible subjects, and how the individual has

---

[32] Lacey, *In Search of Criminal Responsibility*, 33.
[33] Lacey, 'Character, Capacity, Outcome', 29.   [34] Ibid.   [35] Ibid.
[36] Horder, 'Criminal Culpability', 207.
[37] See Lacey, *In Search of Criminal Responsibility*.

'shown himself [*sic*], through his action, to be the sort of person who deserves the kind of criticism implied by the imposition of criminal responsibility'.[38] The notion that these apparently contradictory conceptions of responsibility coexist within criminal liability is further evidence that, although these can be conceptualized as distinct patterns of responsibility attribution, they dynamically interact, shaping and conditioning each other according to tendencies found in a particular context. One of the main findings of Lacey's analysis of criminal responsibility is that, in its long history, she could identify an impulse in criminal law to move from the cautious to the extreme version of character, which 'surfaces at key points in the history of English criminal justice' and 'has large practical and normative implications for the extent to which criminal law exhibits an inclusionary versus an exclusionary temper, and for how far it is seen as addressing free and equal subjects as opposed to managing a threat posed by particular categories of subject'.[39] With regards to my conceptual framework, this finding indicates that the dynamic relationship between responsibility and dangerousness is not only a persistent aspect of criminal subjectivity, but also one of the main forces behind changes and transformations in the framework of criminalization.

The dynamic understanding of criminal subjectivity, besides addressing the relation between capacity and character responsibility, is also helpful to an exploration of the other two patterns of responsibility attribution, outcome and risk. Outcome focuses on the causation of harmful consequences, drawing on a conception of responsibility which maintains that 'even though we are related to unintended outcomes differently than to intended results, they nonetheless engage our agency in some morally relevant way'.[40] This conception, which Tony Honoré deems 'the basic form of responsibility in any society',[41] can be seen to lie behind many offences that expand an individual's responsibility beyond the scope of her/his original conduct, such as those involving constructive liability,[42] and offences that privilege the avoidance of harm over the notion of fault, such as strict liability offences.[43] Risk responsibility, by its turn, is closely associated to character and outcome responsibility, but represents the unique shape that these forms of responsibility attribution

---

[38] V. Tadros, *Criminal Responsibility* (Oxford: Oxford University Press, 2005), 49.

[39] Lacey, *In Search of Criminal Responsibility*, 36–7.

[40] Lacey, 'Space, Time and Function', 239.

[41] T. Honoré, 'Responsibility and Luck: The Moral Basis of Strict Liability' (1988) 104 *Law Quarterly Review*, 530–53, 552.

[42] Examples of constructive liability can be found in the offence of malicious wounding and inflicting grievous bodily harm, contrary to the Offences Against the Person Act 1861, s. 20 and constructive manslaughter under the common law.

[43] See Lacey, *In Search of Criminal Responsibility*, 45.

take within the contemporary context of insecurity and risk prevention in the criminal law. Both of these patterns of responsibility can be seen to be related to the ambivalence in criminal subjectivity, but in a different way than the contrast between capacity and character. While capacity and character can be taken to be making normative statements about what kind of subject the criminal is, outcome and risk responsibility can be interpreted as directly addressing the conditions for individual autonomy, through the reduction of harm and the prevention of dangerousness.

Since it seemingly permeates all the different forms of responsibility attribution, an analysis of the dialectics between responsibility and dangerousness offers a more malleable conceptual framework than understanding responsibility as composed of distinct patterns, which can offer a more nuanced account of the different shapes which criminal liability can take. For instance, even though offences which rely on subjective categories of fault can be aligned to capacity responsibility, and therefore be in principle linked to notions of responsible subjectivity, they can also reflect the tension between responsibility and dangerousness. One example is that of inchoate offences which emphasize subjective fault in lieu of substantive harm; one way of understanding the rationale behind responsibility for these offences is 'that acting on the intention to cause harm to others represents a rejection of the legal order', and that 'people who display an attitude of hostility toward the norms of the system show themselves to be dangerous'.[44] The same tension can be identified in instances of accomplice liability, especially those arising from joint criminal enterprises. And even though sometimes a denial of capacity can imply an exclusion from criminal liability, when this lack of capacity nevertheless implies a semblance of dangerousness to the individual, such excuse from liability can nevertheless be coupled with restrictive consequences not unlike those resulting from punishment, such as in the 'defence' of insanity.[45]

Furthermore, the different patterns of responsibility attribution can also be understood as a reflection of the dynamics of criminal subjectivity, by means of an analogy between these dynamics and the interaction between trust

[44] G.P. Fletcher, *Basic Concepts of Criminal Law* (New York: Oxford University Press, 1998), 179–80, cited in N. Lacey, 'The Resurgence of Character: Responsibility in the Context of Criminalization' in R.A. Duff, S.P. Green (eds), *Philosophical Foundations of Criminal Law* (Oxford: Oxford University Press, 2011), 151–78, 163.

[45] Insanity is particularly interesting as an example of dangerousness since, although it denies capacity and therefore the possibility for criminal liability, it also clearly displays a concern with public safety and social control, as evidenced by the extended powers given by the special verdict. For a comprehensive critical analysis, See A. Loughnan, *Manifest Madness: Mental Incapacity in Criminal Law* (Oxford: Oxford University Press, 2012).

and reassurance. Under this perspective, capacity grounds individual trustworthiness, while character highlights the extent to which the criminal failed to adhere to standards of trust, thus failing to reassure others. Outcome and risk, by their turn, focus on securing the conditions for trust, by aiming at reducing harm and the risk of harm in society. This analogy also reveals an important insight through which the criminal law's pursuit of individual liberty and its role as an instrument of social order can be seen to be actually connected: the criminal law has a '*reassurance function*'[46] in society. This function works on two levels. First, the criminal law strives to prevent harm and social insecurity more broadly, so that the members of society can feel secure in the exercise of their autonomy and in their trust in others. Second, the reassurance function of the criminal law has a symbolic dimension, in that by labelling those who fail in their duty of reassurance as dangerous others, the criminal law also reassures those who are not criminalized of their status as responsible subjects, and of the normative position of responsible subjectivity in society. As Zygmunt Bauman and Tim May have suggested, 'The boundaries between "us" and "them" provide for the maintenance, via distinction, of identity.'[47] In other words, reassurance also possesses a socio-political dimension related to trust, in that the possibility for individuals to be trusted and to act in a trustworthy manner in society depends on the regulation, and often exclusion, of non-reassuring conducts and untrustworthy individuals from socio-political life.

THE LIBERAL IMAGINARY OF CRIMINAL LAW: CITIZENSHIP, CIVILIZATION, AND THE PROBLEM OF INSECURITY

The interdependence between trust and reassurance provides a useful prism through which the problems surrounding responsible subjectivity can be examined, as it reveals both the dynamic relationship between responsibility and dangerousness, as well as the extent to which this relationship is mediated by the environment of citizenship. It is this environment that determines the degree of trust that can be expected of individuals, as well as the amount and quality of reassurance that is necessary to preserve the conditions for trust in society. The notion that trust has limits and conditions problematizes

---

[46] B. Ackerman, 'The Emergency Constitution' (2004) 113 *Yale Law Journal*, 1029–91, 1037 (emphasis added).
[47] Z. Bauman, T. May, *Thinking Sociologically* (Oxford: Blackwell Publishing, 1990), 183.

the universalistic conception of individual liberty underpinning the liberal model of criminal law. At the same time, it can also offer the grounding for a more nuanced defence of that same model, by suggesting that it is possible to organize the criminal law around an expressivist conception of individual autonomy, provided that individuals are adequately reassured. This is why theorists emphasize that the ideal environment of criminal law is that of a liberal democracy: because it implies that these socio-political conditions enable an appropriate balance between trust and reassurance, so that even if there are tensions within criminal subjectivity, responsible subjectivity could—and should—still figure prominently as the normative position.

From this perspective, it is possible to engage with the argument that preventive criminal laws still uphold and respect a notion of individual autonomy, by arguing that the conception of autonomy which they espouse is not grounded on the correct balance between trust and reassurance. Peter Ramsay's work offers an analysis of how the rise of preventive measures and criminal offences is related to the emergence of what he calls the theory of vulnerable autonomy.[48] According to Ramsay, the rationale for preventive measures and criminal offences in England and Wales can be derived from a perspective on autonomy that gained particular prominence at the end of the twentieth century, through the influence of political theories such as Hayek's neo-liberalism or Giddens' Third Way.[49] The main premise of this perspective is the 'construction of normal, representative citizens as vulnerable in their mutual interdependence, and, therefore, required to be active in their attention to each other's need for reassurance'.[50] This view on autonomy can be seen to encourage welfare and mutual cooperation, as it promotes 'the idea that a commitment to social justice requires that society protect individuals with regard to their autonomy-related vulnerabilities'.[51] However, it also has an equal potential to foster distrust, as it suggests that, due to their vulnerability, individuals cannot afford to trust each other unless they are sufficiently reassured. The theory of vulnerable autonomy thus reinforces the reassurance function of criminal law, stressing the need for the state to regulate individual behaviour more actively and directly. In doing so, it arguably raises the bar of reassurance too high, so that criminal offences that are grounded on this perspective, such as pre-inchoate offences, seem to be justified solely on the

---

[48] See P. Ramsay, *The Insecurity State: Vulnerable Autonomy and the Right to Security in the Criminal Law* (Oxford: Oxford University Press, 2012).

[49] See ibid, chapter 5.   [50] Ibid, 84.

[51] J. Anderson, A. Honneth, 'Autonomy, Vulnerability, Recognition, and Justice' in J. Christman, J. Anderson (eds), *Autonomy and the Challenges to Liberalism: New Essays* (Cambridge: Cambridge University Press, 2005), 127–49, 138.

notion that the conduct covered by these offences 'fails to reassure others about the future conduct of the defendant'.[52] The focus on future conduct means that what is effectively at stake is the defendant's capacity to behave as a responsible subject, so that '[t]he conduct that these offences prohibit is not harmful or even dangerous acts, but *acts that constitute the dangerousness of the actor.*'[53] In other words, the normative core of preventive criminal offences is that they normalize the prevalence of dangerousness over responsibility within criminal subjectivity.

While this critique captures with precision what seems to be problematic about the effect of the preventive turn upon the liberal notion of autonomy, it also conceptualizes the preventive paradigm in a way that is coherent with the environment of citizenship, in which autonomy is presented as conditioned by bonds of interdependence maintained within a specific socio-political community. Indeed, as discussed in the previous chapter, an anticipatory perspective on criminalization can be rationalized as a response to a failure of the liberal model to preserve the necessary environment for democratic citizenship. This is evidenced by the political theories that espouse the vulnerable conception of autonomy, which share a criticism of the unconditional distribution of rights which was advocated under the welfare state during the mid-twentieth century, and propose that this distribution should be replaced by a notion of active citizenship[54] that conditions rights upon the due exercise of responsibilities. In his historical analysis of these developments, Ramsay argues that the theory of vulnerable autonomy was directly influenced by changes in socio-political conditions, most significantly the unravelling of the welfare state and the social rights which it guaranteed. Political and economic crises led to a period of a heightened sense of insecurity, and this in turn led to the need for ideas of individuality and autonomy to be reimagined in order to preserve their value within that context. Under this perspective, the shift from a strong conception of autonomy to a notion that establishes its vulnerability can be understood as an 'axiomatic proposition' that has become dominant in political discourse and public policy precisely because it 'offers a normative basis for the duties of citizenship in circumstances in which others have failed'.[55] The link between autonomy and citizenship thus alludes to the existence of a structural level underpinning the shifts in criminal subjectivity,

---

[52] Ramsay, 'Democratic Limits to Preventive Criminal Law', 216.

[53] Ibid (emphasis added).

[54] See N. Rose, *Powers of Freedom: Reframing Political Thought* (Cambridge: Cambridge University Press, 1999), 166.

[55] Ramsay, *The Insecurity State*, 112.

one which is shaped by the forms in which the socio-political community is imagined and organized, and the ways in which these forms change and transform over time.

David Garland has long submitted that changes in the field of crime control cannot be dissociated from their social and cultural context.[56] The transformations occurring in the criminal law should thus be seen as intimately associated with socio-political developments, which in turn lead to 'shifts in the cultural underpinning' of criminal justice institutions.[57] Under this perspective, it is fair to assume that the patterns of liability expressed through preventive criminal offences 'suggest the possibility that, behind these new responses to crime, there lies a new pattern of mentalities, interests, and sensibilities' which reflect shifts in 'the social, economic and cultural arrangements of late modernity'.[58] In this sense, the predominance of dangerousness in the framework of criminal subjectivity of the preventive turn can be partly explained by the socio-political conditions of post-industrial,[59] advanced liberal societies, in which a heightened concern about risk and uncertainty, together with pervasive feelings of ontological insecurity[60] and anxiety, prompts the state to seek to 'protect our subjective feelings of security more directly'.[61] The result is the deployment of a 'precautionary logic'[62] which 'has significant and worrisome implications for the criminal law'.[63] However, while part of this explanation is linked to the specific circumstances of the last few decades, the other part relies on the notion that the normative basis for preventive criminal offences is essentially an attempt to justify a pre-existing normative framework under different structural and cultural conditions. In other words, the preventive turn does not represent a completely new paradigm for the justification of certain criminal offences, but rather symbolizes a different interpretation of normative concepts that are part of the liberal framework of criminal law, in order to legitimize them under the present context.

There are significant insights that can be taken out of this realization. The first is that there are elements of the normative framework of the liberal model that persist within that of the preventive turn, and which indeed serve as the basis for the latter's normative justification. Second, the specific form

---

[56] D. Garland, *The Culture of Control: Crime and Social Order in Contemporary Society* (Oxford: Oxford University Press, 2002). See also D. Garland, *Punishment and Welfare: A History of Penal Strategies* (Aldershot: Gower, 1985).

[57] Garland, *The Culture of Control*, 6.   [58] Ibid, 6–7.

[59] See Z. Bauman, *Modernity and Ambivalence* (Cambridge: Polity Press, 1991).

[60] See A. Giddens, *Modernity and Self-Identity: Self and Society in the Late Modern Age* (Cambridge: Polity Press, 1991).

[61] Ramsay, *The Insecurity State*, 2.

[62] R. Ericson, *Crime in an Insecure World* (Cambridge: Polity Press, 2007), 21.

[63] Ibid, 35.

or configuration that these elements take in each model is a result of the interaction between a specific normative framework and the socio-political conditions in which it has to be actualized; the welfare state and the post-war period in the case of the liberal model, and the advanced or neo-liberal moment in the case of the preventive turn.[64] Third, if the previous assumptions are correct, then the normative position of autonomy and trust put forward by the liberal model is itself intrinsically vulnerable, since it seems that it can only be sustained as long as specific conditions are in place.

Although not explicitly recognized, the liberal conception of autonomy has an aspect of vulnerability. As previously mentioned, the liberal model does allow special cases to undermine the presumption of trust, under the justification that individual autonomy sometimes has to accommodate the needs of welfare.[65] However, because the duty of assurance is only seen to exceptionally displace the burden of trust in the liberal model, the vulnerability of autonomy is also presented as something exceptional, and not normalized as it appears in preventive criminal offences. But if the liberal model depends on structural conditions, it becomes clear that it is these conditions, and not the notion of autonomy in itself, that determine whether or not this vulnerable aspect of autonomy is exceptional or prominent, and the precise degree of reassurance required by civil trust becomes a matter of socio-political contingency. In neglecting this dynamism, the liberal model may be seemingly promoting the idea that autonomy should never be too vulnerable to social insecurity, and that reassurance should only be prioritized in those few instances involving a particularly dangerous crime or individual. However, if the liberal model is reliant on the environment of democratic citizenship, by upholding a static relation between trust and reassurance and by individualizing vulnerability, liberal criminal law may actually be enhancing the vulnerability of autonomy instead of restricting it, and opening itself up to challenge once the structural conditions grounding its assumptions are found to be faltering or lacking.

The problems surrounding the liberal model of criminal law can be examined by contextualizing them within what Charles Taylor called a social imaginary.[66] The notion of a social imaginary is a way of thinking about society which identifies its underlying normative framework as fluid and dynamic, thus being more aware of the malleability of social images and expectations than more fixed theoretical explanations. In thinking of a social imaginary, says Taylor, 'I am thinking, rather, of the ways people imagine their social

---

[64] See Ramsay, 'The Responsible Subject as Citizen'; A. Norrie, 'Citizenship, Authoritarianism and the Changing Shape of the Criminal Law' in B. McSherry, A. Norrie, S. Bronitt (eds), *Regulating Deviance* (Portland: Hart, 2009).
[65] See Chapter 1.   [66] See Taylor, *Modern Social Imaginaries*.

existence, how they fit together with others, how things go on between them and their fellows, the expectations that are normally met, and the deeper normative notions and images that underlie these expectations.'[67] At the core of these underlying normative notions and images lies a 'moral order' which provides social practices and institutions that adhere to it with 'a widely shared sense of legitimacy'.[68] One of the particular aspects of a modern social imaginary is that this sense of legitimacy is predicated on a mainly instrumental idea of social order, which is deemed legitimate to the extent that it can conform to the moral order and actualize its normative expectations.[69] Taylor traces the conceptual foundations of the moral order arising in modernity to notions elaborated in the work of seventeenth-century political philosophers such as John Locke, which laid down a basic structure that, albeit suffering many redactions over time, has retained a stable normative core, constituted by what he calls 'an ethic of freedom and mutual benefit'.[70] Within the modern social imagination, these two notions—freedom and mutual benefit—are largely inseparable, even if their balance can be configured in different ways.

Within a liberal imaginary, for instance, just as in the case of the relation between autonomy and welfare, freedom presents itself as the higher principle, but mutual benefit appears as a necessary condition for freedom, so that individual freedom has to be adequately organized and distributed through a particular set of political arrangements if the liberal social order is to retain its sense of legitimacy. In order to guarantee the enjoyment of freedom by all citizens, the state is thus entrusted with the provision of 'certain common benefits [to its citizens], of which security is the most important'[71]—security both from outside threats and from one another.[72] Security guarantees the exercise of freedom in the same way as reassurance is a requirement for trust, by contributing 'to certainty: freedom from doubt, fear, and anxiety about danger'.[73] What is particular about the liberal model of society, however, is that at the same time as mutual benefit is considered a necessary condition for individual freedom, freedom in itself is also taken to have the potential to generate mutual benefit. In other words, the liberal imaginary suggests that the self-interest of an individual, if pursued responsibly, can generate social outcomes and thus benefit the interests of others.[74] It is based on this premise that the need for security in liberal societies is traditionally understood to

---

[67] Ibid, 23.   [68] Ibid.

[69] See also C. Wright Mills, *The Sociological Imagination* (New York: Oxford University Press, 1959).

[70] Taylor, *Modern Social Imaginaries*, 21.   [71] Ibid, 4.

[72] I. Loader, N. Walker, *Civilizing Security* (Cambridge: Cambridge University Press, 2007), 42–3.

[73] Ericson, *Crime in an Insecure World*, 216.

[74] The conceptual foundations of this idea are discussed in detail in Chapter 4.

be limited, and that institutionalized practices of coercion like the criminal law are seen to be justified only to the extent that they respect individual freedom, invading the individual sphere only so far as it is strictly necessary.[75] The idea that individual freedom, when allowed to flourish, is conducive to mutual benefit gains particular momentum under circumstances of socio-economic prosperity and integration, in which the liberal conception of freedom acquires 'an inescapably "social form" '[76] that ameliorates liberal society's reliance on the provision of security by the state. It is on this specific normative and structural arrangement, linked to the notion of democratic citizenship, that the liberal model of criminal law and its burden of trust appear to be predicated.

What is often neglected in the liberal imaginary, however, is that the same freedom that potentially leads to mutual benefit still remains the greatest threat to it. From the moment individual freedom was established as the cornerstone of society in modernity, it possessed an inherent ambivalence: if harnessed, individual freedom can be the engine of progress; if left unattended, on the other hand, it can lead to violence and war. This ambivalence is as much a facet of modern social and political thought as the other aspects of the moral order enunciated by Taylor, and its conceptual foundations can also be traced back to seventeenth-century political philosophy, in the work of John Locke and, mainly, that of Thomas Hobbes.[77] So at the same time as individual freedom can generate mutual benefit, it still necessitates a specific condition of cooperation in order for it to be properly exercised. Freedom, it seems, needs to be directed towards mutual benefit, otherwise it becomes a source of uncertainty, and the main cause of social and political insecurity. The idea of crime is perhaps the primary symbolic expression of this insecurity.[78]

Just as with the reciprocity between autonomy and welfare and that between trust and reassurance, therefore, there is also an essential tension between the two main tenets of the modern moral order, which is not only preserved but actually exacerbated by the liberal imaginary's emphasis on individual freedom. For, if freedom is the main value to be promoted, but it is also the main source of insecurity, then the promotion of individual freedom has to be highly and constantly regulated, lest it undermines mutual benefit. Thus while a central tenet of liberal society requires it to make sure that individual freedom is protected from any undue interference from the

---

[75] See Rose, *Powers of Freedom*, 10.   [76] Ibid, 83.
[77] The conceptual foundations of this ambivalence in modern political thought are analysed in detail throughout Chapters 3, 4, and 5.
[78] See Ericson, *Crime in an Insecure World*.

state, this protection intrinsically entails that the state 'must curtail freedom through security measures in order to promote conditions in which freedom can flourish'.[79] It is for this reason that the primary social function of the ethics of freedom and mutual benefit enunciated by Taylor is to follow and maintain a specific notion of *order*. In his most recent book, Farmer suggests that the main function of the criminal law should be understood precisely as that of securing a specific form of social order, which he calls civil order.[80] The particular quality of civil order is that it is intrinsically linked with the project of modernity and its civilizing process.[81] Civilization, by its turn, has to be understood as possessing both a normative and a sociological dimension. Although it is often used in a normative sense, to mean a standard of progress and of living that societies should attain or sustain, which is often contrasted with the status of non-civilized or 'barbaric' societies, the idea of 'being civilized' in reality has a very specific history and development, linked to the history of Europe and the values that evolved around the notion of modernity.[82] 'Civilization' should thus be understood as 'a particular configuration of selfhood, violence, and law' produced by 'the modernizing process'.[83] The image of order that comes out of this process, by its turn, is committed to preserving and reproducing this particular configuration, a function to which the institution of the criminal law appears to be dedicated.

Just like the social order resulting from a particular social imaginary, the idea of civil order is also fluid; as Farmer indicates, 'there is no single or simple concept of civil order which it is the aim of the criminal law to secure or produce'.[84] Rather, civil order is the result of the interaction between ideas of selfhood and social and political organization, and the cultural, historical, and structural context in which these ideas have to be actualized. The dynamic character of civil order means that it is a product of the civilizing process at the same time as it seeks to produce it. Likewise, the civilizing process should not be understood as leading to an inevitable or linear progress, but rather as fragile and contingent. While the idea of civilization is usually deployed to imply a specifically developed degree of trust, social interdependence, and self-control in a particular society, as relatively stable outcomes of the civilizing process, the reality is that developments in these characteristics can always find themselves interrupted or even reversed under specific circumstances.

---

[79] Ibid, 217.

[80] Farmer, *Making the Modern Criminal Law*.

[81] See N. Elias, *The Civilizing Process* (Oxford: Blackwell, 1994).

[82] See J. Pratt, 'Norbert Elias, the Civilizing Process, and Punishment' (2016) *Oxford Handbooks Online*, 1–28.

[83] Farmer, *Making the Modern Criminal Law*, 55.   [84] Ibid, 63.

For instance, the current increase in distrust and insecurity, and the predominance of social control over self-control exacerbated by recent transformations in the framework of criminal law, might suggest such a moment of reversal in English society. However, these 'decivilizing' moments, rather than being considered 'interruptions' as Elias first supposed,[85] are perhaps best understood as inherent facets of the civilizing process itself. As John Pratt has argued, the 'deep structural embeddedness' of the civilizing process in modern societies means that we cannot simply assume that this process is only linked to the so-called positive outcomes which it is supposed to produce, and that we are instead 'likely to find civilizing and decivilizing forces both competing with and simultaneously shaping and reshaping each other'[86] within its remit. In other words, the civilizing process is not an inexorable march towards specific outcomes in society, but rather an agonistic struggle between a specific social imaginary and the structural and cultural conditions in which it has to be actualized.

Some time ago, Freud stated that our ideas of civility conceal a 'conflict of ambivalence' born of the tension between creative and destructive tendencies within human sociability.[87] Similarly, we can conceive that what we call 'civilization' actually involves 'ambivalent power dynamics, which work to repress the negative forces it embodies in [favour] of a purely progressive perspective on social development'.[88] The pursuit of civil order is a direct manifestation of these power dynamics, of the effort to contain the ambivalence of the civilizing process and to preserve and develop what are deemed to be its positive outcomes. The reassurance function of the criminal law has a fundamental role to play in the maintenance of civil order. That is why Farmer argues that the aim of the criminal law in securing civil order is ultimately about securing trust, not only 'between individuals, but also the trust of individuals in the order of the law'.[89] However, in order to maintain this trust in a social environment where 'the "individual in society" is seen as the source of order',[90] the insecurity that is inherent to individual freedom must be adequately regulated and curtailed.

One way to do that, which is closely aligned with the notion of responsible subjectivity, is to posit that individual autonomy is to a large extent independent from its context, so that the high degree of trust and self-control

---

[85] Elias, *The Civilizing Process*, 14.
[86] Pratt, 'Norbert Elias, the Civilizing Process, and Punishment', 6.
[87] S. Freud, *Civilization and its Discontents* (Mansfield: Martino Publishing, 2010), 121.
[88] H. Carvalho, A. Chamberlen, 'Punishment, Justice, and Emotions' (2016) *Oxford Handbooks Online*, 1–31, 16.
[89] Farmer, *Making the Modern Criminal Law*, 301.   [90] Ibid, 58.

presupposed by the notion of civilization is not seen to be contingent upon structural conditions. This individualized notion of autonomy and responsibility produces an essentialist notion of civilization, in which the degree of individualization achieved by the civilizing process is presented as a permanent outcome of civilized societies. Under this perspective, civilized individuals are responsible subjects, and if an individual is found not to adhere to this conception of subjectivity, this is a strong indication that the individual in question is not actually civilized. This notion of individuality, which Elias calls the 'we-less I',[91] effectively promotes a 'divorce of the individual from her history'[92] by masking social conditions and interdependencies. But if we are to fully examine the perplexities surrounding criminal law after the preventive turn, we need to deconstruct the essentialism within the liberal model and its conception of responsible subjectivity, and to engage with their boundaries and limitations.

THE BOUNDARIES OF RESPONSIBLE SUBJECTIVITY: BETWEEN INSECURITY AND REASSURANCE

It seems that the main outcome of the intense vulnerability of autonomy in the preventive turn is that it inverts the relation between trust and assurance predicated by the liberal model: instead of assuming that we can trust each other unless an exceptional situation leads to a lack of assurance, preventive criminal offences maintain that we cannot trust others unless we are sufficiently (re)assured. However, the embeddedness of the liberal model of criminal law within the specific socio-historical context of liberal modernity means that the normative values and aspirations promoted by this model are inevitably conditioned by structural transformations and limitations within this context. As a consequence, the trustworthiness of individual autonomy under the liberal model is also inherently vulnerable, since the burden of trust is grounded not on a natural robustness or resistance on the part of autonomy, but on the assumption that specific structural conditions are in place, which are necessary to sufficiently assure autonomy of its security. As such, this burden can only be maintained within the framework of criminal law under particular circumstances; when these circumstances are not in place or are undergoing changes or moments of crisis, the very logic of the

---

[91] N. Elias, *The Society of Individuals* (New York: Continuum, 1991), 201.
[92] U. Beck, *Risk Society: Towards a New Modernity* (London: Sage, 1992), 135.

liberal model requires autonomy to be reassured in a more direct, preventive manner.

It thus needs to be recognized that what the liberal model poses as a relatively stable socio-political environment, the environment of liberal democratic societies, is in reality mostly an idealization of specific socio-political and historical conditions, which are then universalized and abstracted from their own contingency by the liberal social order. This process of abstraction, in which the subject of law is essentialized[93] as a responsible subject, and in which difference and dangerousness are made exceptional, is an attempt to deal with and contain the inherent ambivalence of the liberal notion of individual autonomy and freedom. Ambivalence, according to Bauman, is 'the possibility of assigning an object or an event to more than one category'.[94] Ambivalence is the main enemy of any process of classification; to classify, according to Bauman, 'means to set apart, to segregate' in order 'to give the world a *structure* ... to sustain the order and to deny or suppress ... contingency'.[95] Ambivalence upsets this process of classification by generating disorder. The main problem, however, is that any effort to classify is inherently artificial, so that the more one tries to classify something, to give it a distinct identity, the more ambivalent this classification is likely to become. Ambivalence is thus essentially a 'side-product of the labour of classification', so that the more we try to suppress ambivalence, the more we classify; and the more we classify, the more we 'give yet more occasion for ambiguity'.[96] For Bauman, therefore, the 'struggle against ambivalence is ... both self-destructive and self-propelling. It goes on with unabating strength because it creates its own problems in the course of resolving them.'[97] This discussion on the limitations of the attempts to produce order by repressing ambivalence appropriately reflect both the tensions and limitations found in the liberal model and the currently inexorable march of prevention, arguably because they are both manifestations of the same issues within the modernizing, civilizing process.

In this regard, there is one important aspect of the socio-economic structure of liberal societies which is particularly relevant for an understanding of the ambivalence within the liberal model: its structural violence.[98] The

---

[93] See S.L. Bartky, *Femininity and Domination: Studies in the Phenomenology of Oppression* (New York: Routledge, 1990); K. Woodward, *Identity and Difference* (Milton Keynes: Open University, 1997).

[94] Bauman, *Modernity and Ambivalence*, 1.   [95] Ibid (emphasis in original).

[96] Ibid, 3.   [97] Ibid.

[98] J. Habermas, 'Fundamentalism and Terror: a Dialogue with Jürgen Habermas' in G. Borradori (ed), *Philosophy in a Time of Terror* (Chicago: University of Chicago Press, 2003), 25–44, 35. See

genealogical origins of the notion of the free individual are deeply connected not only to Enlightenment ethics and philosophy, but also to the rise of capitalist society. The socio-political interests tied to this model of society depended on the certainty of legal and economic relations, on the management of risk, and on the protection of individual rights—particularly that of private property.[99] The free and autonomous individual not only reflects these interests and promotes the image of the rational legal system necessitated by the nascent liberal society, but does so 'through a language that is universal and general, and cast in terms of respect for the individual before it'.[100] But while this conception of human being emphasized individual autonomy and agency, it also obscured the fact that the society it legitimated also sustained significant levels of political and socio-economic inequality. 'There was a fundamental disparity between the economic and social substance of the emerging relations of production and their juridical and economic expression.'[101] As a result, the idea of the responsible legal subject embedded within the individual of liberal law is fundamentally a one-sided representation of real individuals and their concrete circumstances.

According to this perspective, the idea of legal subjectivity which arises from notions of free individuality and responsible agency can be conceptualized as abstract because, although grounded on actual values and institutions, it is unable to fully incorporate the breadth and complexity of the human condition. 'Juridical individualism', Alan Norrie argues, 'can be designated as ideology because it is inadequate to the reality of human life and obscures its true basis in fundamental social relations and individual characteristics of men and women.'[102] There is thus an inevitable rupture between juridical individualism and concrete individuality. This fission significantly compromises the claim to normative validity upheld by notions of individual autonomy and liberty within the criminal law, since they can only properly recognize and reflect a small portion of the many interests and needs existent in society. Furthermore, the gap between the formal conception of responsible legal subjectivity and juridical relations, and the limited mutual benefit which actually exists in society, inevitably feeds into feelings and conditions of insecurity and anxiety. Insecurity, by its turn, is always potentially disruptive to the very conception of autonomy which engenders it, as well as to

---

also J. Galtung, 'Violence, Peace, and Peace Research' (1969) 6(3) *Journal of Peace Research*, 167–91; P. Farmer, 'An Anthropology of Structural Violence' (2004) 45(3) *Current Anthropology*, 305–25.

[99] See C.B. MacPherson, *The Political Theory of Possessive Individualism: Hobbes to Locke* (Ontario: Oxford University Press, 2011).

[100] Norrie, *Crime, Reason and History*, 23.

[101] Ibid.   [102] Norrie, *Law, Ideology and Punishment*, 11.

the juridical relations which depend upon this conception, so that it has to be perennially protected, kept within boundaries in which it can properly operate.

These boundaries take the shape of a specific social imaginary that predicates images of civil order which manage normative expectations within a conflictive socio-political environment. The pervasiveness and normative predominance of legal subjectivity in liberal societies, coupled with the inherent insecurity of the legal subject, have given rise to socio-political settings which are endemically concerned with the issue of security. Indeed, according to Foucault, individual freedom has to be understood as 'both ideology and technique of government',[103] as its ideological formulation cannot be de-coupled from the socio-political framework and the forms of social control generated and maintained around it, on which it depends. The liberal model of society can thus be termed 'a society of security',[104] in the sense that it is a socio-political paradigm which, due to the need to maintain human agency within acceptable standards, relies extensively on the use of mechanisms of security. These mechanisms are deeply reliant on forms of classification, through which places, activities, and people are routinely assessed and declared safe and acceptable, risky, deviant, or dangerous. Classifying, furthermore, inherently 'consists in the acts of inclusion and exclusion'; entities can only be made into a class 'as far as other entities are excluded, left outside. Invariably, such operation of inclusion/exclusion is an act of violence perpetrated upon the world, and requires the support of a certain amount of coercion.'[105] Invariably, therefore, the effort to maintain an environment of trust in the exercise of freedom within a specific community, particularly one which preserves in its midst a high degree of structural violence, will involve the exclusion of those manifestations of individual freedom that do not conform to such expectations. Within these lines, the dangerousness within criminal subjectivity is not just the other side of responsibility in criminal law; it is also a *product* of individual responsibility[106] as a technique of civil order, the expression of a cultural form of dealing with ambiguity by turning it into anomaly.[107]

From this perspective, the main function of criminalization is the 'normalisation' of human behaviour,[108] reassuring individuals of the security of juridical relations. The legal system is one of the most powerful instruments

---

[103] Foucault, *Security, Territory, Population*, 48.   [104] Ibid, 11.

[105] Bauman, *Modernity and Ambivalence*, 2.

[106] See M. Lianos, M. Douglas, 'Dangerization and the End of Deviance: the Institutional Environment' in D. Garland, R. Sparks (eds), *Criminology and Social Theory* (New York: Oxford University Press, 2000), 103–26.

[107] See Douglas, *Purity and Danger*.   [108] Foucault, *Security, Territory, Population*, 7.

which the state possesses in order to convey the experience of security to its citizens.[109] Roger Cotterrell examines this function of the legal system through the notion of 'legal security', a normative notion 'based on the belief that power is being used in unseen ways to protect the citizen from unknown others ... who might pose threats through unpredictable or irresponsible action, and from ... authorities that might otherwise seem uncontrolled or unaccountable'.[110] This experience of legal security, an essential aspect of civil order, cannot be sustained within a liberal social imaginary without the expectation of responsible subjectivity promoted by the liberal model. Through its reassurance function, the criminal law reinforces the normative primacy of legal subjectivity, by communicating to the political community that responsible citizens are not criminals, that dangerous offenders are *different* from responsible citizens, and that the criminal law punishes and regulates in order to protect one and contain the other. Due to the abstract character of responsible subjectivity, and to the inherent structural violence of liberal societies, this exclusionary dimension of civil order appears as a necessary condition for the experience of legal security and trust.

CONCLUSION

Having both an inclusionary aspect and an exclusionary purpose, criminal subjectivity is Janus-faced, as this conception is required to advance an ideological conception of human nature and agency at the same time as it has to function as a violent and coercive instrument of order and social control. It is thus best conceptualized as being informed by two dynamically related conceptions. While responsibility represents the normative position for legally permitted agency, dangerousness is the concept underpinning the repressive dimension of the criminal law. Possessing a specifically exclusionary socio-political function, dangerousness as a normative notion defines the scope of human agency which cannot be allowed to be freely exercised in the political community, justifying the coercive power of the state on the grounds that the freedom which is at the core of criminal law must be secured. Dangerousness supplements responsibility as a means of managing and normalizing the socio-political environment of liberal society, necessitated by the abstract character of juridical individualism. Through this relation, the expressive aspect of legal subjectivity—the autonomous, law-abiding individual—is legitimately

---

[109] See Loader and Walker, *Civilizing Security*.
[110] R. Cotterrell, *Law's Community* (Oxford: Oxford University Press, 1995), 5.

contained within the boundaries of legally sanctioned behaviour—abridged by the values and institutions of the political community—which are then guarded by law's repressive apparatus. Dangerousness then symbolizes the scope of human agency which lies beyond these boundaries, and which must be excluded, repressed, and controlled.

Criminal subjectivity is thus conditioned by the interaction between these two normative ideas, so that the subject of criminal law is both held against the ideal of autonomous agency and always potentially dangerous to the conditions for mutual benefit in society. While the idea that some criminal offenders are dangerous and therefore in need of containment can in itself be a source of social insecurity and anxiety, the deployment of dangerousness *as a normative concept* by the criminal law fulfils a reassuring function. Dangerousness both destabilizes and reinforces the model of legal subjectivity. It effectively re-interprets an insecurity which is endemic to liberal society's socio-political structure into something which originates 'outside' of it, in individuals, ideas, and groups which are dangerous precisely because they have deviated from the standard of responsible agency, because they essentially do not belong to the project of liberal society. So although insecurity remains a threat to social cohesion, it is ideologically deployed as something which the liberal state has to manage and address, instead of something which it has itself generated and sustained.

However, the reassuring function of criminal law is a rather precarious solution to the ripples generated within liberal society by its endemic structural violence. The gap between the liberal model of responsible subjectivity and the complexities of actual social experience makes it nearly impossible to reconcile the legal forms which it inspires with the concrete environment in which they operate. And since it is inherent to the normative liberal framework of criminal law and punishment, the tension between responsibility and dangerousness is something that liberal law maintains without being able to resolve. Even when effectively repressed, this political conflict is always bound to resurface, so that the primacy of individual responsibility in the liberal model is intrinsically insecure, as the criminal law 'is primarily the child of its age and the state of civil society at the time'.[111] As a result, criminal responsibility both promotes and hinders individual freedom, being unable to either fully rationalize the law or implement its principles and promises. Instead, this tension becomes constitutive of the legal framework, both expressed and repressed by normative categories within the liberal legal order.

---

[111] G.W.F. Hegel, *Hegel's Philosophy of Right* (New York: Oxford University Press, 1967), 140.

3

Liberty, Insecurity, and
the Conceptual Foundations of Reassurance

To speak impartially, both sayings are very true:
that *man to man is a kind of God*;
and that *man to man is an arrant wolf*.[1]

The idea of individual freedom which informs notions of responsibility and subjectivity in the framework of criminal law not only does not exist independently of its context, but also actually represents one of the cornerstones of the conceptual history of modernity and its civilizing process. Indeed, modern notions of free individuality and rational agency cannot be separated from a reconceptualization of the state, theorized in legal and political thought out of the need to re-imagine political society and authority in a way that could break with the old traditions and hierarchies, and provide the necessary basis for the establishment of a new moral and social order. Even today, the autonomous individual of criminal law, albeit heavily influenced by the abstract universality of its Kantian origins,[2] can only be fully understood if examined in connection with its socio-political environment, and the images of community that arise from it. This is because, once this environment comes into the picture, the abstract idea of freedom needs to be shaped and conditioned in order to fit the context of its actualization. Kant himself, for instance, postulated that a civil state was a state founded on the principles of freedom, equality, and independence of each member of society—freedom to live according to one's own conception of happiness, equality of subjection to the civil law, and independence in terms of political participation as a citizen.[3] Even for Kant, therefore, individual freedom could not be actualized in society without being subjected to a specific legal order and tied to a specific

[1] T. Hobbes, *Man and Citizen* (Indianapolis: Hackett Publishing, 1991), 89 (emphasis in original).
[2] See A. Norrie, *Punishment, Responsibility and Justice* (Oxford: Oxford University Press, 2000).
[3] I. Kant, 'On the Common Saying: "This May Be True in Theory, But It Does Not Apply in Practice"' in I. Kant, *Political Writings* (Cambridge: Cambridge University Press, 1991), 61–92, 77.
The Preventive Turn in Criminal Law. First Edition. Henrique Carvalho. © Henrique Carvalho 2017. Published 2017 by Oxford University Press.

community through political participation in it. When we talk about freedom in society, therefore, we are talking about a specific, conditioned expression of this freedom, limited by authority and shaped by the socio-political environment in which the individual participates; that is, freedom in society is best understood through the conception of liberty. The development of the notion of liberty in modern political thought is particularly illuminating to an engagement with the ambivalence of individual autonomy and liberty in the contemporary framework of criminal law.

This chapter initiates the task of unearthing and examining the conceptual foundations of this ambivalence, looking at how, from its very inception in modern political thought, the idea of individual liberty had an intrinsic relation with insecurity, so that the moment the modern state is conceived with the free individual at its core, it is also inevitably charged with the task of restraining and regulating that very same freedom. For these purposes, I rely on the work of Thomas Hobbes as the starting point from which to examine the normative importance of individual liberty to modern political societies, as well as its relation to liberal legal systems.[4] As the first modern political theorist to advance a model of society based on the liberty and equality of individuals and on the importance of a formal system of civil laws enacted and enforced by political authority for the security of socio-political relations, Hobbes arguably laid down foundations that deeply influenced the long tradition of legal and political thought that followed it, including liberal theory. The value of an analysis of Hobbes's contributions lies precisely in the complexity of his thought and in the ambivalent attitude which Hobbes himself had towards the idea of individual liberty. The notably remarkable diversity of interpretations given to Hobbes's work is testament to this complexity: Hobbes has been considered anything from one of the founders of the liberal tradition to one of its greatest enemies, a staunch defender of absolutism and arbitrary rule. Hobbes's relation to the liberal tradition, together with the range of interpretations regarding the precise role which his work has with regards to it, suggests to me that his theory is particularly useful to examine the extent to and the manner in which both individual freedom and authoritarian government are connected to the conceptualization of the modern state, and to the contemporary challenges underpinning its penal system.

More specifically, my main argument in this chapter is that the current state of insecurity predicated by the preventive turn follows a Hobbesian

---

[4] See the references discussed throughout this chapter, and more generally D. Dyzenhaus, T. Poole (eds), *Hobbes and the Law* (Oxford: Oxford University Press, 2012).

logic, but that this logic does not necessarily break away from or compromise the liberal framework of individual responsibility and justice—at least not in the way that is commonly proposed in recent scholarship. Instead, I explore how an analysis of Hobbes's work indicates that the liberal promotion of individual justice and the neoliberal need for preventive and authoritarian measures both potentially stem from the same conception of individual liberty and autonomy. This problematic ambivalence in the individualism which lies at the core of liberal law is evident in Hobbes's work, so that, as Alice Ristroph indicated, 'Hobbes's account of criminal law and punishment offers broader lessons about the promise, and limits, of liberalism.'[5] In this chapter, I present an investigation of these lessons.

Hobbes's theoretical model reveals and magnifies the basic assumptions behind the criminal law's role as an instrument of social order, as well as the influence that this role exerts over the need in liberal society to preserve and justify punishment. His conceptualization of human nature as intrinsically insecure and in perennial need of reassurance; of political society as the only solution to this insecurity; and of political power as an indispensable condition for the establishment and preservation of society is deeply embedded within the role played by criminal law in the liberal civil order. This identification, in turn, sheds some light upon the model of society which lies at the core of the contemporary normative framework of criminal law. The way in which Hobbes connects all these elements with and through his account of punishment, highlighting its central place within political society, provides a unique theoretical model through which to examine the challenges posed by the preventive turn.

In the first part, I address the issue of insecurity in responsible legal subjectivity, by delineating and discussing the implications of a paradox contained in Hobbes's account of punishment. I look at how this paradox is a reflection of an intrinsic logic within Hobbes's political theory, which engenders a conceptual separation between the subjectivity of those who follow and respect the law, and that of those whose agency reaches beyond its boundaries. This fissure in the law's relation with its subjects compromises the justification for punishment in Hobbes's theory, but it paradoxically also constitutes the very reason punishment is seen as necessary in the first place, representing the main motivation behind the authority of the state in his model of society. I explore this model of society in the second part of the chapter, discussing the main elements in Hobbes's political theory. I examine Hobbes's conception of human nature and the way in which it grounds the passage from the state

---

[5] A. Ristroph, 'Criminal Law for Humans' in D. Dyzenhaus, T. Poole (eds), *Hobbes and the Law* (Oxford: Oxford University Press, 2012), 97–117, 98.

of nature to political society, in order to argue that the endemic insecurity found in the natural condition of mankind implies that the state of nature is never fully transcended, instead remaining at the core of Hobbes's political society and constituting the main basis for crime and the need for punishment, as well as the primacy of political authority over individual autonomy and liberty. In the third and final part, I discuss the influence that Hobbes's logic carries in contemporary criminal law, and how the paradox found in punishment is reflected in the contemporary ambivalence towards individual liberty displayed by the preventive turn. I conclude by stating that a critical examination of Hobbes's influence in modern and contemporary legal thought is an indispensable step towards an understanding of the current crisis of legitimacy in the law, as well as the possibility of moving beyond it.

THE PARADOX OF PUNISHMENT

If Hobbes's political conclusions are taken as a starting point, it is difficult to think of him as anything other than a defender of absolutism, let alone as one of the founders of liberalism[6] and 'originator of modernity'.[7] But Hobbes was more nuanced a theorist, and his postulates more thoughtful and influential, than his staunch defence of absolute authority would suggest. Indeed, Hobbes 'is often credited as inventing the very idea of the modern state',[8] understood as a political community concerned with upholding peace and security through law and grounded on the consent of its citizens. Furthermore, the notion that political authority is necessary for the maintenance of the principles and liberties of civil society is a corollary not only of modern societies in general, but also of liberal societies in particular.[9] The relation between Hobbes's political theory and the premises and institutions of the modern state is nowhere clearer than in his account of punishment and criminal law, an aspect of his work that has received surprisingly little attention over the years, in spite of its centrality to his political paradigm as a whole.

Hobbes thought very carefully about punishment and wrote extensively about the substantive content of the criminal law, even criticizing

---

[6] See J. Hampton, *Hobbes and the Social Contract Tradition* (Cambridge: Cambridge University Press, 1986); C.B. MacPherson, *The Political Theory of Possessive Individualism: Hobbes to Locke* (Ontario: Oxford University Press, 2011).

[7] L. Strauss, *What is Political Philosophy?* (Chicago: University of Chicago Press, 1959), 172.

[8] I. Loader, N. Walker, *Civilizing Security* (Cambridge: Cambridge University Press, 2007), 42.

[9] Ibid. See also M. Oakeshott, 'Introduction to Leviathan' in M. Oakeshott, *Hobbes on Civil Association* (Indianapolis: Liberty Fund, 1975), 1–79, 67: 'Indeed, Hobbes, without being himself a liberal, had in him more of the philosophy of liberalism than most of its professed defenders.'

jurisprudents of his time such as Edward Coke in his *Dialogue on the Common Laws of England*.[10] His account of the form and content of the criminal law advanced many principles and rules that remain at the core of criminal legal theory and doctrine to this day, from a prohibition on *ex post facto* laws and the need for proportionality between the seriousness of crime and the degree of punishment, to the need to uphold the principle of legality and for trial and conviction to precede punishment.[11] The modern quality of these aspects of Hobbes's conception of the role of punishment in society highlights the importance of examining the nuances in his thinking and their implications for the general outlook of his political theory. In light of this, 'the inattention to Hobbes's account of punishment is regrettable'.[12] It is particularly regrettable that so little attention is given to the fact that Hobbes's framework, 'both familiar and strange'[13] to modern criminal law theory, displays an unsettling ambivalence with regards to the justification for punishment. For Hobbes, punishment seems to be both necessary and problematic. The necessity of punishment is clear from the very purpose of the state, as individuals only agree to forego their natural liberty and subject themselves to the commonwealth and its law with 'the foresight ... of getting themselves out from that miserable condition of war, which is necessarily consequent ... to the natural passions of men, when there is no visible power to keep them in awe, and *tie them by fear of punishment to the performance of their covenants*, and observation of [the] laws of nature.'[14] The main function of punishment and criminalization in this perspective is therefore that it reassures the members of the community that everyone will either respect the boundaries set by the law or be punished for breaching them, since this reassurance is a fundamental condition of the commonwealth.

But, while it appears that the state depends on the proper enforcement of the law for its preservation, it is also clear that, for Hobbes, individuals must subject themselves to it voluntarily. Like most liberal theorists, Hobbes grounded the legitimacy of political authority on the consent of its subjects: individuals establish the commonwealth through a covenant in which they consent to lay down their right to self-government, effectively transferring it to the sovereign. However, the voluntary nature of this exchange

---

[10] T. Hobbes, *A Dialogue Between a Philosopher and a Student of the Common Laws of England* (Chicago: University of Chicago Press, 1972).

[11] See Ristroph, 'Criminal Law for Humans', 97–100; See also T. Hobbes, *Leviathan* (Oxford: Oxford University Press, 1996), 193–4.

[12] A. Ristroph, 'Respect and Resistance in Punishment Theory' (2009) 97 *California Law Review*, 601–32, 606.

[13] Ristroph, 'Criminal Law for Humans', 97.

[14] Hobbes, *Leviathan*, 111 (emphasis added).

generates a problem for punishment, as Hobbes postulates that an individual only consents to such transference of right

in consideration of some right reciprocally transferred to himself; or for some other good he hopeth for thereby. For it is a voluntary act: and of the voluntary acts of every man, the object is some good to himself. And therefore there be some rights, which no man can be understood by any words, or other signs, to have abandoned, or transferred. As first a man cannot lay down the right of resisting them, that assault him by force … . *The same may be said of wounds, and chains, and imprisonment* … . And lastly the motive, and end for which this renouncing, and transferring of right is introduced, is *nothing else but the security of a man's person*, in his life, and in the means of so preserving life, as not to be weary of it.[15]

Since security is the main reason individuals establish the state in the first place, they cannot possibly be expected to allow anyone, much less the sovereign, to do anything that could put their own lives and security at risk. For Hobbes, 'no man is supposed bound by covenant, not to resist violence; and consequently it cannot be intended, that he gave any right to another to lay violent hands upon his person'.[16] But if the right to punish inevitably involves the sovereign's right to 'lay violent hands' upon anyone who breaks the law, how could any of the subjects of the commonwealth possibly authorize it? There is an obvious tension between these two aspects of Hobbes's theory; remarkably, this is a tension of which Hobbes himself was keenly aware. He highlights its existence right after the definition of punishment in *Leviathan*, when he states that 'there is a question to be answered, of much importance; which is, by what door the right, or authority of punishing in any case, came in'.[17] His answer is as perplexing as it is illuminating:

It is manifest therefore that the right which the commonwealth … hath to punish, is *not grounded on any concession, or gift of the subjects*. But I have also showed formerly, that before the institution of commonwealth, every man had a right to every thing, and to do whatsoever he thought necessary to his own preservation; subduing, hurting, or killing any man in order thereunto. And this is the foundation of that right of punishing, which is exercised in every commonwealth. For the subjects did not give the sovereign that right; but only in laying down theirs, strengthened him to use his own, as he should think fit, for the preservation of them all: so that it was not given, but left to him, and to him only; and (excepting the limits set him by natural law) as entire, as in the condition of mere nature, and of war of every one against his neighbour.[18]

---

[15] Ibid, 88–9 (emphasis added).   [16] Ibid, 205.   [17] Ibid.
[18] Ibid, 205–6 (emphasis added).

What is most perplexing about Hobbes's solution to the problem of punishment is his admission that the right to punish is not directly authorized by the members of the commonwealth. Indeed, such is the apparent incompatibility between punishment and individual self-interest for Hobbes that, in his model, individuals always retain the right to resist punishment. So although the sovereign's power to punish is indirectly grounded on the consent of the citizens, this power in itself is not an ordinary part of the social contract—even though it is one of the necessary conditions for its possibility. Punishment is both indispensable for the integrity of political society and an act of violence upon the individual who is punished, 'an evil inflicted by public authority' in response to 'a transgression of the law; to the end that the will of men may thereby the better be disposed to obedience'.[19]

There thus appears to be an intrinsic self-contradiction in Hobbes's account of punishment, a paradox that threatens to undermine the legitimacy of the institution and even the very reason the commonwealth is established, for 'while the Sovereign is supposed to protect men from the state of nature, the Sovereign's primary tool for achieving this is itself a weapon of war and a logical conduit back into the natural state'.[20] Hobbes's perplexing honesty about the place of punishment in his theory reveals that the power to punish is not entirely in harmony with the principles of political society, being rather reminiscent of the violence of the state of nature, from which individuals sought to escape in the first place. This is rather 'surprising in its implication that punishment, while necessary, is at best imperfectly legitimate',[21] and raises the possibility that, ultimately, 'the institution of the Commonwealth is a self-defeating proposition'.[22] Both Norrie and Ristroph have deployed this internal tension in Hobbes's account of punishment as a potential challenge to the role of criminal law in contemporary society, seeing it as a manifestation of a conflict between the respect for individual autonomy and the need for political authority which lies at the heart of the socio-political landscape of modernity, and that threatens to compromise the legitimacy of the criminal law. But, if this paradox only hinders the effectiveness of punishment, it would be difficult to explain why Hobbes identified a gap in his theory and still decided not only to preserve it, but also to emphasize it. There must be something more to Hobbes's normative framework that can clarify how punishment can remain so important in spite of being so problematic. A possible

---

[19] Ibid, 205.
[20] A. Norrie, 'Thomas Hobbes and the Philosophy of Punishment' (1984) 3 *Law and Philosophy*, 299–320, 308.
[21] Ristroph, 'Criminal Law for Humans', 98.
[22] Norrie, 'Thomas Hobbes and the Philosophy of Punishment', 307.

answer can be found in an analysis of the specific dynamics operating within the relationship between the state and its subjects—especially those subjects who disobey the law.

The Nature of the Criminal

The treatment of the criminal in Hobbes's theoretical framework raises interesting reflections for the perplexities found in the contemporary framework of criminal law and criminalization. For Ristroph, the main critical potential within Hobbes's account of punishment lies in the notion that not only do individuals not authorize the sovereign's power to punish, but they are also entitled to actively resist it. 'If the state has legitimate authority to punish, how can the subject have a right to resist?'[23] Although it can be deemed little more than a 'blameless liberty' which does not incur any obligation on the state to respect it, the right to resist punishment, 'even if unenforceable, ... seems to undermine any account of the justification for punishment'.[24] Ristroph uses the disruptive potential within the right of resistance in Hobbes's theory to suggest that, if taken seriously, it may indicate 'that punishment cannot be fully reconciled with the criteria for political legitimacy set forth in modern liberal theory. Instead, punishment creates a dilemma for liberals: physically coercive punishments may be socially necessary, but they are also acts of violence, persistent traces of the rule of the stronger in a system otherwise committed to rule by consent'.[25] Awareness of this problem, by its turn, should according to her encourage us to be more cautious with regards to punishment, and to strive to treat criminals with more respect.

Ristroph's account of the right to resist punishment and its implications for the legitimacy of the criminal law is compelling. However, although this aspect of Hobbes's theory does suggest that the justification for punishment in liberal society might be problematic, it did not pose a problem for punishment being one of the most important elements of Hobbes's model of political society, in spite of its liberal aspects. The reason for this is arguably that this conflict between the right to punish and the right to resist, at the same time as it creates difficulties for a normative justification for punishment, engenders a strong *motivation* for the state to punish. Ristroph's work is very helpful in examining how this other dimension of the paradox of punishment operates.

According to Hobbes's solution to the question of punishment, the sovereign's right to punish is akin to the right of nature, the right to self-government

---

[23] Ristroph, 'Respect and Resistance', 603.   [24] Ibid.   [25] Ibid, 604.

that every individual possesses before the establishment of the common-wealth, based on the essential right to self-preservation. As discussed below, the main reason the state of nature is rife with insecurity is that the self-interests of individuals are constantly clashing, and the absence of common judgment entitles individuals to pursue their own self-interest to the ultimate consequences, generating endemic potential conflict. In order to stop this cycle of violence, individuals relinquish their right to self-government for the state to exercise in the name of all: 'an individual's right to do violence as he judges necessary for his own security becomes, in political society, the sover-eign's right to punish'.²⁶ Punishment is thus analogous to the natural liberty an individual possesses to use one's judgment according to the requirements of one's preservation, which necessarily includes 'the natural right to use vio-lence pre-emptively, even against someone who does not pose an imminent threat'.²⁷ The need to care for one's own security therefore implies the right to use violence for purposes other than direct self-defence, and the criminal law can be seen as an exercise of this right in the name of the commonwealth. From this perspective, the right to punish is not something reciprocal, given to the sovereign by individuals' subjection to its authority, but a consequence of the need to protect the commonwealth and its members against crime. It is the potential dangerousness of crime, not the exchange of rights and duties in the social contract, which grounds the right to punish. Punishment is thus not within the political covenant, but rather a condition for its establishment and maintenance, and 'a manifestation of the *sovereign's* [as representative of the commonwealth] right to self-preservation'.²⁸ It is interesting to note that, even if not directly authorized by the citizens of the commonwealth, punish-ment is still grounded on individual liberty, that is, on the need to secure the conditions for its exercise and preservation.

This analogy between the sovereign's right to punish and an individual's natural right to self-preservation may seem controversial, particularly since the sovereign as an entity only exists after the establishment of the common-wealth, so that it would in theory not possess any right of nature to begin with. Ristroph tries to 'alleviate this tension' by proposing that the state of nature should not be understood as a reference to some pre-political historical moment, but rather as a 'term of art' referring to 'the always-possible situation in which political authority is absent'.²⁹ In these terms, the condition of the state of nature can always be recreated under particular circumstances, so that punishment would occur in what she calls 'a recurrent, specific state of nature,

²⁶ Ristroph, 'Criminal Law for Humans', 110.   ²⁷ Ibid.
²⁸ Ristroph, 'Respect and Resistance', 613.
²⁹ Ristroph, 'Criminal Law for Humans', 112.

not an original or universal one'.[30] In this specific state of nature, the unity of
political society is absent, and sovereign and criminal face each other as two
natural subjects, both aiming towards their own self-preservation. Ristroph
highlights that, from this perspective, it becomes clear that punishment does
not appear to the criminal as the expression of an authorized, legitimate political authority, but rather as 'a violent threat to safety and freedom',[31] itself not
very different from the crime against which it poses itself as a response.

From this perspective, it would be possible to conclude that 'the criminal has as much right to resist punishment as the sovereign has to impose
it',[32] and thus make it harder for us to 'pretend that we punish prisoners for
their benefit rather than our own'.[33] But the violent character of punishment
is not the only thing that Ristroph's interpretation elucidates. For, within
this framework, although punishment operates in a specific state of nature
where everyone involved has an equal claim to self-preservation, it is also evident that it was the crime, not the punishment, which gave rise to this state.
Punishment is thus presented as a *reaction* to a specific state of nature—a
rupture in the peace and security of political society—generated by crime or
the risk of crime. Hobbes's peculiar characterization of the right to punish
as a manifestation of the state's right to self-preservation invests punishment
with a normative dimension which appears to legitimate it, even if imperfectly. The fact that individuals do not authorize the sovereign to punish them
does not eliminate or weaken the notion that those who commit crimes are
breaching the terms of the social contract and may thus be endangering the
community tied to it. The idea that crime occurs in political society, and that
it potentially threatens this society's existence, seems to provide punishment
with all the legitimation it needs.

Hobbes's acknowledgement of the right of resistance does not appear to
diminish the motivation to punish either, for when compared to the importance he attributes to punishment, without which 'there can be no security',[34]
a blameless liberty to resist gives individuals little cause for consolation. This
is because the notion that punishment occurs in a specific state of nature
emphasizes that a crime can set the criminal apart from the political community of the state, and effectively against it. Hobbes's logic appears to indicate
that crimes, up to the extent of their wrongfulness and harmfulness, have the
capacity to distance individuals from society and present them as dangerous
others. In this sense, at the same time as the right to resist reveals the violent nature of punishment, it also emphasizes how the criminal's liberty and

---

[30] Ibid.   [31] Ristroph, 'Respect and Resistance', 619.
[32] Ristroph, 'Criminal Law for Humans', 112–13.
[33] Ristroph, 'Respect and Resistance', 621.   [34] Hobbes, *Leviathan*, 87.

self-preservation, in the moment of punishment, finds itself at odds with that of the state, in conflict with it. Most importantly, by portraying the right to punish as analogous to the right of liberty, which is itself based on the right to self-preservation, Hobbes invests punishment with the same aura of blame-lessness ascribed to natural liberty, justifying punishment on the basis of the self-preservation of the commonwealth.

There are two important implications that this analysis of the right to pun-ish as something akin to the right of nature brings to the role of criminaliza-tion in society. The first is that the possibility that crime can give rise to a specific state of nature suggests that the reassurance provided by the state and its sovereign against the insecurity of human nature in Hobbes's work is neither permanent nor inviolable. Instead, crime represents for Hobbes the always-present possibility that the state of nature may creep back into the midst of political society. The second is that, as a result of the vulnerability of the security engendered by the social contract, there appear to be two quali-tatively different forms of interaction between individuals and the political authority in his society: one comprising the peaceful relation between citizens and the laws of the community, and another representing the violent conflict enacted through crime and punishment. Hobbes's account of punishment thereby exposes 'a fissure between the law itself and the remedies for its viola-tion'.[35] What this rupture mainly does with regards to the role of punishment in society, however, is not to compromise its legitimacy by raising questions as to its justification, but rather to reinforce the socio-political motivation for punishment in lieu of the difficulties in normatively justifying it. The real dilemma that Hobbes's political theory presents for liberals is therefore not that 'physically coercive punishments may be socially necessary, but they are also acts of violence';[36] instead, it is that even though punishment is pervaded with violence and clearly at odds with the aspirations of liberal society, it is still posed and maintained to be socially necessary. Likewise, the main prob-lematic arising from the paradox of punishment is not that it constitutes a challenge for the prominence of the penal power of the state in contemporary liberal societies, but rather that it constitutes one of its foundations.

Liberties in Tension: The Natural and the Legal Subject

At the core of Hobbes's political theory, there is the idea that human rela-tions are naturally fraught with insecurity. Without a common authority to

---

[35] Ristroph, 'Criminal Law for Humans', 115.
[36] Ristroph, 'Respect and Resistance', 604.

maintain the law and punish transgressions, it seems virtually impossible for individuals to trust each other.[37] Individual liberty is only appropriately secured with the establishment of a commonwealth, as the social contract unites the will of its participants around a common interest, which is then preserved by the sovereign. Within this framework, relations between human beings are fundamentally different in these two moments: individuals in the state of nature pose a continuous threat to each other and likewise see each other as a threat, while those in political society—since they partake in a common, public interest—display a peaceful and trustworthy exercise of liberty which is therefore protected and promoted by the state. While this contrast is presented by Hobbes and commonly understood to reflect a rather persistent shift in socio-political conditions, the passage from the state of nature to political society, the paradox of punishment indicates that political relations in society are not nearly as stable as it might have appeared at first sight. This is mainly because these relations depend on certain normative expectations held with regards to the attitudes that individuals have towards each other. In the state of nature, individuals are expected to fully exercise their right to self-preservation regardless of the danger such exercise might pose to the liberty of others, while in political society, citizens are expected to accommodate their liberty to the limits established by the law, so that their autonomy poses no threat to others. Since it is precisely the juridical boundaries of liberty that are forsaken by the criminal's actions, under this logic, criminals effectively behave not as responsible subjects who belong to the political community, but as dangerous subjects who put themselves in a state of nature with (or rather against) the state—a threat that must be regulated by the criminal law and minimized by punishment.

The aforementioned fissure between the law and the remedies for its violation is therefore a reflection of a fissure in the law's representation of its subject, caused by a radical normative conceptualization of individuals' attitudes towards the law. It is this conceptual distinction between those who obey the law and those who break it, more than anything else, which allows Hobbes to explicitly preserve the apparent paradox in his theory of punishment. While Hobbes does not expect individuals to authorize the sovereign to punish them and even concedes that they have a right to resist punishment, he expects that those who will actually be punished are those who have placed themselves, through their crimes, outside of the social compact. Meanwhile, most members of the commonwealth are expected to see their liberty in harmony with

---

[37] For a comprehensive discussion of the role of diffidence, or distrust, in Hobbes's theory, see A. Ristroph, 'Hobbes on "Diffidence" and the Criminal Law' in M.D. Dubber (ed), *Foundational Texts in Modern Criminal Law* (Oxford: Oxford University Press, 2014), 23–38.

the public interest, so that Hobbes's citizen, although not actually *giving* the sovereign the right to punish, acknowledges the necessity and legitimacy of punishment to the point that the citizen 'obligeth himself [*sic*], to assist him that hath the sovereignty, in the punishing of another'.[38] This is because the law-abiding citizens of the commonwealth will see the sovereign's exercise of power as in league with their own self-interest.

The tension present in punishment's logic therefore possesses a dialectic aspect, engendered by two distinct and contradictory models of subjectivity, whose political nature conditions the relations between the individual, the community, and its law. It is this dialectic, first explored in modern thought by Hobbes's theory, that causes the 'impasse'[39] found in the justification for punishment, which is reflected in contemporary frameworks of criminal law. As previously discussed, the ideal of individual justice maintained by most accounts of criminal responsibility legitimates punishment on the grounds that it treats individuals as rational and autonomous beings who can recognize the normative character of the law and act accordingly.[40] This cognitive connection between acceptance of the norm and breaking of the norm is deemed essential in order to hold the individual responsible before the law. But the capacity to obey the law—which appears inherent to an individual in political society—is in stark contrast with the propensity for crime commonly associated with the image of the criminal—which is much closer to the image of an individual in the state of nature, Hobbes's natural subject. The notion that both kinds of subjectivity are inherent to the framework of criminal law compromises the very conceptual distinction that erects and justifies the authority of the sovereign and the power to punish, since they are grounded on the promise that the establishment of political society puts an end to the danger of the state of nature. In this sense, Norrie is right to infer that the normative validity of 'the conception of man as a free moral agent is only tenable so long as the naturalistic conception is "forgotten"'[41]—that is, so long as we accept that punishment can fulfil its purpose of tying individuals to the performance of their covenants.

However, as the paradox of punishment elucidates, at the same time as the natural subject is 'forgotten' when it comes to asserting the legitimacy of the criminal law, it remains an essential element of the logic of criminalization, resurfacing whenever the state responds to crime. Hobbes thus 'cannot

---

[38] Hobbes, *Leviathan*, 205.

[39] Norrie, 'Thomas Hobbes and the Philosophy of Punishment', 318.

[40] See A. Ashworth, J. Horder, *Principles of Criminal Law*, 7th ed. (Oxford: Oxford University Press, 2013), 23–6.

[41] Norrie, 'Thomas Hobbes and the Philosophy of Punishment', 319.

resolve the contradiction that exists between his juridical conception of man, which makes the contract a possibility and gives it its moral force, and his nat-uralistic conception of man which threatens to undermine the essential com-ponent of Sovereign power and right, punishment'.[42] By the same token, we cannot expect his right of resistance to rescue or protect the criminal from the necessity and importance that this logic concedes to punishment. But 'while Hobbes cannot solve this problem … , he can at least help us understand why the problem exists.'[43] Most importantly, Hobbes's theoretical framework can help us examine why the paradox of punishment persists, in a more repressed and pervasive way, in contemporary criminal law. For, while '[t]he juridical element at the heart of the Hobbesian theory of punishment is at war with what he understood to be the natural springs of human behaviour',[44] this war is not a mere reflection of a philosophical paradox, but a necessary implica-tion of the model of society in which this paradox is generated. What first appears as a logical problem is actually an enduring aspect of a specific notion of civil order used to engender a socio-political condition in which individual autonomy needs to be permanently managed and disciplined by the state's authority.

THE NATURAL CONDITION
OF INSECURITY

Before we can examine to what extent Hobbes's account of punishment reflects a persistent problem in contemporary criminal law, it is necessary to analyse it within the context of his broader political theory, and particularly in relation to this theory's most essential feature: its individualistic concep-tion of human nature and society. Hobbes's theory is particularly relevant to an examination of contemporary criminal law because the way in which he conceptualized political society, both as a *reflection* of human nature and as a *reaction* against it, is the key to understanding how insecurity is intrinsic to law's conceptualization of its subject, and is the main motivation behind the authority of the state and the force of law. In this section, I explore how, at the heart of Hobbes's political theory, there lies an individual who is quite autonomous when it comes to the determination of personal goals, but in dire need of reassurance when it comes to social relations. Individual liberty, at the same time as it is the motor of society, is also rife with insecurity.

---

[42] Ibid, 308.   [43] Ibid, 318.
[44] A. Norrie, *Law, Ideology and Punishment* (Dordrecht: Kluwer Academic Publishers, 1990), 37.

Hobbes's radical individualism is evident throughout his work—and nowhere clearer than in *Leviathan*, where the whole of political society is conceptualized in function of the individual, and described in individualistic terms: the commonwealth is an 'artificial man; though of greater stature and strength than the natural, for whose protection and defence it was intended'.[45] The state is for Hobbes an artificial construct, made with the specific purpose of protecting and securing its subjects, and created in their own image. Furthermore, Hobbes's 'resolutive-compositive'[46] method understands individuals as isolated entities with their own nature and purpose, and society as the direct result of their interaction. Individuals are the 'constitutive causes'[47] of society, in function of which it operates.

Aimed at understanding individuals as ends in themselves, this method 'regards individual human beings as conceptually prior not only to political society but also to all social interactions'.[48] Individuals are thus taken to autonomously generate their desires and interests, independently of social or historical causality. In Hobbes's framework, '[t]he fundamental characteristics of men are not products of their social existence …. Thus man is social because he is human, not human because he is social.'[49] These human beings are predominantly guided by self-interest, acting according to their own 'exclusively self-interested'[50] sense of pleasure or displeasure. They are also endowed with reason. However, reason for Hobbes does not act as a hindrance to desire; instead, rationality serves self-interest by allowing individuals to deliberate on the consequences of actions and circumstances and choose the best path to satisfy their desires. 'Rationality would therefore be regarded by [Hobbes] as having instrumental value.'[51] There is a certain aspect of 'inertness'[52] in reason, in that it steers action but is not in itself the source of action.

Hobbes's individuals are therefore complex, embodied[53] beings guided both by reason and by passions, with self-interest as their driving force. Paramount to every individual's self-interest is the desire for self-preservation, and it is

---

[45] Hobbes, *Leviathan*, 7.

[46] Hampton, *Hobbes and the Social Contract Tradition*, 7–8.   [47] Ibid, 6.

[48] Ibid.

[49] D. Gauthier, 'The Social Contract as Ideology' (1977) 6 *Philosophy and Public Affairs*, 130–64, 138.

[50] Hampton, *Hobbes and the Social Contract Tradition*, 24. See also D. Gauthier, 'Taming Leviathan' (1987) 16(3) *Philosophy & Public Affairs*, 280–98, 285.

[51] Hampton, ibid, 35.   [52] Ibid, 16.

[53] Ristroph, 'Hobbes on "Diffidence" and the Criminal Law', 27. For a comprehensive discussion of the importance of embodiment for an understanding of punishment, see A. Chamberlen, *Embodying Punishment: Emotions, Identities, and Lived Experiences in Women's Prisons* (Oxford: Oxford University Press, forthcoming).

this desire, along with the rationality steering its pursuit, that grounds the Hobbesian conception of individual autonomy. Individuals have the freedom to govern their own lives, and for Hobbes this constitutes both a fact and a norm: human beings are naturally free, and their natural freedom entitles them to pursue their own interests in any way they deem best. The highest expression of this autonomy is the right of nature, 'the liberty each man hath, to use his own power, as he will himself, for the preservation of his own nature; that is to say, of his own life; and consequently, of doing any thing, which in his own judgment, and reason, he shall conceive to be the aptest means thereunto'.[54] In a philosophically controversial move,[55] Hobbes derives from a naturalistic conception of individual freedom the normative right of human beings to exercise their autonomy guided only by their own judgment. For the first time in modern history, individual autonomy and liberty acquire an important socio-political dimension.

Furthermore, human beings are not only inherently free, but also inherently equal. This equality is first displayed as one of ability,[56] from which Hobbes infers also an 'equality of hope in the attaining of our ends'.[57] There undoubtedly is a strong emancipatory aspect in Hobbes's postulate of natural equality, in that whatever differences there might be between individuals, for him, they possess 'no *political* significance'.[58] The conjunction of natural liberty and equality constitutes the essence of Hobbes's state of nature, a state where all individuals have the right and the capacity to determine their own fate. It is in the 'natural condition of mankind'[59] where individual autonomy is most expressive; it is also, however, where it is most insecure. Human nature is the source of both liberty and insecurity, and the right of nature is the greatest expression of one as well as the other. Since individuals have the right to do anything they deem necessary in order to guarantee their self-preservation and to pursue their self-interest, any disagreement or conflict of interests proves problematic, as all of those involved have an equal right to whatever claim they advance. As a result, 'if any two men desire the same thing, which nevertheless they cannot both enjoy, they become enemies; and

---

[54] Hobbes, *Leviathan*, 86. It should be stressed that the right of nature is not a right in the sense that it entails a corresponding duty on the part of others, but more in the sense of a 'blameless liberty', which cannot be removed or sanctioned by others. See Ristroph, 'Respect and Resistance', 602–3.

[55] MacPherson, *The Political Theory of Possessive Individualism*, 13.

[56] '[T]he difference between man, and man, is not so considerable, as that one man can thereupon claim to himself any benefit, to which another may not pretend, as well as he' (Hobbes, *Leviathan*, 82).

[57] Ibid, 83.

[58] Hampton, *Hobbes and the Social Contract Tradition*, 25 (emphasis in original).

[59] Hobbes, *Leviathan*, 82.

in the way to their end ... endeavour to destroy, or subdue one another'.[60] Unhindered self-interest inevitably generates competition, and the awareness of this condition fosters diffidence, or distrust. Since individuals are naturally distrustful,[61] in the state of nature 'there is no way for any man to secure himself, so reasonable, as anticipation; that is, by force, of wiles, to master the persons of all men he can, so long, till he see no other power great enough to endanger him'.[62] Under these circumstances, the state of nature inevitably leads to violence and war.

'Conflict is endemic in Hobbes's world',[63] and thus so is insecurity. This is a consequence of the 'self-destructive character of judgment'[64]—namely, as a result of Hobbes's radical individualism, the freedom possessed by individuals leads to an incapacity for them to trust each other's judgment, or to respect each other's liberty. Consequently, human beings 'have no pleasure, (but on the contrary a great deal of grief) in keeping company, where there is no power able to over-awe them all'[65]—that is, where there is no authority to reassure them. The natural liberty and equality of individuals imbue them with the right to govern their own lives, according to their own judgment; but 'where every man is his own judge, there properly is no judge at all'.[66] This trap contained in individual liberty is, ironically, a reflection of Hobbes's emancipatory project. His 'refusal to impose moral differences on men's wants' is the main reason behind the influence exerted by his work, the essence of 'his revolution in moral and political theory'.[67] The irony is that the same liberty that frees individuals from the constraints of tradition eventually shackles them to the power of the sovereign. While the state of nature may give human beings the freedom to make their own judgments, it affords them no reassurance that their choices will be respected by others. Since every individual is free to make her/his own judgments and decisions, no one can accuse another of doing wrong. And, even if someone desires something that belongs to or interferes with someone else's liberty, these urges 'are in themselves no sin. No more are the actions, that proceed from those passions, till

---

[60] Ibid, 83.   [61] See Ristroph, 'Hobbes on "Diffidence" and the Criminal Law', 30.

[62] Hobbes, *Leviathan*, 83.

[63] T. Poole, 'Hobbes on Law and Prerogative' in D. Dyzenhaus, T. Poole (eds), *Hobbes and the Law* (Oxford: Oxford University Press, 2012), 68–96, 69.

[64] R. Tuck, quoted in Poole, ibid, 69–70.

[65] Hobbes, *Leviathan*, 83. For a detailed and fascinating discussion of the cause of conflict in Hobbes's state of nature, see Hampton, *Hobbes and the Social Contract Tradition*, 58–96.

[66] T. Hobbes, *Human Nature and De Corpore Politico* (Oxford: Oxford University Press, 1994), 95.

[67] MacPherson, *The Political Theory of Possessive Individualism*, 78.

they know a law that forbids them.'[68] Political authority is necessary in order to establish a standard of common judgment, to which all individuals must adhere. 'Where there is no common power, there is no law: where no law, no injustice.'[69]

Hobbes's account of the state of nature establishes a dialectical move where absolute liberty results in a complete lack of security, which by its turn compromises the very liberty that originates it. By the same token, the conceptual independence of human beings from socio-political constraints results in their absolute dependence on the state and its sovereign authority. This dependence is unavoidable, for 'during the time men live without a common power to keep them all in awe, they are in a condition which is called war; and such a war, as is of every man, against every man.'[70] The lack of trust intrinsic to Hobbes's conception of liberty thus turns the state of nature into a state of insecurity. As a consequence, individual autonomy—when unprotected by political authority—gives individuals no reassurance, only anxiety. 'In such condition,' all there can be is 'continual fear, and danger of violent death; and the life of man, solitary, poor, nasty, brutish, and short.'[71]

The Artificial Quality of Security

The solution to the adversities of the state of nature is to find some way to establish a standard of judgment, and a means to uphold it. As Hobbes suggests over and over throughout his work, the institution of a common authority is the way out of the insecurity of the natural condition of mankind. As it became clear, however, cooperation does not come naturally to individuals, and thus the establishment of political society must be a conscious effort, an artificial construct. The crafting of a commonwealth requires for Hobbes two conditions, one internal and one external to its prospective members. The internal condition is for individuals to restrain their own liberty so that they refrain from invading the liberty of others; the external condition is for this restraint to be kept in check by the threat of punishment. Both conditions are necessary, for at the same time as autonomy must be respected, it must also be restricted. So while individuals themselves must voluntarily lay down their natural right through the social contract, since the insecurity of liberty

---

[68] Hobbes, *Leviathan*, 85.   [69] Ibid.

[70] Ibid, 84. It should be noted that for Hobbes this does not imply that individuals would always be fighting with each other: 'the nature of war, consisteth not in actual fighting; but in the known disposition thereto, during all the time there is no assurance to the contrary' (ibid). In other words, the state of war is essentially a state of dangerousness.

[71] Ibid.

arises precisely from the lack of boundaries in human nature, these boundaries must be artificially crafted and reinforced.

It should be highlighted that, for Hobbes, human beings have a natural disposition to try to avoid conflict. This disposition originates in the laws of nature, 'qualities that dispose men to peace, and obedience'[72] endowed by reason. The problem of the state of nature is not that individuals do not seek peace; human beings are not necessarily brutes in the absence of authority. But without the reassurance of a standard of judgment that sets limits to natural liberty, peace becomes very difficult to achieve, as 'individuals seeking self-preservation will pose threats to one another'.[73] In the state of nature, insecurity tends to escalate, giving individuals increasingly greater reasons to use their right of nature pre-emptively and violently against each other.[74] Thus while the fundamental law of nature is 'to seek peace, and follow it',[75] this law is qualified by the lack of trust in natural liberty, so that Hobbes's general rule of reason is 'that every man, ought to endeavour peace, as far as he has hope of obtaining it; and when he cannot obtain it, that he may seek, and use, all helps, and advantages of war'.[76] This rule is a true separator of waters, not only distinguishing two radically opposite forms of social behaviour—the safe pursuit of peace and the blameless pursuit of war—but also determining the ultimate frontier that divides nature from political society, brutishness from civilization: the hope for peace, which can only be obtained through security. Since natural autonomy is the source of insecurity, security necessitates the curbing of this blameless liberty. This is the second law of nature, which rules 'that a man be willing, when others are so too, as far-forth, as for peace, and defence of himself he shall think it necessary, to lay down this right to all things; and be contented with so much liberty against other men, as he would allow other men against himself'.[77] Liberty must be restrained.

As human beings only transfer or renounce rights with the expectation of getting something in return, the curbing of liberty must be collective and reciprocal, and go as far as peace requires, in order to keep it 'within the limits of peaceful competition'.[78] However, 'the laws of nature ... of themselves, without the terror of some power, to cause them to be observed, are contrary to our natural passions, that carry us to partiality, pride, revenge, and the like'.[79] These laws, 'in the condition of mere nature ... are not properly laws',[80] because 'they are but conclusions, or theorems concerning what

---

[72] Ibid, 177.   [73] Ristroph, 'Respect and Resistance', 608.
[74] Hobbes, *Leviathan*, 87.   [75] Ibid.   [76] Ibid.   [77] Ibid.
[78] MacPherson, *The Political Theory of Possessive Individualism*, 95.
[79] Hobbes, *Leviathan*, 111.   [80] Ibid, 177.

conduceth to the conservation and defence of themselves; whereas law, properly is the word of him, that by right hath command over others'.[81] It is the civil law that must determine the boundaries of individual liberty, for they must represent a common standard of judgment. And, in order to overcome the partiality of natural liberty, law necessitates a quality that is absent in the state of nature: authority.

The establishment of a commonwealth requires the institution of a power that is able to uphold common judgment, and reassure individuals of their security against each other's autonomy. Without such reassurance, 'every man will, and may lawfully rely on his own strength and art, for caution against all other men'.[82] Since in the state of nature it is the multitude and equal worth of desires that lead to insecurity, the aim of the commonwealth is to establish a political authority 'that may reduce all their wills, by plurality of voices, unto one will: which is as much to say ... *to bear their person*'.[83] The sovereign *personifies* the members of the community, exercising the right of nature in the name and for the protection of all citizens, and thus unifying their self-interest into a single will—a *public interest*. Therefore, intrinsic to the social contract is the establishment not only of political society, but also of a standard of justice. After the restraining of individual liberty and the unification of every individual will into a common will, the social contract effectively *is* justice, and so 'to break it is unjust',[84] and thus blameworthy and deserving of punishment.

Furthermore, once the commonwealth is established, there appears to be an effective transformation in the way individuals exercise their autonomy, in that it ceases to be unfettered and becomes conditioned by the public interest expressed through the sovereign's law.[85] Autonomy is *juridified* by the social contract, being both limited and protected by the law. Furthermore, this juridification of autonomy is deeper than a mere convenience, as it includes the assimilation of a politico-juridical form of morality, the public interest manifested in the civil law. This is arguably a reflection of Hobbes's embodied conception of human nature. Since self-interest is informed by reason and conditioned by passions, from the moment individuals feel secure under the sovereign's aegis and subject their wills to the will of the commonwealth, their autonomy is not merely restricted, but is effectively transformed. In other words, the establishment of the commonwealth gives rise to, and relies

---

[81] Ibid, 106.   [82] Ibid.   [83] Ibid, 114 (emphasis added).

[84] Ibid, 95. See Poole, 'Hobbes on Law and Prerogative', 75: 'Law gives the commonwealth its standard of right and measure of justice.'

[85] See D. Dyzenhaus, 'How Hobbes met the "Hobbes Challenge"' (2009) 72(3) *Modern Law Review*, 488–506.

upon, a distinct form of subjectivity, one which is linked to the expectation of responsibility promoted by the civil law.

However, as suggested above, the boundaries between natural and juridical liberty are more unstable and uncertain than Hobbes's theory would super-ficially indicate. Even after the establishment of the normative framework of political society, individuals still are in many ways unable to fully overcome the insecurity of the state of nature. The most obvious evidence of this issue is that punishment in the commonwealth is not simply an abstract threat, but a fully functional and rather pervasive aspect of the social order. The same can be said of crime, and the existence of crime poses an interesting problem for the normative justification of political society. Why is it that, even though all the conditions for individuals to behave as legal subjects are present, they keep invading each other's liberty? A possible answer to this question can be explored by revisiting the natural condition of mankind. The alignment between individual autonomy and political society is mainly established through the laws of nature, but their prudential quality means that they are but 'convenient articles of reason, upon which men [*sic*] *may be* drawn to agreement'.[86] Reason conditions human behaviour, but primarily as a tool to assist individuals in their pursuit of self-interest, itself guided by pas-sions. Beyond reason, therefore, political society also relies on 'passions that incline men to peace'.[87] These, according to Hobbes, are 'fear of death; desire of such things as are necessary to commodious living; and a hope by their industry to obtain them'.[88] It slowly becomes evident that there is more to the social contract than pure rationality and the repudiation of the insecurity of the state of nature. Political society also involves a particular exchange, which privileges some interests over others.

Although the security provided by the state clearly has some common appeal to all individuals (as they all fear death), it is especially desirable to those who, beyond self-preservation, also pursue a commodious living—and even more appealing to those who have actual hopes of obtaining it. Thus while the juridical boundaries of autonomy may be deemed necessary for peace and somewhat beneficial to all individuals, it can only fully satisfy some of them. There will likely be many people for whom the sovereign's law may appear excessively restraining, hindering their desires, and for whom the pro-tection they receive in exchange may feel like a poor bargain. And, as Hobbes anticipated, human beings only pursue peace as far as they have hopes of obtaining it. If the juridification of autonomy depends on embodied satisfac-tion as well as on rational deliberation, it is nowhere nearly as permanent or

---

[86] Hobbes, *Leviathan*, 86 (emphasis added).   [87] Ibid, 109.   [88] Ibid.

uniform as the shift from state of nature to political society implies. Moreover, the notion that the self-interest of some individuals is not fully satisfied by the social contract has consequences not only to the liberty of these individuals, but also to those citizens whose self-interest can be fully satisfied by the commonwealth but only insofar as the commonwealth can provide the peace and security it promised, and whose will is personified by the sovereign. If necessity, self-interest or the working of some passion leads someone beyond the sovereign's law and outside the boundaries of society, reason predicts that both individual and state may 'seek, and use, all helps, and advantages of war'.[89] This is because the conditionality of autonomy attests not only to the possibility of crime, but also to its dangerousness, and to the vulnerability of autonomy against this dangerousness.

Thus Hobbes himself implicitly indicated that the conflict and insecurity of the natural condition of mankind could not be completely dispelled, but instead merely managed, by the state. This is why the criminal law is not just a formal guarantee for the security of juridical autonomy, but a pervasive instrument of social order, permanently required in order to keep the insecurity of natural liberty at bay. This is not to say that there is no difference between political society and the state of nature; on the contrary, this reasoning only reinforces the importance of civil order to political society. However, it becomes clear that this order does not entirely overcome the natural condition of mankind; instead, it conditions, regulates and relies on aspects of the state of nature for its continued legitimation.

The establishment of political society in Hobbes's work initiates a dynamic and complex relationship between individual autonomy and state authority. Individuals remain, at heart, natural individuals; the tendency to disagreement and conflict is always underlying the civil order in society, capable of manifesting itself. 'Civil life is fragile and only law conjoined with power can hold it together.'[90] Furthermore, the endemic insecurity of human nature means that crime is not only possible, but expected, so that criminalization and punishment are posited as necessary even if their justification is problematic. The juridical moment of consent is only formally required, for although individuals do not actually give the sovereign the right to punish them and would undoubtedly individually resist its exercise, juridical autonomy (responsible subjectivity) cannot exist without the threat (and security) of punishment.

The perspective on human nature grounding this understanding has seemed far-fetched to many, an opinion which Hobbes himself anticipated.[91] Hobbes's materialism, along with the lack of trust that accompanies it, is

---

[89] Ibid, 87.   [90] Poole, 'Hobbes on Law and Prerogative', 94.
[91] In response to such possible claims, he argued that even 'civilised' social mores suggested a common distrust among individuals: 'when going to sleep, he locks his doors; when even in his

rigorous and unavoidable, so that insecurity is always present beneath the surface of autonomy, both within and outside of political society. But, though the philosophical consistency of Hobbes's work can be (and has been) criticized, it is quite possible to accept such criticism and still maintain that his postulates on individual autonomy and liberty enjoyed a significant and long-lasting influence[92] over the liberal tradition of legal and political thought. This is because such influence did not arise from the impeccability of his logic, but from the ideological thrust of his individualistic framework.

THE VULNERABILITY
OF INDIVIDUAL LIBERTY

There is an inextricable link between the paradox of punishment in Hobbes's work and an individualistic perspective on the human condition. It is this conception of human beings as atomized and self-interested individuals that naturalizes distrust and grounds the insecurity behind the motivation for punishment, and this is nowhere clearer than in the theoretical framework set out by Hobbes, 'the theorist par excellence of human vulnerability'.[93] This vulnerability is at the core of Hobbes's political theory, justifying both the liberty of the individual and the authority of the state. 'Without the performance of covenant, we would be back in the state of nature.'[94] This same logic legitimates the state's right to punish, as punishment reinforces the integrity of the community by reassuring citizens of the security of their liberty.

The reassurance function of state authority, however, cannot completely overcome the natural condition of insecurity, so that the vulnerability that Hobbes finds in human nature is also an inherent aspect of the political community. Because dangerous behaviour is always a possibility, and since it threatens the integrity of the common judgment sustained by the state, it follows that punishment is indispensable for the preservation of juridical autonomy: 'covenants, without the sword, are but words, and of no strength to secure a man at all'.[95] Therefore, not only individuals themselves, but also

---

house he locks his chests; and this when he knows there be laws, and public officers, armed, to revenge all injuries shall be done him ... Does he not there as much accuse mankind by his actions, as I do by my words?' (Hobbes, *Leviathan*, 84–5).

[92] C. Gearty, 'Escaping Hobbes: Liberty and Security for our Democratic (Not Anti-Terrorist) Age' in E.D. Reed, M. Dumper (eds), *Civil Liberties, National Security and Prospects for Consensus* (Cambridge: Cambridge University Press, 2012), 35–61, 43. See also C. Gearty, *Liberty and Security* (Cambridge: Polity Press, 2013).

[93] Ristroph, 'Respect and Resistance', 607.

[94] R. Shiner, 'Hart and Hobbes' (1980) 22(2) *William and Mary Law Review*, 201–25, 208.

[95] Hobbes, *Leviathan*, 111.

the very notion of responsible legal subjectivity that lies at the core of political society, and even political society itself, are vulnerable to natural liberty and its primary social expression, crime. The lack of trust engendered by Hobbes's individualistic conception of autonomy and liberty infiltrates (and motivates) the whole of his political theory.

In political society, therefore, individuals are always dependent on the authority of the state, as it alone can guarantee that conduct is being regulated, crime is being prevented, and the conditions for responsible legal agency are being protected. Hobbes's theory displays a privileged concern towards security, on which his very conceptions of political society and juridical liberty rely. This logical connection between individual liberty, political authority, and security, manifested within the paradox of punishment, is an intrinsic conceptual and normative element of the modern state. It is this link that conveys the importance of understanding Hobbes's work to a study of contemporary issues concerning law and society, as his theoretical model exposes a specific logic that is embedded within 'our very "social imaginary" ',[96] and that significantly influences changes and transformations in the contemporary socio-political framework, reflected by the preventive turn.

In this sense, there are two main lessons that can be taken from Hobbes's account of punishment and political society, in relation to the contemporary condition of criminal law. The first relates to the artificial nature of juridical liberty and public interest in Hobbes's theoretical framework. The conceptual distinction drawn by Hobbes between the exercise of individual liberty in the state of nature and in political society, together with the link between natural liberty and crime, suggests not only that these two expressions of subjectivity are in conflict with each other, but also that natural, or dangerous, subjectivity is the presumptive position, while responsible subjectivity is the normative position with regards to individual autonomy. In other words, while individuals in political society are supposed to behave as responsible legal subjects, restraining their liberty to the limits of the law, they are all in fact, or at least potentially, natural subjects who may, out of self-interest, become dangerous to the project of political society. Under this perspective, if an individual is accused or suspected of committing a serious crime, the state is more inclined to expect this person to be dangerous than to be a trustworthy, law-abiding citizen who would otherwise not have committed this offence against the community, or who was falsely accused. The artificial quality of juridical liberty both necessitates and undermines the peace and security promised by

---

[96] Loader and Walker, *Civilizing Security*, 44. See also C. Taylor, *Modern Social Imaginaries* (Durham: Duke University Press, 2004).

the state authority, preserving a latent threat that maintains a fragile 'balance between freedom and insecurity'.[97] This balance sustains both the normative primacy of juridical liberty and the need for punishment through an uneven distribution of insecurity in society, which is mainly subjectively felt by those identified as responsible legal subjects, and objectively experienced by those who behave in a way considered deviant or dangerous, or whose social position associates them with one of the many 'suspect communities'.[98] When structural socio-political conditions for trust and solidarity are lacking in a particular moment, within this framework political authority appears as the only thing that can preserve social cohesion, and thus any suspicion of disharmony between an individual's autonomy and the public interest is enough to undermine the expectation that such individual can be expected to behave within juridical boundaries.

The second lesson, however, is that the vulnerability of the state with regards to the insecurity generated by human relations does not necessarily compromise the state's authority, but on the contrary can also ground and reinforce it. In Hobbes's theory, political society is not presented as a failed project; instead, an absolute state is postulated as the only hope of managing the endemic insecurity of human nature, a formidable power aimed at containing a formidable threat. Within Hobbes's logic, the state may have to be authoritarian at times, and the liberty of many individuals is bound to suffer from this, but this unfortunate situation is not created by the state—it is the consequence of the fickleness of human nature, which the state is precisely trying to contain however it can. The fissure created by the paradox of punishment is 'mended' by the socio-political distribution of its conflicting conceptions of subjectivity: the state's primary function is to promote and preserve juridical liberty, something which can only be achieved through the repression and coercion of natural liberty. As seen above, the trap contained in Hobbes's theory lies in that the authoritarian vein of his model of political society stems precisely from his emancipatory postulates. Since respect for individual liberty is conceptualized as connected with and dependent upon the need to protect liberty from its own vulnerabilities, the primacy of individual autonomy inevitably leads to its subjection to political authority.

---

[97] Gearty, *Liberty and Security*, 20.

[98] See C. Pantazis, S. Pemberton, 'From the "Old" to the "New" Suspect Community: Examining the Impacts of Recent UK Counter-Terrorism Legislation' (2009) 49 *British Journal of Criminology*, 646–66. For more general comments on the social distribution of insecurity in contemporary liberal societies, See L. Wacquant, 'Crafting the Neoliberal State: Workfare, Prisonfare, and Social Insecurity' (2010) 25(2) *Sociological Forum*, 197–220, 208; see also L. Wacquant, *Punishing the Poor: The Neoliberal Government of Social Insecurity* (London: Duke University Press, 2008).

Hobbes, Insecurity, and Preventive Criminal Law

In making these claims, I am in a sense both supporting and disagreeing with the view of recent theorists, such as Richard Ericson[99] and Peter Ramsay,[100] who have critically analysed the current preventive turn in the law. While, like them, I see that the substantive changes occurring to the criminal law in the past few decades are deeply problematic, and intimately connected to the efforts by the liberal state to produce and maintain authority, my approach to the relationship between the current framework of preventive and regulatory laws and the normative premises of the liberal legal and political tradition is slightly different. For both Ericson and Ramsay, it seems that the growing preventive apparatus of the criminal law gives form to a waning of political authority experienced by the preventive state as it, in employing this apparatus, is openly and fundamentally questioning the force and the validity of its own authority. Both scholars, furthermore, use Hobbes's theory to substantiate their claim that a preventive state acts as a state that does not recognize its own authority, drifting apart from Hobbes's ideal of the state as the ultimate source of reassurance for the civil order.

Ramsay's perspective on the preventive turn is grounded on the acute perception that the legitimacy of contemporary preventive measures relies on the assumption that citizens have a right to security which must be actively guaranteed by virtue of the vulnerable character of their autonomy, 'an assumption ... that is radically at odds with Hobbes's account of Leviathan's sovereignty'.[101] Although Hobbes conceptualizes individuals as intrinsically vulnerable, it is precisely this vulnerability which the state, through its authority, is supposed to eliminate. Sovereignty seems to be justified in Hobbes's theory as the power necessary to remove individuals from the insecurity and vulnerability of the state of nature, 'to keep them in awe, and tie them by fear of punishment to the performance of their covenants'.[102] Preventive measures, by their turn, strongly imply that the state is 'declaring the normal vulnerability of its subjects', a move which 'undermines its own authority in a way that would be intolerable to Leviathan, or indeed any sovereign worthy of the name'.[103] According to Ramsay, while Hobbes's state seeks to escape the state of nature through the force and authority of the sovereign's law, the insecure law of the preventive turn 'converts at least some of the conditions of the state of nature into the normal conditions of civil society',[104] thus amounting 'to an authoritative statement of the law's lack of authority'.[105] Ramsay's reasoning

---

[99] R. Ericson, *Crime in an Insecure World* (Cambridge: Polity Press, 2007).
[100] P. Ramsay, *The Insecurity State: Vulnerable Autonomy and the Right to Security in the Criminal Law* (Oxford: Oxford University Press, 2012).
[101] Ibid, 215.　　　[102] Hobbes, *Leviathan*, 111.
[103] Ramsay, *The Insecurity State*, 5.　　　[104] Ibid, 217.　　　[105] Ibid.

relies on Ericson's perception that, through the use of preventive measures, '[t]he Hobbesian Leviathan as a state that expresses the liberal imaginary of physical security and prosperity begins to break down.'[106] Furthermore, both Ramsay and Ericson highlight that the authority of the Hobbesian state, 'though it appears to be the "negation" of the liberal idea of freedom under the rule of law, is in reality "its very presupposition"'.[107] From the assumption that preventive measures compromise the authority of the state, therefore, it would follow that '[t]he hollowing out of the state's sovereign authority' essentially constitutes 'an abandonment of liberal tradition'.[108]

While I entirely agree that the authority of the state is the very presupposition of the liberal idea of freedom—and Hobbes's theory especially emphasizes that—and that the hollowing out of the state's sovereign authority compromises the liberal framework to a significant degree, I do not believe that the current state of insecurity in the law represents a breakdown of the Hobbesian model of political authority. But neither do I subscribe to accounts such as David Garland's, which suggest that the present 'culture of control' represents a novel 'Hobbesian solution'[109] to the problem of authority, or Simon Hallsworth and John Lea's argument that the 'security state' aims at 'reconstructing Leviathan'[110] as an *alternative* to the liberal welfare state. What I argue instead is that both freedom and insecurity are part of Hobbes's political model, and the relation between these two conceptions is such that political authority relies on the preservation of one as well as the other within the liberal imaginary. So while Leviathan is predicated on the promise of putting an end to the insecurity of the state of nature, the management of its political authority—including the criminal law, one of its main instruments—depends on a conception of human nature that betrays the concrete feasibility of this promise. In other words, the core of Hobbes's normative framework lies not in the security of the sovereign state, but in the insecurity of the natural condition of mankind. When preventive measures are legitimately deployed in the name of the protection of individual freedom and rights, they are fuelled by this logic, which is not only essentially Hobbesian, but also an intrinsic element of the normative structure of the liberal civil order.

---

[106] Ericson, *Crime in an Insecure World*, 202.

[107] Ramsay, *The Insecurity State*, 218, paraphrasing F. Neumann, 'The Concept of Political Freedom' in W. Scheuerman (ed), *The Rule of Law Under Siege: Selected Essays of Franz Neumann and Otto Kircheimer* (University of California Press, 1996), 213.

[108] Ramsay, ibid.

[109] D. Garland, *The Culture of Control: Crime and Social Order in Contemporary Society* (Oxford: Oxford University Press, 2002), 202.

[110] S. Hallsworth, J. Lea, 'Reconstructing Leviathan: Emerging Contours of the Security State' (2011) 15(2) *Theoretical Criminology*, 141–57, 141.

The most significant conclusion which can be derived from this analysis, and which diverges from Ramsay and Ericson's interpretation of Hobbes's work, is that, although the main function of the Hobbesian state is to eliminate the insecurity of the state of nature, this is a task that Hobbes was keenly aware that Leviathan could never fully achieve. Instead, Hobbes's radical (and abstract) individualism implies that insecurity is intrinsic to human nature, and it permeates his entire socio-political framework, so that some of the conditions of the state of nature are also, by definition, normal conditions of civil society. While the state is supposed to suppress insecurity and reassure individuals of the conditions for legal subjectivity, the structural violence inherent to the liberal model of society means that political society is always a tentative compromise, bound to become volatile under conditions of social erosion. This dialectical relation between nature and society is exposed, not generated, by the justificatory framework of the preventive turn. The preventive turn is thus a manifestation, not subversion, of the social imaginary grounding the authority of the liberal state, so that the main problem expressed by preventive criminal laws is not that they are anti-liberal, but that they reveal and magnify the cracks and contradictions in the liberal legal framework. Hobbes's political model thus suggests that the vulnerability of the authority of the liberal state stems directly from the vulnerability that is inherent to responsible subjectivity, and that is now only coming to the fore under advanced liberal socio-political conditions.

CONCLUSION

Hobbes's controversial perspective on the nature, function, and justification of punishment reveals a 'philosophical problematic' which is not only 'fundamental to an understanding of the modern philosophy of punishment',[111] but also essential to a proper examination of the contemporary state of insecurity in criminal law. This paradox reflects the dialectical relation between criminal law's normative justification and its pragmatic necessity, which perennially compromises the security of individual autonomy. Hobbes's philosophical account of political society provides an analytical framework through which to understand these contradictions, and moreover constitutes one of the main philosophical and ideological grounds for them, as one of the conceptual bases of the liberal social imaginary.

---

[111] Norrie, 'Thomas Hobbes and the Philosophy of Punishment', 299.

There is a perennial relationship between liberty and insecurity within the liberal framework, which directly affects conceptions of responsibility and punishment within criminal law and justice. This relationship, just like that between the liberal ideas of freedom and state authority alluded to by Ramsay and Ericson, has in Hobbes's work its main philosophical foundation. It is the ambivalence within individual liberty that prevents any attempt to recast or safeguard the proper balance between liberty and security from escaping a Hobbesian logic. The normative legitimation of state authority and of its power to punish relies on the existence of a politico-ideological conflict between the juridical and the natural elements of human behaviour. The paradox of punishment, more than a moral or a logical problem, reflects the abstract character of the prevalent model of political community and the conception of subjectivity underpinning it. And as long as the notion of civil order underpinning the criminal law continues to advance the idea of human emancipation while still preserving violent conditions of structural inequality, the ambivalence within individual liberty and autonomy will remain unaddressed and unresolved. Hobbes himself admonished that, when attempting to trail a path between the defence of liberty and the preservation of authority, ''tis hard to pass between the points of both unwounded.'[112]

---

[112] Hobbes, *Leviathan*, 3.

4

Mutual Benefit, Property, and the Conceptual Foundations of Trust

> Men living together according to reason, without a common Superior on Earth, with Authority to judge between them, is properly the State of Nature.
>
> … And were it not for the corruption, and vitiousness of degenerate Men, there would be no need of any other; no necessity that Men should separate from this great and natural Community, and by positive agreements combine into smaller and divided associations.[1]

The Hobbesian theoretical framework examined in the last chapter lays the ground for the insecurity which I argue drives the dialectical relationship between responsibility and dangerousness within criminal subjectivity. Hobbes's radical individualism effectively isolates and exposes the relation between individual autonomy and state authority which results in the coercive power of the state being conceptualized as necessary in order to reassure citizens of the maintenance of civil order. However, while Hobbes's theory can highlight how the current preventive turn in criminal law is implicated within the liberal legal tradition, it is less helpful in exposing the full complexity of the relation between trust and reassurance, which is fundamental to the dynamic aspect of criminal subjectivity. The intrinsic vulnerability of individual autonomy, laid bare in Hobbes's account of society and currently grounding the preventive turn, usually appears in the liberal imaginary in less radical forms, suppressed and alleviated by notions of civility which reassure the normative position of trust in liberal societies. The subject of liberal criminal law is conceived primarily as a citizen, presumed innocent until proven guilty, and only exceptionally treated as a dangerous offender. This management of insecurity through images of trust is an essential element of the ambivalence of individual autonomy, which needs to be properly analysed. In this chapter, I propose that such an analysis can be conducted by

---

[1] J. Locke, *Two Treatises of Government* (Cambridge: Cambridge University Press, 2010), 280, 352.

The Preventive Turn in Criminal Law. First Edition. Henrique Carvalho. © Henrique Carvalho 2017. Published 2017 by Oxford University Press.

contrasting Hobbes's theoretical framework with that of another seventeenth-century political theorist, John Locke.

Locke is celebrated as one of the main exponents of the liberal political tradition,[2] for being the first modern political theorist to conceptualize a model of society which, against the vulnerability and arbitrariness of human nature posited by authors such as Hobbes and Robert Filmer, was grounded on the belief that natural liberty and individual autonomy not only require but also generate mutual benefit and security, thus being the main basis for a prosperous and peaceful society. Although both Hobbes and Locke are said to have promoted notions of individual liberty and rights that took them away from 'the strictures of natural law' and placed them within the individual, thus initiating a tradition of subjective natural right,[3] Locke's perspective is considered distinctive in that he directly associated these natural rights with duties. Indeed, Locke inferred rights from the duties he found to be held under the law of nature, so that duties effectively came before rights in his account.[4] For Locke, 'Truth and keeping of Faith belongs to Men [*sic*], as Men, and not as Members of Society.'[5] Locke's account also explicitly advanced that individuals held rights against the state—and that the state had a duty to respect these rights. His perspective on the intrinsic value and trustworthiness of individual liberty, seen as the main corollary of Locke's socio-political model, has become a cornerstone not only of liberal political theory but, to a large extent, also of the normative idea of modern society as a whole.[6] The central aspects of this theoretical model provide a structural framework for the notion of civil order within the liberal imaginary which, I argue, is largely reflected on the normative structure of the liberal model of criminal law.

With this in mind, I pursue a close examination of Locke's political theory as put forward in his *Second Treatise of Government*. I do this in order to construct a conceptual framework in which the elements and connections identified in Locke's model of society can elucidate the problems and limitations found in liberal criminal law, due to its ideological basis and its dependence on specific socio-political conditions. I start by looking at how Locke's unique account of the state of nature, grounded on the idea of the interdependence between law and liberty, attempts to resolve issues found in

---

[2] See J. Waldron (ed), *Liberal Rights: Collected Papers 1981-1991* (Cambridge: Cambridge University Press, 1993), 1.

[3] E. Curran, 'An Immodest Proposal: Hobbes Rather than Locke Provides a Forerunner for Modern Rights Theory' (2013) 32 *Law and Philosophy*, 515–38, 518. See also B. Tierney, 'Historical Roots of Modern Rights: Before Locke and After' (2005) 3(1) *Ave Maria Law Review*, 23–43, and Peter Laslett's introduction to the *Two Treatises of Government*.

[4] Curran, ibid, 521.   [5] Locke, *Two Treatises of Government*, 277.

[6] See C. Taylor, *Modern Social Imaginaries* (Durham: Duke University Press, 2004), 15, and more generally the discussion explored in Chapter 2 above.

earlier conceptions of human nature, such as Hobbes's. Drawing a comparison between the main premises in Locke's and Hobbes's theoretical models, the first section investigates how Locke strived to preserve the emancipatory aspects of Hobbes's revolution in moral and political theory, at the same time as he tried to do away with its more radical elements. My main argument is that, in order to do that, Locke naturalizes the juridical boundaries of individual liberty that, for Hobbes, could only exist after the establishment of political society, a move that has significant implications for the justificatory framework of punishment in his theory.

However, in spite of these efforts, a deeper analysis of Locke's state of nature reveals an intrinsic, albeit repressed, instability that hints at the presence of a latent insecurity underpinning his theoretical model, which is what ultimately motivates the establishment of political society—just as it did in Hobbes's theory. Pursuing this intuition, the second part of the chapter explores the extent to which, as C.B. MacPherson suggested, '[i]n making one structural alteration in Hobbes's theoretical system that was required to bring it into conformity with the needs and possibilities of a possessive market society, Locke completed an edifice that rested on Hobbes's sure foundations.'[7] I argue that, rather than simply rejecting Hobbes's model of society, the Lockean framework can be seen to actually complement it by reassuring its ideological setting. In so doing, however, Locke also preserves the subjection of individual liberty to the power of political authority. The last section applies the theoretical analysis developed throughout the chapter towards an understanding of the conceptual structure of criminal subjectivity, particularly with regards to the normative primacy of responsible subjectivity within the liberal model of criminal law. I conclude by suggesting that this comparative critique of Hobbes's and Locke's theories highlights a conceptual relation between individual liberty and insecurity, which remains embedded within the framework of criminal law, is linked to its tensions and contradictions, and lies behind the perplexities involving the preventive turn.

LAW AND LIBERTY: LOCKE'S NATURALIZATION OF TRUST

In the introduction to his Second Treatise, Locke proposes that his specific objective in that book is to examine political power. He conceptualizes this

---

[7] C.B. MacPherson, *The Political Theory of Possessive Individualism: Hobbes to Locke* (Ontario: Oxford University Press, 2011), 270.

power as having three main aspects: the power to make laws and to set penalties for the violation of these laws (that is, to criminalize); the power to regulate and preserve property; and the power to employ 'the force of the Community' in the execution of laws (which includes the power to punish) and in the defence of the community against external threats.[8] Also, from the outset, Locke is very clear that the purpose of his treatise is to offer an alternative to accounts of government that define it as 'the product of Force and Violence';[9] Locke is thinking here specifically of his declared opponent, Robert Filmer. But, as we will see, the same objections Locke makes against Filmer's perspective could be directed to Hobbes's account of political authority. Just as in Hobbes's work, however, the 'fundamental basis'[10] of Locke's political theory lies in his account of the state of nature, the 'State all Men [*sic*] are naturally in',[11] where the origins and justificatory framework for political power can be found. Also similarly, Locke's nature is 'a State of perfect Freedom' where individuals pursue their interests as they deem fit, 'without asking leave, or depending upon the Will of any other Man', and a state of perfect equality, where individuals co-exist 'without Subordination or Subjection'.[12] The starting point of Locke's political theory thus carries the same emancipatory impulse seen in Hobbes's conceptualization of natural liberty.

However, there is a significant distinct quality in Locke's state of nature, in that it is not characterized by the absence of a standard of judgment. For Locke, the state of nature may be a state of perfect liberty, 'yet it is not a State of License', for it 'has a Law of Nature to govern it, which obliges every one'.[13] This law, even in the absence of political authority, is 'a real law, offering obligatory commands rather than prudential advice'.[14] Its commands, moreover, are universal and self-evident: 'Reason, which is that Law, teaches all Mankind, who will but consult it, that being all equal and independent, no one ought to harm another in his Life, Health, Liberty, or Possessions.'[15] While Hobbes presumes an absolute right from the natural equality of individuals, Locke derives first of all an obligation, constituting this natural equality as the foundation for justice. For Locke, therefore, freedom and equality already enjoy a harmonious balance in the state of nature, and they do so

---

[8] Locke, *Two Treatises of Government*, 268. See also J. Tully, *An Approach to Political Philosophy: Locke in Contexts* (Cambridge: Cambridge University Press, 1993), 14.

[9] Locke, ibid.

[10] R. Harrison, *Hobbes, Locke, and Confusion's Masterpiece: An Examination of Seventeenth-Century Political Philosophy* (Cambridge: Cambridge University Press, 2003), 175.

[11] Locke, *Two Treatises of Government*, 269.   [12] Ibid.   [13] Ibid, 270–1.

[14] Harrison, *Hobbes, Locke, and Confusion's Masterpiece*, 169.

[15] Locke, *Two Treatises of Government*, 271.

because they are naturally embedded in a form of order. In Locke's orderly conception of nature, law and liberty are intrinsically connected. 'So that, however it may be mistaken, *the end of Law* is not to abolish or restrain, but *to preserve and enlarge Freedom*: For in all the states of created beings capable of Laws, *where there is no Law, there is no Freedom*.'[16] In linking law and liberty, Locke provides what is possibly the first comprehensive conceptual expression of the ethics of freedom and mutual benefit which for Taylor stands at the core of the modern moral order.[17]

Thus natural liberty does not give individuals a licence to do what they please, but only the right 'to be free from any Superior Power on Earth, and not to be under the Will or Legislative Authority of Man, but to have only the Law of Nature for his Rule'.[18] However, Locke is aware and accepts that law requires a power to enforce it. In arguing for the natural existence of law, he is not assuming that law can bind individuals without political power; rather, he is advancing the unique claim that there is political power in the state of nature.

For the Law of Nature would, as all other Laws that concern Men in this World, be in vain, if there were no body that in the State of Nature, had a Power to Execute that Law, and thereby preserve the innocent and restrain offenders, *and if any one in the State of Nature may punish another, for any evil he has done, every one may do so.*[19]

In one elegant twist, Locke's 'very strange Doctrine'[20] secures natural liberty within juridical boundaries by giving every individual the reciprocal power to enforce these boundaries. So while for Locke, just like for Hobbes, natural liberty is about self-government—'not to be subject to the arbitrary Will of another, but freely follow his own'[21]—for Locke this does not mean the lack of a standard of justice, for that would make natural liberty self-defeating. 'For who could be free, when every other Man's Humour might domineer over him?'[22] For Locke, therefore, individuals are naturally self-governing 'because they are capable of exercising political power themselves'.[23] This seemingly simple distinction regarding the natural condition of individual liberty is the cornerstone of Locke's political theory, and influences the whole of his model of political society, from its justification to its shortcomings.

It seems that political power is Locke's answer to the problem of insecurity which abounded in Hobbes's state of nature, as it reassures the liberty of

---

[16] Ibid, 305–6 (emphasis in original).
[17] See Taylor, *Modern Social Imaginaries* and Chapter 2 above.
[18] Locke, *Two Treatises of Government*, 283.   [19] Ibid, 271–2 (emphasis added).
[20] Ibid, 272.   [21] Ibid, 306.   [22] Ibid.
[23] Tully, *An Approach to Political Philosophy*, 15.

individuals through the reciprocal exercise of judgment and, particularly, the reciprocal power to punish. However, although Locke's doctrine addresses the inherent insecurity of individual liberty, it does not fully resolve it; for even if everyone shares a single standard of judgment, they might still disagree on how to actualize or enforce it. As Hobbes suggested, 'where every man is his own judge, there properly is no judge at all'.[24] Why would Locke have hopes that mutual self-government would lead to cooperation and order, instead of conflict and war? Part of the answer is that he did not actually have such hopes; as we will see, the problem of private judgment is the main reason why individuals choose to abandon the state of nature and establish political society. Nevertheless, Locke's account of political power does suggest that he saw individuals as naturally trustworthy. The main grounds for this assumption is the interrelation between law and liberty, which maintains that individuals are only free when they act within juridical boundaries. Locke naturalizes these boundaries by tying them to rationality: the law of nature, for Locke, is not merely rational; it is *reason*, so that the prudential aspect of individual self-interest is conceptualized as bound with that of other human beings, dependent upon peaceful coexistence. Whenever individuals exercise their natural liberty, they do so in accordance with the law, and 'the fundamental Law of Nature' is 'the preservation of Mankind'.[25] Likewise, although political power is shared among all individuals, it is bound by this fundamental law so that it can be used 'only for the Publick Good'.[26] It is this conjoining of law and liberty that effect the most significant transformation in individual liberty, from Hobbes to Locke. By naturalizing the juridical boundaries of liberty, Locke also naturalizes the essence of responsible legal subjectivity: Locke's natural individual is a responsible subject.

All the basic elements of individual responsibility seem to be present in Locke's natural conception of individuality. For example, individuals are assumed to have the capacity to act according to the law, because they know what the law requires of them and can foresee the consequences of their actions. And, because they can be expected to act responsibly, they can also be held responsible for their agency, and punished if necessary. The existence of punishment in the state of nature, however, implies the existence of crime. And, if acting within the boundaries of natural liberty is to act according to the law, which is dictated by reason, then crime has to be conceptualized as an act that eschews rationality, and which in doing so threatens the trust which lies at the basis of human relations. 'In transgressing the Law of

[24] T. Hobbes, *Human Nature and De Corpore Politico* (Oxford: Oxford University Press, 1994), 95.

[25] Locke, *Two Treatises of Government*, 358.   [26] Ibid, 269.

Nature, the Offender declares himself to live by another Rule, than that of reason and common Equity, which is that measure ... set to the actions of Men, for their mutual security.'[27] It is already possible to find traces of the ambivalence of criminal subjectivity in Locke's account of criminal behaviour, for while Locke claims that the criminal acts against rationality, there is an element of voluntariness in crime, in that the criminal is aware that her/his actions go against the law of nature. At the same time, in doing so, the criminal 'becomes *dangerous* to Mankind, the tye, which is to secure them from injury and violence, being slighted and broken by him'.[28] There is thus a clear aspect of dangerousness in Locke's account of crime, which highlights its social dimension, and the possibility of crime is undoubtedly one of the reasons why individuals in the state of nature have to pay the cost of vigilance and subject themselves to the reciprocal use of political power.

The main reason why, at first sight, the dangerousness of crime does not appear to be overwhelming in Locke's state of nature is that Locke conceptualizes criminal behaviour as exceptional. The idea that law and punishment do not intrinsically require a public authority in order to be effective relies on the assumption that they are naturally promoted by a majority of responsible individuals against an exceptional minority of dangerous offenders. It is the natural predominance of responsible subjectivity, grounded on the symbiosis between law and liberty, which allows Locke to provide his state of nature with a presumption of trustworthiness, by reassuring individual liberty.

The Reassurance of Property

There is another challenge to Locke's natural presumption of trustworthiness, posed by Hobbes's theory, which must be examined before this analysis can proceed. For Hobbes, the main factor behind the inherent insecurity of the state of nature was not the lack of desire for peace or the lack of knowledge of the rational limits of individual liberty, but the intense struggle for self-preservation and self-interest. Whenever two people desired something which only one of them could possess, competition would feed into distrust, and conflict would inevitably ensue. Locke himself acknowledged that an individual's primary duty was towards her/his own preservation, and it was only when this minimum security was guaranteed that an individual 'ought ... as much as [possible], to preserve the rest of Mankind'.[29] If Locke's juridical conception of individual liberty is to be maintained, then, it has to be

---

[27] Ibid, 272.   [28] Ibid (emphasis added).   [29] Ibid, 271.

established that the self-interest of individuals can be pursued in harmony, or at least kept 'within the limits of peaceful competition',[30] even before the existence of a political authority. Locke's answer to this problem is to posit that the juridification of natural liberty is grounded on the natural existence of private property.[31]

Locke's account of property begins with the idea that although the world belongs to humanity's common use, in order for individuals to be able to enjoy the fruits of the earth, 'there must of necessity be a means to appropriate them some way or other before they can be of any use, or at all beneficial to any particular Man'.[32] Appropriation is done through the use of labour power: since 'every Man has a Property in his own Person',[33] labour extends this property to whatever individuals transform or affect through their physical energy. Since it is essential for survival, this basic kind of appropriation is a natural right, independent from the consent of others. This 'original Law of Nature for the *beginning of Property*, in what was before common',[34] constitutes labour power as 'the means of individuating the common into individual possessions to be used for preservation'.[35] Locke maintains that the privatization of property does not pose a risk to the preservation of others, insofar as it follows two rules. First, an individual can only appropriate as much as can be enjoyed, so that nothing is spoiled or needlessly destroyed. Second, individual appropriation must remain 'within the bounds, set by reason of what might serve for his use',[36] so that there is always as good and enough for others. 'The measure of Property, Nature has well set, by the Extent of Mens Labour, and the Conveniency of Life.'[37] The beginning of property thus constituted a right that was regulated,[38] set within boundaries meant to avoid spoilage and scarcity, and therefore was seen as in league with the perfect freedom and equality of individuals.

However, Locke is aware that individuals do not only seek property for immediate survival, but rather constantly look for ways in which to guarantee the 'Support and Comfort of their being'.[39] The best way to achieve these goals, which Locke called 'the chief matter of Property', concerned the use and possession of land.[40] The appropriation of land complicates the careful

---

[30] MacPherson, *The Political Theory of Possessive Individualism*, 95.

[31] It should be noted that, although Locke's account of property focuses mainly on material goods, the general connotation given by Locke to property is much broader, referring to the 'Lives, Liberties and Estates' of individuals (Locke, *Two Treatises of Government*, 350).

[32] Locke, ibid, 286–7.   [33] Ibid, 287.   [34] Ibid, 289 (emphasis in original).

[35] Tully, *An Approach to Political Philosophy*, 27.

[36] Locke, *Two Treatises of Government*, 290.   [37] Ibid, 292.

[38] Tully, *An Approach to Political Philosophy*, 28.

[39] Locke, *Two Treatises of Government*, 286.   [40] Ibid, 290.

balance of private property enunciated by the two provisos set by Locke, since it not only allows the possession of a large quantity and quality of goods by association (whatever is produced on the land), but also limits the liberty of others more directly, by depriving them from using the land for their own purposes. From the outset, then, it would seem that land would be problematic for Locke's account of private property. In another surprising twist, however, Locke suggests that the opposite is actually true, that the privatization of land is beneficial, and more conducive to peace and cooperation than its common use. This is because 'he who appropriates land to himself by his labour, does not lessen but increase the common stock of mankind',[41] since by cultivating the land, individuals make the land more productive than it would be if it was left uncultivated.

By inextricably linking the fruits of labour to the desire for private property, Locke is able to propose 'that the Property of labour should be able to over-balance the Community of Land. For 'tis Labour indeed that puts the difference of value on every thing'.[42] This last quote contains an interesting double meaning. On the one hand, Locke is attempting to justify the appropriation of land through the notion that it makes land more valuable—not just to the proprietor, but to humanity in general. On the other hand, Locke is also implying that individuals do not appropriate land because they need it or because it can 'increase the common stock of mankind', but because land is valuable. The very value of land, in its turn, is a consequence of its capacity to produce more. The privatization of land gives rise to a second moment in Locke's state of nature, distinguished primarily through its treatment of property with regards to mutual benefit. In the first moment, private property was limited by the need to protect mutual benefit. However, the original limits of the right to property were only tenable 'before the desire of having more than Men needed, had altered the intrinsick value of things'.[43] Once individuals begin to seek accumulation beyond what was necessary for their preservation, Locke needs to modify his account of property if he is to preserve the semblance of peaceful coexistence in his state of nature. He does so by arguing that private accumulation is conducive to mutual benefit.

Locke's argument relies on two premises. The first, already mentioned, is that the appropriation of land actually increases the production of goods. However, this would not on its own prevent the problem of scarcity and spoilage, for since people desire land precisely for its value, it would be unlikely that they would gratuitously share its products. Locke says this would indeed be the case, 'had not the Invention of Money, and the tacit Agreement of Men

---

[41] Ibid, 294.   [42] Ibid, 296.   [43] Ibid, 294.

to put a value on it, introduced (by Consent) larger Possessions, and a Right to them'.[44] Money thus completes Locke's defence of private property. Since appropriation actively enhances the value of things and the common stock of mankind, then private property is preferable to common property; and since money can be exchanged for goods and labour, and accumulated without spoiling, it allows for the distribution of wealth without hindering the desire for accumulation. Relying on these two assumptions, Locke advances the claim that individuals have tacitly 'agreed to disproportionate and unequal Possession of the Earth'.[45] Furthermore, he poses this consensus as 'natural', in the sense that it emerges from human rationality, without conflict or imposition. 'This partage of things, in an inequality of private possessions, men have made practicable out of the bounds of Societie, and without compact.'[46] In doing so, Locke provides his account of individual liberty with a structural quality. For even if some individuals pursue their self-interest beyond the boundaries of their perfect equality, the social function of private property reassures other individuals that such pursuits do not threaten their own security, but rather can potentially increase their own comfort—as long as they are rational. If some individuals do not desire or succeed in accumulating property, they can still work for money and buy the goods they need for their comfort and support.

Due to its social function, private property effectively becomes the main guarantor of trust in Locke's state of nature, grounded as it is on the notion that human relations can be reassured of their security against the disruptive potential of individual interest as long as they are focused on rational accumulation. 'We can see in Locke's formulation how much he sees mutual service in terms of profitable exchange. "Economic" (i.e., ordered, peaceful, productive) activity has become the model for human behaviour and the key to harmonious coexistence.'[47] Furthermore, since natural liberty is conceptualized as both in harmony with individual self-interest and conducive to mutual benefit, this conception reinforces the idea that individuals do not depend on the power of a common authority to convince them of the importance of restraining their agency to juridical limits, nor of the wrongfulness of transgressing those limits. This image goes hand in hand with the idea that criminal and overall dangerous behaviour is exceptional, and therefore not an overwhelming risk to the natural harmony of human relations. There is, however, a problem with this picture: if Locke's conception of the criminal is followed to the letter, then punishment should only be aimed at rare

---

[44] Ibid, 293.   [45] Ibid, 302.   [46] Ibid.
[47] Taylor, *Modern Social Imaginaries*, 15.

occasions in which individuals go to such lengths as to forsake reason and threaten society as a whole. In other words, the exceptionality of crime would suggest that punishment itself would have a minor role in society. But that is not the case. Rather, punishment appears in Locke's work as an essential aspect of political power, necessary so that '*all Men* may be restrained from invading others Rights, and from doing hurt to one another, and the Law of Nature be observed'.[48] So at the same time as crime appears to be exceptional, punishment is posited as a pervasive instrument of social order. It seems that Locke's account of punishment has its own paradox.

The Ideological Conditions for Trust

One way to engage with this tension in Locke's theory is to understand Locke's state of nature, as C.B. MacPherson has suggested, as 'a curious mixture of historical imagination and logical abstraction from civil society'.[49] In *The Political Theory of Possessive Individualism*, MacPherson argues that the key to properly grasp both Hobbes's and Locke's political theories is to understand their postulates as identifying and building towards a specific model of society—which MacPherson identified as a possessive market society, but which arguably provided the foundations for contemporary liberal democratic societies. Hobbes lived in a period of extreme political turmoil, and concluded from his own experience the need for a strong and undisputed political authority.[50] In theorizing the state of nature, then, Hobbes was not hoping to find some universal truth about human nature, but to convey a message about the human condition in modernity that could 'persuade his readers of his political conclusions'.[51] For this purpose, he did not need to speculate about what happened with all societies throughout history in order to conceptualize his state of nature; he only needed to look 'just below the surface of [his] contemporary society'.[52] What he saw was a highly competitive environment, riddled with conflict and wars over property and dominance. There, just one step away from civilization, Hobbes found his natural subject. MacPherson aptly described Hobbes's state of nature as 'a two-stage logical abstraction in which man's natural proclivities are first disengaged from their civil setting and then carried to their logical conclusion in the state

---

[48] Locke, *Two Treatises of Government*, 271 (emphasis added).
[49] MacPherson, *The Political Theory of Possessive Individualism*, 209.
[50] See J. Hampton, *Hobbes and the Social Contract Tradition* (Cambridge: Cambridge University Press, 1986), 1: 'It would be difficult to find a time in history more tumultuous than the period … from approximately 1640 to 1660.'
[51] Ibid.　　　[52] MacPherson, *The Political Theory of Possessive Individualism*, 26.

of war'.[53] The essence of Hobbes's conception of human subjectivity comes from the first stage of this abstraction, which originates from 'the historically acquired nature of men [*sic*] in existing civil societies'.[54] This notion of human nature and psychology proved particularly attractive to the 'rising commercial classes'[55] of early modernity, which desired both to legitimate their claim to property and to reject the old hierarchies of medieval society. The individual freedom and equality which Hobbes theorized were to become hallmarks of the liberal tradition.

The core of Hobbes's argument lies in how he conceptualized the social acquired behaviour of individuals as part of their nature *at the same time* as he removed this behaviour from the socio-political environment which conditioned its existence. The result is a conception of human beings whose very nature makes them incapable of living in peace without a political authority. What made this conception of subjectivity so powerful, and the reason why it is still relevant today, is that Hobbes did not come to conceptualize individuals in the state of nature as savages or brutes who never came into contact with civilization. On the contrary, his argument could only be effective if the dangerousness of natural subjects lay just below the surface of civilized society. 'Natural man is civilised man with only the restraint of law removed.'[56] However, there was one significant shortcoming in Hobbes's theory: he conceptualized a natural equality among human beings that was too radical, and which therefore 'did not allow for the existence of politically significant [inequality]'.[57] This is what led Hobbes to postulate the necessity for an absolute sovereign, which proved unacceptable to the same rising commercial classes that were attracted by his depiction of human psychology, so that in the end the bulk of Hobbes's political model was largely rejected in preference for models of representative government, such as the one proposed by Locke.

Locke's conception of human nature also proved more attractive because he managed to preserve the image of the self-interested individual at the same time as he refused to completely abandon traditional natural law conceptions of morality, which promoted the intrinsically orderly and rational nature of human beings. In order to avoid Hobbes's authoritarian conclusions, Locke attempted to naturalize both individual liberty and law, so that Locke's natural subject was a civilized individual with only the reassurance of political authority removed. Instead of being reassured by an absolute sovereign, Locke proposed that individuals could mutually cooperate on the basis of the sharing of political power and of the structural conditions provided by private property. The result of this amalgamation was a theoretical framework

---

[53] Ibid.   [54] Ibid, 22.   [55] Ibid, 25–7.   [56] Ibid, 29.   [57] Ibid, 93.

which, although more prone to fall into contradiction, provided liberal political theory with a normative moral basis for law and society which Hobbes's
radical individualism lacked.

Locke's naturalization of the structural bases for responsible subjectivity and trust also brings into the state of nature another element of society
which was missing from Hobbes's account: structural inequality. MacPherson
argues that this inequality, when linked to Locke's conception of individual liberty and rationality, fully reveals the ideological dimension of Locke's
theory. This can be seen in the way that Locke connects his treatment of
property with his broader conception of individual liberty and rationality.
In Locke's theory, private property appears as the primary expression of individual liberty, meaning that it is rational and morally justified. Furthermore,
the importance of property (particularly land and money) to the exercise of
freedom and, especially, to the security of mutual benefit, implies that private
accumulation is not only a natural and legitimate manifestation of human
rationality, but effectively its highest expression. However, if rationality is
tied to property accumulation, and if property is unequally distributed, then
it can be inferred that Locke's state of nature also espouses an inequality of
access and capacity to reason. As MacPherson suggests, 'when ... unlimited
accumulation becomes rational, full rationality is possible only for those who
can so accumulate'.[58] Just as Locke's account started from formal equality in
order to legitimize substantial inequality with regards to property, the same
conclusion can be reached with regards to the exercise of individual liberty
more broadly.

Thus '[t]he initial equality of natural rights ... cannot last after the differentiation of property', since 'the man without property in things loses that
full proprietorship of his own person which was the basis of his equal natural
rights'.[59] It is important to note that the inequality of rationality implied in
this account is mainly ideological, in the sense that it does not suppose that
some individuals are biologically less rational than others, but rather that they
are incapable of exercising their rationality in full accordance with the dictates
of the law due to their socio-economic situation. The full thrust of Locke's
account of property thus highlights the structural conditions for his notion of
individual liberty: the state of nature is a state of perfect freedom, but only in the
sense that it is a state where each individual's freedom perfectly fits their capacity for rationality, measured by the alignment between their self-interest, their
means, and the values upheld by society's civil order. The promise of a notion
of individual liberty that is trustworthy and free from the shackles of political

---

[58] Ibid, 232.   [59] Ibid, 231.

authority is thus contingent upon the condition that liberty follows a specific logic.

This interpretation of Locke's theoretical framework, although somewhat far-fetched, can help explain the paradox in Locke's account of punishment. Since individuals without large possessions cannot 'be accounted fully rational',[60] they cannot be trusted to exercise their agency in complete conformity with the law, so that their freedom must be restrained. The stratified condition of Locke's natural liberty means that although most individuals will strive to behave as legal subjects, and only an exceptional few will behave in flagrant disregard for the bonds of mutual cooperation, the rationality employed by those who do not accumulate property (most probably the majority of the population) cannot be expected to be perfectly employed. Such imperfect exercise of liberty has the potential to become dangerous, so that it has to be properly regulated through political power. It is because of this need for regulation, conditioned by the notion that Locke's perfect liberty presupposes an imperfect, limited, and unequal distribution of autonomy, that Locke's state of nature, however orderly, requires a pervasive framework of punishment.

THE INCONVENIENCES OF INSECURITY: FROM PUNISHMENT TO PREVENTION

From the perspective developed in the previous section, it is possible to re-examine Locke's framework of crime and punishment, and draw some links between his account and the liberal model of criminal law. Different from the Hobbesian framework, where individual liberty was intrinsically insecure, and its exercise always potentially dangerous, in Locke's theory the primacy of responsible subjectivity is more firmly reassured, mainly because it is not arbitrary—that is, it is not artificially established through political society, but stems naturally from human agency and rationality. However, although responsible subjectivity is the presumptive position, it still needs to be secured and reassured through punishment. At first sight, punishment is directed solely at dangerous others. Locke claims that crime 'consists in violating the Law, and varying from the right Rule of Reason, whereby a Man so far becomes degenerate, and declares himself to quit the Principles of Human Nature, and to be a noxious Creature'.[61] Locke's strong denunciation of crime suggests that he is only considering as crimes those actions that are particularly

---

[60] Ibid, 238.   [61] Locke, *Two Treatises of Government*, 273.

serious, offences which are usually located at the normative core of the criminal law, such as crimes against the person, property, and public order.

Furthermore, Locke's emphasis on dangerousness implies that he does not see criminals as responsible subjects. Indeed, when discussing how the law should treat murderers, Locke states that such criminals have 'renounced Reason', so that they 'may be destroyed as a Lyon or a Tyger, one of those wild Savage Beasts, with whom Men can have no Society nor Security'.[62] In these cases, it seems that the only purpose of punishment is to incapacitate these savage individuals, so that they can do no (more) harm. Here Locke's account of punishment draws very close to Hobbes's, where punishment is presented mainly as a matter of self-preservation. However, only a few pages before his discussion of murder, Locke presents us with a markedly different picture, stating that punishment should only be delivered in order 'to retribute to [the criminal], so far as calm reason and conscience dictates, what is proportionate to his Transgression, which is so much as may serve for *Reparation* and *Restraint*'.[63] Now, Locke paints a rather different picture of punishment, arguing that it should be a measured, rational, and proportionate endeavour. Furthermore, punishment in this moment also affects the criminal in a rather different way, as it is not delivered merely in order to incapacitate and to prevent harm, but to 'make him repent the doing of [the crime], and thereby deter him, and by his Example others, from doing the like mischief'.[64] In this passage, not only is the criminal presented as a rational, moral, and responsible subject, but punishment itself also possesses a communicative aspect, in that it is partly targeted at deterring other responsible subjects from committing further crimes.

Seen as a whole, Locke's criminal subject appears to be inherently ambivalent: s/he is presented both as a responsible subject who can be addressed rationally and who therefore deserves to be treated with respect, and as a dangerous subject who cannot be expected to behave responsibly and who therefore needs to be contained. In addition, this problem of ambivalence in Locke's work seems to go beyond his notion of the criminal, affecting the entirety of his conception of individual liberty. This ambivalence, which remains latent throughout his account of the state of nature, is exposed when he starts to make his case for the necessity of political authority. Towards the end of the chapter on the state of nature, he concedes that this state is not without its inconveniences. The main problem he identifies, surprisingly, is that of insecurity. For although individuals have the natural right to freely exercise their liberty, 'the Enjoyment of [this right] is very uncertain, and

---

[62] Ibid, 274.   [63] Ibid, 272 (emphasis in original).   [64] Ibid.

constantly exposed to the Invasion of others'—a risk which 'must certainly be Great, where Men may be Judges in their own Case'.[65] Ironically, the problem of insecurity in the state of nature stems from the same notion which Locke deployed to reassure his natural liberty: the reciprocity of political power. In echoing Hobbes's words that the absence of a common judge hinders the possibility of justice, Locke admits that political power in the state of nature falls prey to the volatility of private judgment. Furthermore, the main hindrance to the trustworthiness of private judgment appears to be the problem of self-interest, as 'Men being biased by their Interest ... are not apt to allow of [the law of nature] as a Law binding to them in the application of it to their particular Cases.'[66] However, it has become clear from Locke's account of property that self-interest is also what leads to private accumulation, which is the main conduit to mutual benefit.

How can Locke sustain such irreconcilable conceptions of individual liberty, self-interest, and criminal behaviour in his theoretical framework, and claim that the reciprocity of political power is both the source of insecurity in the state of nature, and the solution to it? One way to address these perplexities is to rescue the notion that individual liberty and responsible subjectivity are stratified and unevenly distributed in Locke's theoretical framework. If not all individual agency is fully rational, then what makes self-interest conducive or harmful to mutual benefit depends on whether it is being employed in a rational manner, or whether it is being driven by the 'Defects and Imperfections which are in us, as living singly and solely by our selves'.[67] Indeed, in one passage, when discussing the limitations to the right of property in the state of nature, Locke explicitly recognizes the inequality of responsible subjectivity in his framework: 'For all being Kings as much as he, every Man his Equal, *and the greater part no strict Observers of Equity and Justice*, the enjoyment of the property he has in this state is very unsafe, very insecure.'[68] Unlike in Hobbes's work, insecurity for Locke is not radical, and not shared by everyone in equal measures. Instead, Locke appears in this passage to be specifically referring to those individuals who are fully rational, and who are most concerned about their property, and distinguishing them from 'the greater part' of the population, whose imperfect rationality (and access to property) makes them 'no strict Observers of Equity and Justice'.

The same perspective can be applied to provide a more nuanced interpretation of Locke's framework of punishment and criminal subjectivity. While some crimes will be serious and dangerous, those instances are expected to be exceptional, the product of 'the corruption, and vitiousness of degenerate

[65] Ibid, 276.   [66] Ibid, 351.   [67] Hooker cited in Locke, ibid, 278.
[68] Locke, ibid, 276.

Men'[69] who forsake reason. Instead, most crimes in Locke's socio-political framework are likely to refer to the conduct of those individuals who do not have full access to rationality, and who therefore exercise their liberty imperfectly. These crimes will be either the result of unchecked self-interest, or of an error in reasoning. So although the pervasiveness of punishment in Locke's theory suggests that crime is a normal occurrence in his model of society, this does not necessarily compromise the trustworthiness of human nature. This is so because the structural inequality in Locke's framework implies that although many individuals—probably the majority—will not behave in full conformity with his normative conceptions of liberty and property, and therefore will be no strict observers of justice in Locke's view, only a rare few will actually behave as dangerous subjects. Under these lenses, it is dangerousness, and not crime, that is conceptualized as exceptional by Locke. And while the dangerous criminal is at the core of Locke's justification of punishment, the main function of the criminal law in such a society is likely to be the regulation of social behaviour.

Examined in these terms, Locke's socio-political framework can provide a more complex picture of the role of punishment and criminalization in society than Hobbes's theory, for it allows for a more nuanced understanding of criminal subjectivity. The notion that crime can appear as the expression of a wanton disregard for the law and security of others highlights the preventive function of the criminal law. The idea that crime can be the consequence of a defect or imperfection in an individual's agency, in turn, points to how criminalization has an important regulatory role. Finally, the possibility that self-interest and partiality can lead to a misuse of individual liberty suggests that crime can be the result of a moral mistake, of unfair or wrongful conduct; this time, criminalization and punishment can be seen to possess a mainly declaratory, condemnatory aspect.[70] This complexity has an important reassuring role, as it reinforces the normativity of responsible subjectivity by diffusing the insecurity generated by dangerousness. From this perspective, crime can be potentially dangerous, but it is most of the time an outcome of the 'unsocial sociability'[71] of human beings, that is, a misuse of liberty on the part of otherwise responsible subjects who can be trusted to learn from their punishment not to make the same mistake again. Arguably, then, Locke's account of criminal subjectivity is much closer to the normative conceptions that lie at

---

[69] Ibid, 352.

[70] For the different functions of punishment and criminal law, see A. Ashworth, 'Conceptions of Overcriminalization' (2008) 5 *Ohio State Journal of Criminal Law*, 407–25.

[71] I. Kant, 'Idea for a Universal History with a Cosmopolitan Purpose' in I. Kant, *Political Writings* (Cambridge: Cambridge University Press, 1991), 41–53, 44.

the core of the liberal imaginary of criminal law and the balance the criminal law presumes between trust and reassurance.

Legitimizing the Primacy of Prevention: The War of Law against All

However, in the state of nature, the security of responsible subjectivity is still threatened by the fragility of political power. Although Locke's state of nature has a law to govern it, and individuals in it have the power to enforce this law, this power provides little reassurance if it is not secured by a common authority, as it can always be misused. Even the power to judge and punish finds itself compromised by the imperfections of individual liberty, as 'Passion and Revenge is very apt to carry them too far, and with too much heat, in their own Cases ... as well as negligence, and unconcernedness, to make them too remiss, in other Mens.'[72] And even where a fair judgment might be reached, without such authority, 'there often wants *Power* to back and support the Sentence when right, and to *give* it due *Execution*'.[73] This way, although the possibility of social relations in the state of nature is not universally rejected, the instability of rational agency effectively imbues individual liberty with an aspect of vulnerability. The inevitable outcome of this vulnerability is that liberty must be secured by being subjected to a higher authority which can exercise political power in the name of individuals, and so rid it of its insecurity. Thus while Locke begins his account of human nature by linking law and liberty together, when he later removes the legal aspect from the imperfect liberty of some individuals, it is the law that appears natural and perfect, so that certain forms of human agency become unnatural, and therefore wrongful. This happens because Locke's normative conception of liberty is not a function of human nature, but a reflection of a specific model of society and of the civil order contained in it.

As a result of the insecurity of political power, even though Locke's sociopolitical framework is supposed to reassure responsible subjectivity without recourse to an authoritarian notion of political society, his natural conception of civil order still ends up depending on the power of the state for its security. The implications of this dependence can be examined through Locke's discussion of the state of war. While for Hobbes it seemed that war was the inevitable outcome of the natural condition of mankind, were it not for the establishment of political society, Locke starts his discussion by stressing that 'the State of Nature, and the State of War, which however some Men have confounded, are as far distant, as a State of Peace, Good Will, Mutual

---

[72] Locke, *Two Treatises of Government*, 351.　　　[73] Ibid (emphasis in original).

Assistance, and Preservation, and a State of Enmity, Malice, Violence, and Mutual Destruction are one from another'.[74] For Locke, war takes place when someone forsakes the boundaries of their liberty and declares, 'by Word or Action',[75] the intent to 'take away the Freedom'[76] of another by use of force. 'To be free from such force is the only security of my Preservation: and reason bids me look on him, as an Enemy to my Preservation, who would take away that Freedom, which is the Fence to it.'[77] The danger contained in such aggression confers upon the victim the right of war, which entitles an individual to abandon the limits of her/his own liberty and attack, possibly even kill, an aggressor 'for the same Reason, that he may kill a *Wolf* or a *Lyon*; because such Men are not under the ties of the Common Law of Reason, have no other Rule, but that of Force and Violence, and so may be treated as Beasts of Prey, those dangerous and noxious Creatures'.[78]

The remarkable similarities between Locke's description of the criminal and that of the aggressor in the state of war highlight once more the dangerousness which is inherent to his conception of criminal subjectivity, as well as the preventive aspect of punishment and criminalization. More than that, however, it also emphasizes how the danger of crime makes the criminal appear as a dangerous other, as someone who is not part of the community, but rather a threat to it. It is interesting to note that Locke attempts to maintain a distinction between punishment and the right of war, claiming that while punishment is a measured expression of political power aimed at preserving the boundaries of juridical liberty, subject to certain procedural restraints, war is a reflection of the victim's right to self-preservation, a defensive response to an imminent danger. 'Thus a Thief, whom I cannot harm but by appeal to the Law, for having stolen all that I am worth, I may kill, when he sets on me to rob me, but of my Horse or Coat.'[79] It appears that the main difference between the state of nature and the state of war is that, in nature, there is a minimum sense of order, so that individuals have recourse to the law and are therefore bound to respect its limits, while in war, their self-preservation is directly at risk, so that the juridical boundaries of liberty have no hold.

As Locke wrote, 'Want of a common Judge with Authority, puts all Men in a State of Nature: Force without Right, upon a Man's Person, makes a State of War.'[80] In the state of nature, the appropriate response to criminal behaviour is punishment; in the state of war, individuals can do whatever is necessary to guarantee their preservation. This distinction in the Lockean framework produces a very close analogy to the distinction maintained by liberal criminal law between punishment and prevention, which also exposes the

---

[74] Ibid, 280. [75] Ibid, 278. [76] Ibid, 279. [77] Ibid. [78] Ibid.
[79] Ibid, 280. [80] Ibid, 281.

latter's normative assumptions: while punishment is measured and respects the criminal as a responsible subject, prevention focuses mainly on the individual's dangerousness, and is ultimately unprincipled. However, there are a few details that complicate this picture. The first is that, as Locke's theory indicates, although dangerousness reigns over prevention, it is also part of the framework of punishment. In this sense, punishment itself also intrinsically displays a preventive aspect, which can always potentially overcome its concerns with justice and proportionality. To some extent, therefore, the difference between punishment and war is one of degree, not of quality.

Secondly, although Locke's state of war disturbs the order of the state of nature, it is still far from being the amoral fight for self-preservation in Hobbes's war of all against all. Locke's war is a moral, even juridical, endeavour: it begins with an act of force *without right*, which *entitles* the victim and any supporters to *rightfully* fight any aggressors up to the point of taking their life. Thus war for Locke is not about two sides with equal opposing rights to self-preservation, but about one side exercising their right to self-preservation against another, who forsake their own right by means of their aggression. It is therefore far from a lawless condition; rather, it is 'a juridical decision by arms: the right to judge and proceed against a recalcitrant transgressor by force of arms'.[81] So instead of eschewing or nullifying the law of nature, the right of war constitutes its ultimate means of enforcement, its ultimate guarantee, available whenever it is necessary 'to appeal to Heaven';[82] that is, to seek justice through force. While the right of war initially appears to be triggered by self-preservation, it soon becomes clear that it is the *right* to self-preservation that leads to the right of war, not self-preservation in itself; proof of this is that the aggressor loses her/his right the moment s/he performs the aggression. The core of the right of war is thus the law, the preservation of all through the preservation of right, and not individual self-interest as in Hobbes's theory. For this reason, even though war disturbs the natural social order, it does not completely disrupt it; on the contrary, it constitutes the means towards the restoration of this order. Because it is legalized, the right of war still has its place even after the establishment of political society.

The juridification of war exposes the primacy of legal authority and security over individual liberty and autonomy in Locke's thinking. Moreover, it also illustrates how prevention is justified, even in its excesses, as providing and securing the conditions for the exercise of individual liberty. The distinction between punishment and prevention is mostly strategic and ideological, as dangerousness is an inherent aspect of the way the criminal subject is

---

[81] Tully, *An Approach to Political Philosophy*, 25.
[82] Locke, *Two Treatises of Government*, 282.

conceived within a social imaginary that is predominantly concerned with civil order. While Locke puts great emphasis on the trust embedded within his conception of human nature, the dependence of individual liberty on a specific model of society, with a particular set of structural conditions and normative expectations, demonstrates that it is this particular social order, and not the individual per se, which is Locke's core concern.

Locke's discussion of the state of war and the importance of (rightful) self-preservation completes his justification of the need for individual autonomy to be subjected to political authority. Since the right of war necessitates political power to fulfil its function of restoring law and order, then just like punishment, it finds itself precarious in the state of nature. It is only possible to ensure that conflict reaches an end when it occurs 'between those who are in Society, and are equally on both sides Subjected to the fair determination of the Law; because then there lies open the remedy of appeal for the past injury, and to prevent future harm; but where no such appeal is, as in the State of Nature, ... the State of War once begun, continues'[83] indefinitely. 'To avoid this State of War', Locke continues, 'is one great reason of Mens putting themselves into Society, and quitting the State of Nature'.[84] This last sentence evidences how close insecurity is to the peaceful surface of Locke's model of society, and how important it is for this model's normative justification.

Instead of eliminating the vulnerability of juridical relations, Locke's conception of natural liberty only represses it under an ideological structure which is deeply reliant on socio-political conditions, while still deploying this same vulnerability in order to legitimate the political and juridical authority of the state. By making dangerousness exceptional, Locke may have reassured the primacy of responsible subjectivity and provided a more nuanced and moralized account of punishment. At the same time, however, he also justified war and reinforced the legitimation of political authority, including its preventive and coercive aspects, thus maintaining the reassurance function at the core of the criminal law.

THE ENDS OF POLITICAL SOCIETY: CRIMINAL LAW AND CIVIL ORDER

The juridification of natural liberty in Locke's political theory provides an interesting framework through which to analyse the dynamics of trust and

---

[83] Ibid, 281.
[84] Ibid, 282. Peter Laslett (ibid, editor's notes) calls this sentence 'Locke's closest formal approach to [Hobbes] in his political theory'.

reassurance in criminal subjectivity. As previously discussed, in Hobbes's theory, natural liberty was essentially at odds with any juridical boundary, as individuals in the state of nature were free to act in any way they saw fit for their self-preservation. Individual liberty is only artificially restricted through the establishment of the commonwealth, and this implies that although individuals choose to limit their liberty and empower the sovereign to protect these limits, at heart, they remain natural subjects who can always be at least potentially dangerous, thus highlighting the intrinsic vulnerability of individual autonomy. Locke's conception of human nature, on the other hand, advances an image of natural liberty which is compatible with the premises behind responsible legal subjectivity. For Locke, individual autonomy is inherently harmonious with law and reason, and exercised within juridical boundaries, so that individuals can be expected to behave responsibly. Likewise, the structural and political conditions of society are not at odds with natural liberty, as they exist to promote the conditions for its flourishing. Since the liberty of individuals is not directly in conflict with political authority, the citizens of the community can be expected to normally behave responsibly, and to only exceptionally commit crimes.

The inherent connection between liberty and law, and law and security, means that the civil law mainly promotes and enhances natural liberty— Locke's political society perfects the state of nature, instead of overcoming it. On the other hand, such perfecting is made necessary by the insecurity of political power with regards to the partiality and defectiveness of private judgment. Without the protection of the state, Locke's liberty is perfect only in the abstract, as it necessitates political authority for its complete actualization. 'Civil Government is the proper Remedy for the Inconveniences of the State of Nature.'[85] It is interesting that although the abstract character of liberty originates from its uneven distribution, inequality is not the main problem to be resolved for Locke. Indeed, Locke's model of society requires inequality and is there to preserve it, for the highest expression of rationality and liberty lies in unlimited accumulation. Individual liberty is about competition; the problem is to make sure that this competition remains peaceful— that is, orderly. For this purpose, the main problem of the state of nature is that, while liberty is unequal, political power is equally shared. Thus the same political equality that grounds the law of nature, the perfect liberty of individuals and the reciprocity of political power eventually leads to inequality, and to the need for law and punishment to be enforced and reinforced by a public authority. Locke confers political power to individuals just so that

---

[85] Ibid, 276.

he can justifiably take it away; for 'there, and there only is Political Society, where every one of the Members hath quitted this natural Power'.[86] Likewise, while individuals have to be deemed capable of self-government in order to be considered responsible, once this standard of responsible subjectivity needs to be universalized, individuals need to agree to give up their right to self-government 'to be regulated by Laws made by the Society', which 'in many things confine the liberty he had by the Law of Nature'.[87] So although it appears to remain the same, individual liberty effectively takes a different form under political society, when the regulation of its boundaries is taken from individuals and given to civil government.

Or rather, while individual liberty initially seems to be about the liberty of every individual, after the differentiation of property, liberty has to be defined around the specific rationality of private accumulation and structural inequality. It is this specific rationality which turns out to be the chief end of Locke's conceived society, and it is this specific image of society which comes to generate a standard of judgment that will represent the general will of the community. Different from Hobbes, Locke does not conceive that political society will be fully personified by a sovereign; instead, these two entities, society and sovereign, remain somewhat conceptually distinct. His framework suggests a 'double contractual operation' in which people 'contract with each other in order to have "society", and then this "society" (the people as a whole) decides to have a government, a government it constructs on conditions'.[88] This conceptual structure, setting the foundations for representative government, has a clear emancipatory aspect which resists Hobbes's absolutist conclusions, by retaining political power in the hands of the people, which for Locke represents the real public authority. However, although individuals enter society in order to protect their individual rights and property, it should be noted that society is not mainly concerned with representing the self-interest of its members per se, but rather the *public interest*. The public interest, in turn, is that which is in league with the law of nature, which corresponds with the dictates of individual liberty and rationality. 'In Lockean liberalism the durability of natural law in civil society, combined with the pre-existence of the individual person as *proprietor*, means that natural law has precedence over civil laws and over the rights of individuals, even in their most particularised aspects'.[89] In other words, it is the socio-political framework postulated

---

[86] Ibid, 324.   [87] Ibid, 352–3.

[88] Harrison, *Hobbes, Locke, and Confusion's Masterpiece*, 212.

[89] L. Jaume, 'Hobbes and the Philosophical Sources of Liberalism' in P. Springbord (ed), *The Cambridge Companion to Hobbes's Leviathan* (Cambridge: Cambridge University Press, 2007), 199–216, 202.

by the law of nature that is at the heart of Locke's conception of society. And although individual freedom is central to this framework, this freedom is in actuality a function and an abstract representation of this civil order, an idea in service of the public good.

By turning a specific notion of subjectivity and agency into a normative standard for the whole of society, Locke makes this notion acquire an aspect of universality. 'And thus all private judgment of every particular Member being excluded, the Community comes to be Umpire, by settled standing Rules, indifferent, and the same to all Parties.'[90] However, the structural inequality maintained by Locke's model of society betrays the ideological aspect of this universality, showing that its purpose is to legitimize particular practices and notions. For instance, in his account of property, Locke universalizes access to property in order to legitimize its privatization. And in his account of political power and punishment, Locke privatizes judgment so that he can then justify its universalization. In the end, the property of all becomes the legitimate property of some, while the judgment of some serves as the legitimate judgment of all.

Criminal Subjectivity, Prerogative, and the Contingency of Trust

The relationship between individual freedom, law, and juridical liberty at the heart of Locke's framework of punishment can guide an understanding of how the standard of responsible subjectivity embedded in the liberal model of society can shape and condition, while still preserving, the essential insecurity of legal individualism. Some general insights can be taken from the previous analysis. First, since punishment is naturalized in Locke's theory, it appears moral and legitimate in political society, instead of an arbitrary imposition of power as it might be implied in Hobbes's work. Crime, in turn, is not presented as a consequence of individual liberty, but rather as originating in imperfections of human nature arising either from the anti-social, almost pathological behaviour of some, or from the misguided judgment of those who do not have full access to the rationality of property. Individual self-interest may generate insecurity, but only when it is not restrained by reason or not properly regulated by political power; when it is rational and measured, self-interest actually benefits the public interest, so that it should be encouraged. Because of that, political power and authority can be harmonious with individual liberty, and preserve and enhance it. It is only the imperfect agency of some that may threaten this balance.

Second, in Locke's account, the normative aspects of individual liberty appear to remain the same in the shift from nature to political society. The

---

[90] Locke, *Two Treatises of Government*, 324.

main exception is the right to self-government through political power, which is transferred from individuals to society. Since political power involves the power to criminalize and to punish, the shift from nature to society incurs a transformation in the treatment of criminalization and punishment by Locke, which can assist in further explaining the aforementioned complexity in his account. Initially, the greatest threat to individual liberty seems to be the dangerousness of crime, which is ultimately what justifies the power to punish. However, when arguing for the necessity of political authority, the main problem of Locke's society shifts from dangerousness to the imperfection and partiality of private judgment. At this moment, furthermore, the problem of dangerousness is pushed to the margins of society, into the state of war. Right at the shift to political society, then, dangerousness is effectively 'exceptionalised', and punishment acquires a much more orderly aspect, linked mainly to the regulation of society and to the condemnation of wrongful behaviour. Locke's socio-political framework effectively reassures responsible subjectivity by placing it within a conceptual and contextual structure which allows individuals to be conceptualized as generally trustworthy, and only exceptionally dangerous. Locke's account of punishment in political society, in contrast to war, implies that punishment is mainly addressed at responsible subjects, while war—'a juridical decision by arms'—is reserved for those who behave too dangerously. As previously discussed, it is possible to argue that the distinction between punishment and war in Locke's work can be conceptualized as different expressions of the state's penal power, emulating the distinction often reproduced in criminal law scholarship between punishment and prevention.

Locke's socio-political framework is thus able to provide the conceptual foundations for many of the aspects of the contemporary framework of criminal law, particularly with regards to its interpretation under the liberal model. This is arguably due to the thick notion of civil order implicit in Locke's framework, which advances many notions which lie at the core of the liberal social imaginary. However, if this analogy is correct, then it can also be used to highlight the abstract and contingent character of the trust grounding responsible subjectivity. Although individual liberty plays a primary role in Locke's conception of society, around which his whole socio-political structure is constructed, this liberty is primarily a function of his model of society. The result is that, when the liberty of individuals comes into conflict with the security of the structural conditions of his society, this security is prioritized. The supremacy of security in Locke's framework[91] is made evident by the shifting role of self-preservation in the passage from nature to society. In

---

[91] See M. Neocleous, *Critique of Security* (Edinburgh: Edinburgh University Press, 2008), chapter 1.

the state of nature, when political power rested in the hands of individuals, the rationality of the law of nature had to adequate itself to individual self-interest, so that individuals were bound, only 'when [their] own Preservation *comes not in competition*, ... to preserve the rest of Mankind'.[92] But when political society is established, the political power necessary to guarantee the security of the public interest is transferred to society, to be employed by its civil government. Once political power is freed from the inconveniences of private judgment, the fundamental law of civil government transforms into '*the preservation of the Society*, and (as far as will consist with the public good) of every person in it'.[93] As the public good is the ultimate goal of individual liberty, once the power to protect it is concentrated in government, the protection of society predominates over individual self-preservation.

The primacy of the common good in Locke's theory is grounded on the idea that the establishment of political society promotes formal equality, since 'every single person [becomes] subject, equally with other the meanest Men, to those Laws, which he himself, as part of the Legislative had established: nor could any one, by his own Authority, avoid the force of the Law, when once made'.[94] This equalizing aspect of society, furthermore, extends itself even to those in government, so that unlike Hobbes's sovereign, they too are subject to the law. 'The relation of governance between governors and free citizens is conceptualized, not as sovereign and subjects, as in the absolutist traditions, but rather as a game of conditional and mutual subjection in which each governs the other by subjecting the other to the rule of law.'[95] According to James Tully, 'this agonistic picture of government is [Locke's] most distinctive and enduring contribution to modern political thought'.[96] Indeed, this agonistic picture of government can be seen to resonate with the role given to individual responsibility in the normative framework of criminal law: responsible subjectivity appears as the primary normative concept, binding the power of the state (by subjecting punishment to the ascription of responsibility) as well as the autonomy of individuals (by linking individual autonomy to responsible agency, and therefore subsuming human subjectivity under responsible subjectivity).

In Locke's political society, therefore, the power of government is not posited as absolute, but as subjected to the same public good that binds individual liberty:

---

[92] Locke, *Two Treatises of Government*, 271 (emphasis added).
[93] Ibid, 356 (emphasis in original).   [94] Ibid, 329–30.
[95] Tully, *An Approach to Political Philosophy*, 3.   [96] Ibid.

though Men when they enter into Society, give up the Equality, Liberty, and Executive Power they had in the State of Nature, into the hands of the Society … yet it being only with an intention in every one the better to preserve himself his Liberty and Property … the power of the Society, or *Legislative* constituted by them, *can never be suppos'd to extend farther than the common good*; but is obliged to secure every ones Property by providing against those … defects … that made the State of Nature so unsafe and uneasie.[97]

However, although Locke considered that the sharing of power between governors and citizens would mean that the government could always be scrutinized and regulated by the people, and even deposed if necessary, these hopes significantly downplay both the ideological force of the idea of public good and the asymmetry of power between the state and actual citizens. Both of these issues come together in Locke's account of prerogative. According to this power, although government is normally limited by the civil law, in cases of emergency, 'wherein a strict and rigid observation of the Laws may do harm', the power to decide and to do whatever is necessary 'must necessarily be left to the discretion of him, that has the Executive Power in his hands, to be ordered by him, as the publick good and advantage shall require'.[98] Since the maintenance and promotion of the public good relies on the structural conditions set by the law of nature, and since the primary goal set by these laws is the preservation of the community, whenever these conditions find themselves vulnerable and in danger, Locke has no choice but to bring back the absolute power of the sovereign.

Just like the right of war, this sovereign power upsets the juridical boundaries of individual liberty; however, just like war, this power is ultimately justified as an instrument of justice, necessary for protecting the conditions and integrity of society. Prerogative is thus 'nothing but the Power of doing publick good without a Rule'.[99] The logic of the prerogative highlights and emulates the main paradox contained in the relation between liberal law and prevention, namely, that liberty is seen as the main restraint to the preventive power of the state, but this limitation is effectively trumped by the notion that prevention is necessary in order to preserve the conditions for liberty. What is posited as a situation of balance thus conceals a hierarchy of priorities, managed primarily by socio-political discourse and contingency. As long as it remains tied to images of civil order that preserve socio-political conditions of structural violence, the ideal of individual autonomy and responsibility at the core of the liberal model is at best a compromise, and at worst an

---

[97] Locke, *Two Treatises of Government*, 353.   [98] Ibid, 375.   [99] Ibid, 378.

ideological construction that can legitimize emancipatory and exclusionary measures alike, when circumstances demand it.

CONCLUSION

The vulnerability of liberty to the structural conditions of trust in society reveals the limitations of the pursuit of individual justice grounded upon an abstract conception of individual autonomy and responsible subjectivity. Criminal subjectivity, even in conditions of social stability, remains essentially a function of the maintenance of the ideological framework of liberal society, for the liberal conception of responsible subjectivity is more directly aligned with the civil order grounding these structural conditions than it is with the complexity and diversity of human agency found in the midst of society. For that reason, even when the socio-political environment is such that liberal law can guarantee or expect a high degree of legal security, ultimately this trust rests on insecure foundations. Whenever the structure of trust is threatened or finds itself eroded, the expectation of social compliance disappears, and the need for the reassurance function of the criminal law is reinforced.

This is why the framework of individual responsibility is intrinsically vulnerable to dangerousness. The naturalization of punishment, the moralization of war, and the possibility of the state to justifiably go against its own law by means of the prerogative in Locke's theory offers a conceptual framework through which to analyse these ideas. Moreover, these elements in Locke's socio-political framework also suggest that, when it really mattered, Locke was unable to maintain his trust in human agency, choosing instead to place his confidence in the reassuring potential of his model of society. As MacPherson suggested, 'Locke was indeed at the fountain-head of English liberalism', the 'greatness' of which 'was its assertion of the free rational individual as the criterion of the good society'; its 'tragedy', however, 'was that this very assertion was necessarily a denial of individualism' to a great portion of the population.[100] In this chapter, I aimed to argue that this 'tragedy' is one of the main factors underpinning the ideological trappings and limitations of liberal criminal law.

---

[100] MacPherson, *The Political Theory of Possessive Individualism*, 262.

5

Civil Society, Dangerousness, and the Ambivalence of Liberal Civil Order

The greatest problem for the human species, the solution of which nature compels him to seek, is that of attaining a civil society which can administer justice universally.[1]

After examining the conceptual foundations of both reassurance and trust in the liberal imaginary, in this chapter I turn to a discussion of how the ambivalences and paradoxes found within the liberal imaginary are systematized in modern liberal political and legal thought and how, in doing so, they inform and legitimize a particular notion of civil order. I aim to uncover the normative grounds for the dialectic relation between responsibility and dangerousness in the contemporary framework of criminal law, which allow it to retain its sense of legitimacy and justification even as it defies its own principles and assumes an explicit authoritarian aspect, such as in the case of the preventive turn. I pursue this objective through an analysis of the work of two Enlightenment theorists, G.W.F. Hegel and Jeremy Bentham. More specifically, I explore how these two complex accounts of the role of criminal law in society manage to actualize the primacy of individual responsibility only by recognizing the embeddedness of dangerousness within criminal subjectivity. As a result, the conceptual frameworks laid down by both Hegel and Bentham end up allowing for the legitimacy of the authoritarian and preventive power of the state while still upholding the primacy of responsible subjectivity and of individual autonomy and freedom. What engenders these dynamics is arguably the existence, at the core of both accounts, of an ideal conception of social order and human agency which is conceptualized as an embedded and persistent aspect of modern civil society.

The chapter starts with a discussion of the prevalence in modern political thought of a dichotomy in the conception of society, which legitimates

[1] I. Kant, 'Idea for a Universal History with a Cosmopolitan Purpose' in *Political Writings*, 41–53, 45.
The Preventive Turn in Criminal Law. First Edition. Henrique Carvalho. © Henrique Carvalho 2017. Published 2017 by Oxford University Press.

political authority and law by distinguishing it from unruly and dangerous forces in society that are normally attributed to aspects of human nature. This conception of society finds its most sophisticated account in Hegel's political theory, detailed in his *Philosophy of Right*.[2] The second part of the chapter examines Hegel's account of criminal law and punishment, focusing on the shifts in that account as it travels from an examination of abstract right to the perplexities of crime, law, and punishment in civil society. I argue that, since Hegel cannot eliminate the problems of that society, he needs to posit the possibility of transcending these problems through the political unity provided by the rational state. In so doing, however, Hegel isolates his ideal notion of political community from the structural violence of modern social relations, and thus allows the state to retain its normative position as the guarantor of individual liberty even when it appears arbitrary or authoritarian.

The third part of the chapter looks at Bentham's account of crime and punishment, focusing particularly on the theoretical framework laid out in *The Principles of Morals and Legislation*.[3] My main argument in this section is that Bentham's account of the criminal law and of the role of punishment in society emulates the same dichotomy found in Hegel's political theory, so that it expresses the same ambivalence with regards to criminal subjectivity. I then discuss how the relation between civil and political society in the liberal imaginary allows the criminal law to both uphold the primacy of individual liberty and responsibility, and to justify preventive and authoritarian measures, all in the name of the preservation of civil order.

THE CIVIL DYNAMIC
BETWEEN NATURE AND SOCIETY

Although the political theories presented by Hobbes and Locke differ in many significant ways, I argued in the previous chapters that they espouse elements which share a common background, a specific model of society. This model is grounded on two primary ideas: that of human beings as autonomous, self-interested individuals, and that of political society as the necessary coming together of these individuals under the rule of a public authority. Together, these two ideas constitute the foundations of a tendency, common throughout most of modern political thought, to consider political society—that is, the state—as

---

[2] G.W.F. Hegel (T.M. Knox translator), *Hegel's Philosophy of Right* (New York: Oxford University Press, 1967).

[3] J. Bentham, *The Principles of Morals and Legislation* (Amherst: Prometheus Books, 1988).

the supreme and definitive moment of the common and collective life of man [*sic*] considered as a rational being, as the most perfect or less imperfect result of that process of rationalisation of the instincts or passions or interests for which the rule of disorderly strength is transformed into one of controlled liberty.[4]

According to Norberto Bobbio, this process is conceptualized and theorized 'through the constant use of a dichotomic model, where the state is conceived as a positive moment opposed to a pre-state or anti-state society, which is degraded to a negative moment'.[5] In both Hobbes's and Locke's theories, this dichotomic model appears expressed as the contrast between the state of nature, or natural (pre-political) society, and political society, or the state, formed after the social contract, by means of the establishment of a public authority which can secure and express a common standard of judgment.

Hobbes posited the state of nature as a state of endemic insecurity, which almost inevitably led to a war of all against all, and which could only be overcome by means of political society. Locke, on the other hand, saw natural society as an environment of relative social harmony, which was only disturbed by inconveniences arising from the defective rationality of some and the exceptional wickedness of a few individuals. While political society in Hobbes's framework was an attempt to suppress and eliminate the state of nature, for Locke it was meant to perfect natural society through the inclusion of civil law and common judgment. As previously discussed, the contrasts between the Hobbesian and the Lockean perspectives on the relation between pre-political and political society revealed important insights about the role of criminalization and punishment in society. Since for Hobbes the insecurity of the state of nature meant that there could be no valid law or effective moral judgment, the protection of individual rights and the enforcement of responsible agency were only possible after the establishment of a political power capable of reassuring the limits to individual autonomy through law and punishment. This perspective on human nature implied that individuals could only be trusted to behave responsibly within the protected environment of political society, otherwise they would always be potentially dangerous to each other. Crime in this sense primarily represents an expression of the intrinsic dangerousness of human nature, symbolizing a denial of the terms of the social contract and a recurrence of the natural, pre-political condition of human relations.

---

[4] N. Bobbio, 'Gramsci and the Conception of Civil Society' in C. Mouffe (ed), *Gramsci and Marxist Theory* (London: Routledge, 1979), 21–47, 21.
[5] Ibid, 22.

For Locke, on the other hand, the state of nature was furnished with a basic structure that was in principle able to provide the necessary conditions for trust. As a result, individual right, law, and punishment all had validity even before the establishment of political society. The main purpose of political society and its institutionalization of law was thus not to supress human nature but to regulate it, to correct defects in natural individuals which required the tutelage of the state.[6] While dangerousness was an aspect of Locke's society, it was conceptualized as exceptional; so although criminalization and punishment still had a reassurance function with regards to dangerousness in Locke's socio-political model, their primary function appeared to be the maintenance of social order. Even so, this aspect of order was only fully reassured in political society, as political authority turned out to be necessary in order to ensure that dangerousness remained the exception and not the norm.

The analytical framework provided by an analysis of the political theories of Hobbes and Locke exposes the main conceptual structure arising from the dichotomic model of society. However, while it is with Hobbes and Locke that this tradition of modern political thought, which establishes the roots of liberal theory, is initiated, it is arguably after the Enlightenment, and more specifically in the work of Hegel, that 'the rationalisation of the state reaches its climax'.[7] This is so because, until Hegel, the dichotomy between nature and society was too categorical, and therefore too static; while it is possible to uncover the dynamism in these theoretical accounts, their own models of society maintained—indeed, relied upon—the notion that there was, at some point, a definitive rupture between the natural and the political condition of mankind. As such, these conceptions of society—along with the notions of subjectivity that they sustained—remained too idealized. As was previously discussed, the notion of the state of nature appears mostly as an ideological device in order to justify the necessity of political society. In Hegel's work, on the other hand, the dichotomy between pre-political and political society is for the first time 'represented not simply as a proposal for an ideal model, but as an understanding of the real historical movement: the rationality of the state is no longer just a necessity but a reality, not just an ideal but an event of history'.[8] In other words, Hegel's political philosophy preserves the dichotomic model, but does so by embracing its complexities and ambivalences as different dimensions of modern society. By historicizing this dialectic, Hegel does away with the polar opposition between nature and civilization upheld

---

[6] See M. Oakeshott, *Hobbes on Civil Association* (Indianapolis: Liberty Fund, 1975), 62–3.
[7] Bobbio, 'Gramsci and the Conception of Civil Society', 21.   [8] Ibid, 21.

by the social contract tradition, understanding the pre-political condition of individuals as a moment within the modern socio-political framework. The key to this significant transformation lies in Hegel's re-conceptualization of civil society.

Civilizing Nature

Up until and including the writings of Kant, the terms 'civil society' and 'political society' were essentially synonymous. Kant, who was significantly influenced by Locke's work, postulated in his *Metaphysics of Morals* that 'the condition of the state of nature is not opposed and contrasted with the social condition but with the civil condition. For within a state of nature there can indeed be society, but not a civil society'.[9] In other words, Kant implied that it was only when society was regulated by civil laws and guaranteed by a public authority—that is, when it was a political society—that the standards of civility could be maintained, where individuals could be recognized as citizens and treated as legal persons.[10] Civil society for Kant required the civil state, because it is only the latter which guarantees the boundaries of responsible legal subjectivity and which therefore confines the insecurity of social relations to the pre-political moment.

Perhaps one of the greatest insights in Hegel's political philosophy was to implicitly realize that, given the juridical individualism prevalent in modern and liberal conceptions of society, the essential characteristics of pre-political social relations—including their insecurity—could never be completely dispelled by the power of the public authority. In this sense, Hegel's model of society can be seen to adopt and further develop elements of both Hobbes and Locke's frameworks. On the one hand, Hegel's conception of the pre-political moment as something which is preserved within political society is closer to Locke's notion of the state of nature as a natural society than to Hobbes's radical individualism. Having said that, on the other hand, the pre-political and political moments should not be confused, as the political moment is not merely the perfecting of pre-political relations, but a qualitatively distinct sphere within Hegel's socio-political framework, so that it rejects Locke's idea that political society merely perfects and secures natural society. In Hegel's theory, then, the political moment contains and preserves the pre-political moment (since it is an essential aspect of social relations) but

[9] I. Kant, *Metaphysics of Morals: Metaphysical Elements of Justice Pt.1* (Indianapolis: Hackett Publishing, 1999), 41.

[10] See Bobbio, 'Gramsci and the Conception of Civil Society', 27.

at the same time also transcends it, transforming its conflictive nature into part of a universality, into a political community.[11]

This innovation results in a significantly more nuanced and dynamic account of socio-political relations. First of all, Hegel's conception of the pre-political moment resists the tendency of considering it a 'natural' state, in contrast with civilization. Instead, Hegel explicitly calls this moment 'civil society', making it clear that this conception is part and parcel of modernity, an aspect of society as we know it, contrasted only with the dimension of political society, crystallized in the idea of the state. In doing so, Hegel suppresses the dominance of the notion of political authority which was maintained by the natural law dichotomies. For Hegel, what distinguishes civil society from the state is not the absence of civil laws or the ineffectiveness of punishment. Rather, the main distinction between the pre-political and political moments lies in how the relations between individuals and their socio-political experience are conceived—that is, in individuals' subjectivities. Civil society is conceptualized as dominated by socio-economic relations between competing self-interested individuals and institutions, and civil association appears primarily as a matter of convenience or necessity. The state, in turn, is defined as a space of socio-political relations, where individuals mutually recognize each other as equals and have their autonomy and freedom recognized and actualized by the state.

In this framework, the competitive and economic aspect of human relations—individual self-interest—is effectively civilized, presented not as a matter of natural impulse but as a characteristic embedded in modern society. This civilization of the pre-political moment has an important implication: while for Hobbes and Locke (and Kant) the main defining aspect of the state of nature was the lack of a public authority, for Hegel this authority is already part of the environment of civil society. Since, instead of being located at some mythical or distant moment in time, Hegel's pre-political moment is contained within modern society, it has to presuppose the existence of laws and of a public power that maintains them. In doing so, however, Hegel's reconceptualization of the dichotomic model explicitly acknowledges that the existence of a public authority does not guarantee an end to the conflictive and insecure dimension of human relations. Instead, the establishment of political society relies on the identification between individuals and their political community, a union based on mutual recognition. And while civil society is 'an association of members', in this particular moment this 'association is brought about by their needs',[12] and not by a deeper political common

---

[11] Ibid, 22.   [12] Hegel, *Philosophy of Right*, 110.

purpose. Because of this, although civil society includes a 'legal system—the means to security of person and property—and … an external organization for attaining their particular and common interests'[13] (which Hegel calls 'the external state, the state based on need'),[14] these institutions appear in civil society as a contingent necessity. As a result, the public authority in civil society is experienced by individuals as a state that may protect freedom, but that may also constrain and coerce it.

The main rule of civil society is individual self-interest. Thus, for Hegel, even though there is a public power which is supposed to preserve the conditions for right and property, this authority and its law—due to the lack of political unity—appear either as a means or as an obstacle to individuals' personal ends.[15] Such a situation breeds as much conflict as it does cooperation, since social relations at this moment are primarily a reflection of the pursuit of individual self-interest. The only purpose of the external state in civil society is security, the provision of the necessary conditions for individuals to exercise their subjective freedom. Since individuals see the state only as a matter of support for their personal interests, this means that although relations between individuals may be regulated by the public authority, self-interest in itself remains unrestrained. From this perspective, Hegel seems to recognize that the presence of a public authority and of the structural conditions for individual rights are insufficient to generate the trust and solidarity necessary to turn individual self-interest into a public interest. As a result of this lack, 'civil society affords a spectacle of extravagance and want as well as of the physical and ethical degeneration common to them both',[16] which will only 'be regulated, dominated and annulled in the superior order of the state'.[17] Hegel's conception of civil society is thus one in which the civil order promoted by modern liberal socio-political conditions, laws, and institutions not only maintains the primacy of individual self-interest and structural inequality, but also admittedly also fosters structural violence.

It is thus not the absence of public authority, but the externality and instrumentality of the state in civil society which makes it a conflictive environment. Individuals may acknowledge the necessity and utility of the state, but they do not identify with it or with each other. Therefore, the problem with the pre-political moment of civil society is not that there is no social relationality between individuals, no bonds of interdependence, but that this relationality is fragile because it is subjected to self-interest, and thus becomes vulnerable. Likewise, although the conditions for the actualization of responsible legal

---

[13] Ibid.   [14] Ibid, 123.   [15] Ibid, 124.   [16] Ibid, 123.
[17] Bobbio, 'Gramsci and the Conception of Civil Society', 28.

subjectivity are present—indeed, they are established—in civil society (as there is a system of needs, laws that guarantee individual rights and property, and a public authority to enforce the laws and reassure individual liberty through punishment), without the unity of political society, responsible subjectivity itself becomes more a matter of convenience. This is because, as Hegel puts it,

[i]f the state is confused with civil society, and if its specific end is laid down as the security and protection of property and personal freedom, then the interest of the individuals as such becomes the ultimate end of their association, and it follows that membership of the state is something optional.[18]

In other words, if the ultimate end of society is individual rather than public interest, then responsible subjectivity appears as something contingent, since it is external to the way in which individuals conceive of their role in society. Individuals only 'internalise' their responsible subjectivity when they conceive themselves as citizens; that is, when they fully belong to and identify with the state as a political community.

In civil society, therefore, the external state cannot vouch for the trustworthiness of all individuals, since it is aware that their responsible agency is ultimately an instrument of their self-interest. If at any moment the social order promoted by the state appears as an obstacle rather than a facilitator to the attainment of their interests, individuals may find themselves in competition with the state instead of in cooperation with it. It thus occurs that, in civilizing the pre-political moment in modern political theory, Hegel exposed the ambivalence of individual autonomy—and also, by consequence, the ambivalence of criminal subjectivity.

ABSTRACT RESPONSIBILITY, CONCRETE DANGEROUSNESS: HEGEL'S DIALECTICS OF CRIME AND PUNISHMENT

In order to understand how this ambivalence is actualized in civil society, it is necessary to engage with Hegel's interesting and complex account of crime and punishment. In a nutshell, Hegel's *Philosophy of Right* sets as its main objective to examine how the concept of right gets realized in history and society—how it comes from being an inner principle of the subjective will to acquiring an objective reality. This journey starts in the sphere of Abstract Right, where right is materialized through the individual's subjective will,

---

[18] Hegel, *Philosophy of Right*, 156.

through which the individual sees her/himself as a person with rights. This subjective will is actualized through the notion of property, and confirmed through contracts with other individuals, in which each recognizes the other's personality and rights. These expressions of subjective will can be compromised and put under compulsion by crime, and for this reason Hegel's conception of abstract right includes not only a right to property but also 'a right to coerce, because the wrong which transgresses [my right to property] is an exercise of force against the existence of my freedom in an external thing'.[19] Understood in these terms, in its most basic expression, right seems to involve something similar to a right to self-preservation. However, Hegel's right to coerce only arises as a response to a previous coercion, so that is more closely aligned with Locke's (and Kant's) right to punish than to Hobbes's notion of an amoral right of nature.

The initial act of force against another individual is determined as wrongful, because it 'infringes the existence of freedom in its concrete sense, infringes the right as right'.[20] That is, in attacking someone's freedom and property, a crime attempts against the foundations of personality, and thus it represents 'a negatively infinite judgement … whereby not only the particular (i.e. the subsumption under my will of a single thing …) is negated, but also the universality and infinity in the predicate "mine" (i.e. my capacity for rights)'.[21] For this reason, Hegel conceptualizes the right to coerce not as a representation of a right to be exercised in lieu of the aggressor's rights or against them, but rather in conformity with these rights. This is because, since crime attempts against the foundations of the capacity to have rights, then to negate crime is to protect and preserve these very foundations, which are also the basis and the core of the criminal's rights. 'This', Hegel claims, 'is the sphere of criminal law'[22]—the negation of infringements to freedom in order to preserve right as right, that is, the conditions for the existence of individual rights.

However, it is also worth noting that Hegel claims that abstract right as such, the 'implicit will' within individuals, 'is rather that which has no external existence and which for that reason cannot be injured'.[23] Thus, although crime manifests itself as an infringement of right as such, it is only the externalization of right that is injured, and which must be restored. Because, at this moment, right is still abstract, it is not vulnerable to crime, so that the criminal law is at this moment not about security or prevention. Instead, the wrongfulness of right arises from the notion that to infringe someone's right is to put the normative grounds of individual rights into question, and therefore to undermine everyone's capacity to have rights, including the criminal's. The

---

[19] Ibid, 67.   [20] Ibid.   [21] Ibid.   [22] Ibid, 68.   [23] Ibid, 69.

main point, then, is that the manifestation of an individual's will through a crime is anomalous—the individual cannot really claim a right to whatever is the purpose or outcome of the crime, because a criminal act injures or rejects the very basis of personality. In this sense, the criminal's own subjective will requires the annulment of her/his crime. Hegel summarizes this argument in the following addition to the *Philosophy of Right*'s main text:

A crime alters something in some way, and the thing has its existence in this alteration. Yet this existence is a self-contradiction and to that extent is inherently a nullity. The nullity is that the crime has set aside right as such. That is to say, right as something absolute cannot be set aside, and so committing a crime is in principle a nullity: and this nullity is the essence of what a crime effects. A nullity, however, must reveal itself to be such, i.e. manifest itself as vulnerable. A crime, as an act, is not something positive, not a first thing, on which punishment would supervene as negation. It is something negative, so that its punishment is only a negation of the negation. Right in its actuality, then, annuls what infringes it and therein displays its validity and proves itself to be a necessary, mediated, reality.[24]

This idea of crime as essentially a moral wrong, and of punishment as the 'negation of a negation', is one of the classic foundations for liberal retributive theories of punishment. Crime is then a wrong that is fundamentally self-evident, and which demands its correction by way of punishment. However, there is also a social dimension of criminalization and punishment which is already highlighted at this stage in Hegel's account, which derives from the notion that crime and punishment are also, and perhaps mainly, matters of appearance. This dimension can be seen in the notion that, although crime does not affect right as such, it does injure its manifestation in the rights of the victim. From the perspective of its appearance, then, crime does manifest itself as a conflict between a claim of right by the criminal and the rights of the victim. Punishment is thus also necessary in order 'to annul the crime, *which otherwise would have been held valid*, and to restore the [external appearance of] right'.[25] In other words, punishment is necessary because if the crime goes unpunished, then at least in appearance, it is the right of the criminal which is upheld, and the victim's claim which is annulled. This highlights the fundamental limitation in the sphere of abstract right; namely, that since right as such is still internalized, idealized, there is no external universal regulation of which right-claim is the valid one, and which one is the negation. Without some common notion of the good, the difference between right and wrong is primarily a personal perspective, so that 'acts of punishment in the level of abstract right are acts of revenge', and punishment deteriorates into

---

[24] Ibid, 246.   [25] Ibid, 69 (emphasis added).

vengeance.[26] In order for individual right and freedom to acquire an objective reality, it needs to be linked to a shared, objective notion of the good. This takes us from the section on Abstract Right into the sphere of Morality in *The Philosophy of Right*.

Hegel's discussion of morality involves the definition of a common moral standpoint from which individuals can judge the validity and rightness of their actions. It is here that Hegel develops notions such as intention, purpose, and responsibility, which are integral to a conception of responsible subjectivity. From this discussion, Hegel concludes that morality has to include two dimensions: an element of individual right—the right of individuals to actualize their intentions and to bear responsibility for the consequences of their actions; and a notion of welfare—the interdependence between an individual's purpose and the purpose of others. In the sphere of morality, the notion of the good (the union of right and welfare) is externalized through the individual's conscience, which generates in her/him the notion of duty. For Kant, and for natural law theorists such as Locke, this is where the story of responsibility reaches its end, as once the individual realizes her/his duties towards her/himself and others, s/he is already capable of foreseeing the outcomes of her/his actions and therefore of answering for them. Responsibility, in this sense, is just a matter of actualizing in society the notion of right informed by individuals' inner morality (reason).

For Hegel, however, morality is still an intermediary stage in the dialectics of right. Although individuals develop a notion of the good and externalize it through their subjective will by means of their conscience and sense of responsibility, Hegel claims that the good in itself requires an objective reality. Without it, both good and subjective will remain abstract, and therefore still contingent and contestable. 'Morality needs to be transcended. Its insights should be preserved, but its inadequacies need to be corrected by the study of Ethical Life.'[27] It is thus in ethical life where both abstract right and morality acquire an objective reality, because they are brought together and actualized through social and political institutions. In civil society, the rights and property of individuals are guaranteed by civil laws and by the administration of justice, and welfare and the common good are overseen and protected by the public authority (which Hegel calls 'the police').[28] Punishment, in turn, is elevated from its abstract position as vengeance, taken from the hands of the victim to be delivered by the administration of justice, thereby assuming

[26] T. Brooks, *Hegel's Political Philosophy* (Edinburgh: Edinburgh University Press, 2009), 44.

[27] D. Knowles, *Hegel and the Philosophy of Right* (London: Routledge, 2002), 220. See also Hegel, *Philosophy of Right*, 103.

[28] Hegel, *The Philosophy of Right*, 145.

a concrete, public character. By the same token, crime is also elevated from its status as abstract injury to a concrete manifestation of a wrong which concerns society at large—a public wrong.

This shift, Hegel suggests, incurs a radical transformation in the relationship between crime and right:

Since property and personality have legal recognition and validity in civil society, wrongdoing now becomes an infringement, not merely of what is subjectively infinite, but of the universal thing which is existent with inherent stability and strength. Hence a new attitude arises: the action is seen as *a danger to society* and thereby the magnitude of the wrongdoing is increased.[29]

Thus whilst in the sphere of abstract right, crime was considered primarily an individualized, private matter, because it was mainly linked to the subjective manifestation of right in the person's property. However, when right gets concretized in civil society, the wrongfulness of crime acquires a social dimension, and with it an aspect of dangerousness. In discussing this shift, Hegel provides remarkable insights into the ambivalence of criminal subjectivity in civil society. At first, Hegel says that the public character of crime in civil society does not alter the conception of wrongdoing, in that crime continues to represent a negation of individual right, and therefore is primarily a matter of individual responsibility. On the other hand, immediately after this claim, Hegel concedes that the social dimension of crime 'does alter' the conception of wrongdoing 'in respect of its outward existence as an injury done ... which now affects the mind and consciousness of civil society as a whole, not merely the external embodiment of the person directly injured'.[30] Therefore, crime under concrete conditions has both an internal, individual aspect and an external, social context.[31]

Furthermore, these two dimensions are intrinsically related, so that both condition the notion of crime and the role of the criminal law. As a result, although crime continues to be a matter of individual responsibility, 'its danger to civil society is a determinant of the magnitude of a crime, or even one of its qualitative characteristics'.[32] In this sense, the subject of criminal law is conceptualized as both responsible and inherently, potentially, dangerous. I say 'inherently potentially' because, although there is an inherent dangerousness to the notion of crime in civil society, which conditions the quality and magnitude of any particular crime, 'this quality or magnitude varies with the state of civil society; and this is the justification for sometimes attaching the penalty of death to a theft of a few pence or a turnip,

---

[29] Ibid, 140 (emphasis added).   [30] Ibid.
[31] See A. Norrie, *Law, Ideology and Punishment* (Dordrecht: Kluwer Academic Publishers, 1990), chapter 4.
[32] Hegel, *The Philosophy of Right*, 140.

and at other times a light penalty to a theft of a hundred or more times that amount'.[33] Thus although crime is intrinsically ambivalent in civil society, the specific dynamics between responsibility and dangerousness depend on the present condition of civil society, on the existence and strength of structural elements which provide reassurance as to the primacy of responsible subjectivity—what in the previous chapter was referred to as the structure of trust in society.

Hegel's theoretical framework evidences how, due to the social dimension of crime, notions of individual responsibility cannot be normatively sustained in the framework of criminal law under conditions of civil society without being affected by the dangerousness of crime. Under this perspective, the normative position of individual autonomy in the liberal model of criminal law reveals itself as contingent upon specific socio-political conditions. A strong notion of individual autonomy therefore requires solid structural conditions, where the status of citizenship can appear reassured. In Hegel's words, when

... society is sure of itself, a crime must always be something idiosyncratic in comparison, something unstable and exceptional. *The very stability of society gives a crime the status of something purely subjective which seems to be the product rather of natural impulse than of a prudential will.* In this light, crime acquires a milder status, and for this reason its punishment too becomes milder. If society is still internally weak, then an example must be made by inflicting punishments, since punishment is itself an example over against the example of crime. But in a society which is internally strong, the commission of crime is something so feeble that its annulment must be commensurable with its feebleness. Harsh punishments, therefore, are not unjust in and by themselves; they are related to contemporary conditions.[34]

The emphasized portion of this quote illustrates how the state of civil society conditions the criminal law's very conception of its subject. Under reassured social conditions, crime appears as mainly subjective, an exceptional moral wrong which can be addressed in a measured and parsimonious manner. If social conditions are insecure, however, this is reflected by a sense of vulnerability which heightens the aspect of dangerousness in crime, and the focus of the criminal law shifts from addressing the wrongfulness in crime to preventing or eliminating its harmfulness. Furthermore, since it is conditioned by dangerousness, the individual dimension of crime in such conditions assumes the semblance of a 'subjective willing of evil, and this is what the universal authority must prevent or bring to justice'.[35] Because of this, even when

---

[33] Ibid. T.M. Knox, the translator of this particular version of Hegel's *Philosophy of Right*, notes that this almost exact same phrase was used by Blackstone in his *Commentaries*. See ibid, 359.
[34] Ibid, 274 (emphasis added).   [35] Ibid, 146.

acting in retribution, the criminal law in an insecure civil society acquires a tendency to be more punitive.

The Two Faces of the State

The dimension of dangerousness which Hegel confers to crime within civil society exposes the dynamic and contingent character of criminal subjectivity, portraying how the criminal law 'is primarily the child of its age and the state of civil society at the time'.[36] However, regardless of the state of civil society at any moment, for Hegel, crime is an intrinsic aspect of civil society, so that underlying the dialectics between responsibility and dangerousness there is a fundamental regulatory function that needs to be exerted by the criminal law. 'The point is that the actions of individuals may always be wrongful, and this is the ultimate reason for police control and penal justice.'[37] The reason crime is always a possibility in civil society is because, as previously mentioned, civil society is the sphere of self-interest in Hegel's account of ethical life. For Hegel, although responsible subjectivity is actualizable in civil society, it is only fully realized within the sphere of the rational state, the political moment in Hegel's theoretical framework.

If we recall, the association of individuals in civil society appears as brought about by relations of interdependence, which are guided by individual self-interest and are only managed and regulated by an external state or public authority. It is only in the political moment that this external organization 'is brought back to and welded into unity in the Constitution of the State which is the end and actuality of both the substantial universal order and the public life devoted thereto'.[38] Hegel says that this union is 'brought back' because, as he later reveals, in his political dialectics 'the state as such is not so much the result as the beginning'.[39] In this significant move, Hegel again radically transforms the logic of the dichotomic model, presenting the pre-political moment not as the condition or origin of political society, but as one of its necessary aspects or implications. There is no chronological or structural sequence from civil society to the state; rather, these are two moments contained within the development of political community. For Hegel, then, the solution for the insecurity of social relations does not lie in the assimilation of civil society by the state, but precisely in a proper *differentiation* between these two moments. Appearing to be aware that the structural violence of civil society is inextricably linked to the modern state and its civil order, Hegel concedes that he cannot eliminate the conflicts and inequalities of civil society,

---

[36] Ibid, 140.   [37] Ibid, 146.   [38] Ibid, 110.   [39] Ibid, 155.

so that his state has to somehow overcome these problems by accepting them as part of political life.

Hegel's main argument supporting this transcendence is that the political unity of the state is the ultimate purpose of the individual's participation in society, and as such it is already implicit in civil society. After all, the system of needs has some form of socio-political organization as one of its necessary conditions, especially with regards to civil laws guaranteeing individual rights and property. While in civil society this form of organization may appear as one in which each individual's self-interest has to be negotiated and to compete with others in order to be actualized, the ultimate aim of each individual is to have their freedom fully recognized and reflected in society. And since the state is what turns right and good into an objective reality in society, 'it is only as one of its members that the individual himself has objectivity, genuine individuality, and an ethical life'.[40] That is, it is only as a full member of the community, as a citizen, that an individual can have her/his self-interest, her/his freedom and autonomy, fully actualized. Furthermore, since the rational state represents the realization of the recognition of its citizens as full members of society, then in order to be fully actualized, individual autonomy has to have the state 'as [its] starting point and [its] result'.[41] Responsible subjectivity, therefore, is properly the subjectivity of those individuals who identify their own interest with the values and interests of the state.

There are thus two ways in which the state can appear in the realm of ethical life:

In contrast with the spheres of private rights and private welfare … , the state is from one point of view an external necessity and their higher authority; its nature is such that their laws and interests are subordinate to it and dependent on it. On the other hand, however, it is the end immanent within them, and its strength lies in the unity of its own universal end and aim with the particular interest of individuals, in the fact that individuals have duties to the state in proportion as they have rights against it.[42]

In essence, then, the political moment is the expression and manifestation of a unity that is already latent in civil society, as the basis for the very reason why individuals pursue their interests in society—that is, the hope of fully realizing their subjective will in association with others. 'The state is the actuality of concrete freedom.'[43] To be a citizen and a legal subject is to realize this unity between individual autonomy and state authority. This for Hegel is the aim of concrete individuality, the conception of an individual both as a particular and as a reflection of the universality of the state. Because it is primarily subjective, the shift to political society is attained from the moment

---

[40] Ibid, 156.   [41] Ibid.   [42] Ibid, 161.   [43] Ibid, 160.

individuals realize that the state, instead of being a cumbersome necessity and an occasional obstacle, is actually the expression of their subjective freedom in objective form.

It is important to note that, because the state is already latent in civil society, the attainment of citizenship and the universality of the rational state do not eliminate the particularity of civil socio-political conditions. On the contrary, even in political society, civil society continues to exist as the sphere of socio-economic relations, where individual self-interest and public good exist apart from each other, although 'both are still reciprocally bound together and conditioned'.[44] This means that although the state ultimately belongs to the political moment, to a large extent, it also has to be actualized in and through civil society. Thus at the same time as the state contains civil society, it is also contained within it. This contradictory picture can be explained through an analysis of two aspects of the Janus-faced character of Hegel's state. The first is that, from an objective perspective, the rational state, along with its promise of concrete individual autonomy and freedom, is conceptualized as already embedded in the structures of civil society. For the trained eye, the system of needs, the legal system and the public authority in civil society are already expressions of the unity and security of the constitutional state. 'Civil society in Hegel is the sphere of economic relations together with their external regulations according to the principles of the liberal state, and is at the same time bourgeois society and bourgeois state.'[45] Under this perspective, then, the liberal state is already a reality in the conflictive state of civil society, and there ultimately is no contradiction.

However, there is a caveat, in that the state as a socio-political phenomenon is conditioned by, and therefore contingent upon the subjective experience of individuals, so that its actualization becomes primarily a matter of individual perspective. The attainment of citizenship, in other words, depends on whether individuals are prepared to embrace the reality of civil order, and to actualize the rational state through their agency. In Hegel's words:

The isolated individual, so far as his duties are concerned, is in subjection; but as member of civil society he finds in fulfilling his duties to it protection of his person and property, regard for his private welfare, the satisfaction of the depths of his being, the consciousness and feeling of himself as a member of the whole; and, *in so far as he completely fulfils his duties* ... , he is upheld and preserved.[46]

---

[44] Ibid, 267.   [45] Bobbio, 'Gramsci and the Conception of Civil Society', 28–9.
[46] Hegel, *The Philosophy of Right*, 162 (emphasis added).

Thus although the state may already have an objective reality in political society, this reality has to be constantly negotiated by individuals in civil society; there is no escape from this necessity. Individuals who have the consciousness and feeling of being a member of the community are able to exist in harmony with the state, to be upheld and preserved. However, individuals who remain in isolation from the community, who do not identify with it or who do not fulfil their duties, cannot help but find themselves in subjection.

Hegel's iteration of the dichotomic model can provide significant insights to the tensions and ambivalences embedded in the contemporary framework of criminal law. Hegel's political theory posits that there are two aspects of the liberal state, one conditional and one unconditional. The unconditional aspect is that of the political moment, which conceptualizes the state as a concrete universality, bringing all the members of society together as citizens within its constitution, guaranteeing their rights and placing their duties in complete harmony with their welfare. This aspect of the state does not differentiate between its members, because it is the objective manifestation of right as such, which in turn is the very condition for citizenship. The conditional aspect, however, is that of civil society, where the state appears as an eternal entity, conditioned by the attitudes of individuals and by the current state of society's structure of trust. The main purpose of the external state is to maintain and promote the structural elements of civil society—its civil order—which provide the conditions for individuals to transcend their subjective needs and see themselves as part of a political whole. Furthermore, since the conditions for political society require individuals to respect rights and fulfil their duties, and since the conflictive appearance of the state in civil society is presented primarily as a consequence of the self-centred, particular, and fragmented experience of individuals, the state in civil society does differentiate between individuals, treating them according to the extent to which they fulfil their duties and identify themselves with the public interest.

In conceptualizing that it is the subjective experience of individuals that ultimately determines which aspect of the state is prevalent at any moment, Hegel manages to both acknowledge the contingency of responsible subjectivity and to protect its normative position. On the one hand, individuals are expected to experience their socio-political existence in different ways, since individual subjectivity is complex, and it is actualized in a civil society which is in constant socio-historical flux and replete with structural inequality and violence. On the other hand, these contingencies do not affect the universality of political society, only the way individuals experience it. The constitutional state as an ideal is universally valid, it is only its actualization that is conflictive and fragmented. It is not by chance that Hegel locates the administration of justice and the public authority as elements of civil society, and not of the constitutional state. As a reflection of the state, the administration of justice is ultimately about the externalization of right—Hegel's sphere of criminal law proper. But because this externalization occurs in civil society, the administration of justice is a reflection of the state in its particularity, an actualized aspect of the public good which is nevertheless vulnerable to the state of society and to the danger of crime. However, the potential violence and invasion of individual rights inflicted by the criminal law are conceptualized as mainly appearances which are only visible from the perspective of civil society, and which only occur as a reaction to the violence and fragmentation of that sphere of ethical life. From the perspective of the unity of the rational state, the criminal law is always an expression and actualization of right, which itself is not vulnerable—neither to crime nor to punishment.

Hegel thus conceptualizes his model of society as inherently dialectical, as both civil society—a conflictive space that needs ordering—and political society—the normative ideal that legitimates and justifies civil order. In doing so, Hegel manages to both preserve the structural violence of liberal society and to justify the criminal law as a liberal institution despite its regulatory, preventive, and authoritarian aspects. This is because the criminal law is only an external expression of the liberal state, which in civil society is more a regulative idea than a concrete reality. It is up to individuals (whenever conditions allow for it) to make the transition from civil society to the full citizenship of the liberal state, and therefore to realize that the criminal law is about right, not violence.

The subject of criminal law, therefore, is inherently ambivalent, because the criminal law essentially operates in two distinct spheres. In the first sphere, the subject of criminal law appears as the conflictive and contradictory inhabitant of civil society, an individual who has both the capacity to be responsible and the potential to be dangerous, against whom the criminal law must be directed. In the second, however, the subject of criminal law is contained within the notion of the rational liberal state, and the civil order embedded in it. Since concrete individuality in Hegel's schema is only possible when subjectivity is in identification with the state, it occurs that it is the state itself that occupies and populates the normative position of subjectivity in the liberal civil order, furnishing the standard to which individual agency must adhere and determining the scope and quality of individual autonomy and liberty. The criminal law's image of its subject is thus shaped by the extent to which the individual in question identifies with one of these spheres. Fundamentally, however, the subject of criminal law is ambivalent, because s/he is a subject of two worlds.

INDIVIDUALIZING RESPONSIBILITY, SOCIALIZING DANGEROUSNESS: BENTHAM'S AMBIVALENT CRIMINAL LAW

The essential elements of the dichotomic model of society and state authority, as well as the ambivalence of criminal subjectivity which results from it, can also be identified and explored through Jeremy Bentham's *The Principles of Morals and Legislation*. Bentham's work offers an interesting contrast to Hegel's conception of civil society, because it can be seen as both giving continuity to the political tradition which developed and sustained the dichotomic model, while also breaking away from it. On the one hand, Bentham also placed the self-interested individual at the centre of his model of society, and justified his notion of government on the need to promote individual liberty, security, and welfare. At the same time, he explicitly sought to distance himself from the social contract tradition, rejecting any notion of a state of nature as a distinct moment in social organization.[47] Thus civil order for Bentham was neither the result of an external regulation imposed on human nature, nor the expression of a natural law that pre-existed society; instead, civil order was the reflection of legislation, which was itself 'part of the institutional means by which the modern idea of the social was itself constituted'.[48] This notion of legislation is arguably the key to understanding Bentham's conception of civil society, to examining the essential role that criminal law had in this conception, and to uncovering its underlying and enduring ambivalence.

If a political theory is to be interpreted out of Bentham's *Principles*, it is a theory shaped around the notion of human motivation. At the core of this theory lies Bentham's famous calculating self-interested individual. This individual shared many of the essential elements found in Hobbes's theory. First, Bentham's rational individual was primarily egoistic, moved by passions, and motivated by self-interest. Possibly the most famous of Bentham's statements is that which opens the first chapter of *The Principles of Morals and Legislation*, which states that '[nature] has placed mankind under the governance of two

---

[47] G. Binder, 'Foundations of the Legislative Panopticon: Bentham's *Principles of Morals and Legislation*' in M.D. Dubber (ed), *Foundational Texts in Modern Criminal Law* (Oxford: Oxford University Press, 2014), 79–99, 81.

[48] L. Farmer, 'Reconstructing the English Codification Debate: The Criminal Law Commissioners, 1833-45' (2000) 18 *Law & History Review*, 397–426, 425.

sovereign masters, *pain* and *pleasure*. It is for them alone to point out what we ought to do, as well as to determine what we shall do'.[49] So although these individuals are overly rationalistic, rationality always plays a prudential role, in that it has the purpose of pointing out the most effective and economic means to maximize pleasure and minimize pain. In addition, just like in Hobbes's work, the most important individual interest for Bentham is self-preservation, that is, the avoidance of pain and suffering.

Bentham derived his ideal model of government directly from his conception of human nature, political community being 'a fictitious *body*, composed of the individual persons who are considered as constituting as it were its *members*'.[50] The main implication of this conception is that the purpose of the community is intrinsically tied to the interests of its members, as '[i]t is in vain to talk of the interest of the community, without understanding what is the interest of the individual'.[51] Utility was for Bentham the primary means through which the interest of the individual could be understood, and it can be defined as a mixture between emotional drive and rational motivation. Individuals are driven to pursue pleasure and avoid pain, but they do so by rationally calculating the amount of pleasure or pain that is likely to result from a particular course of action, and then deciding whether or not to pursue it. In this sense, individuals acted primarily on the anticipation of avoiding pain or achieving pleasure through their actions.[52] Following Beccaria, Bentham believed that the certainty of a coherent and public system of laws was the most effective source of authority which could guide individual expectations.

However, in order for a legal system to be coherent and to address the community as a whole, it could not focus on the specific interests of particular individuals; instead, it should look at the public interest. 'The general object which all laws have, or ought to have, in common, is to augment the total happiness of the community.'[53] Likewise, the main principle to guide legislation should be that of public, not private, utility. In other words, the government should produce and execute laws aimed at serving the common good. 'Agreement on collective action could only be achieved by identifying a common interest',[54] that is, an expected benefit to the community as a whole. The main common interest on which Bentham focused his attention, which for him was 'the general object of all laws', was the prevention of

---

[49] Bentham, *Principles of Morals and Legislation*, 1.
[50] Ibid, 3 (emphasis in original).   [51] Ibid.
[52] Binder, 'Foundations of the Legislative Panopticon', 82.
[53] Bentham, *Principles of Morals and Legislation*, 170.
[54] Binder, 'Foundations of the Legislative Panopticon', 82.

'mischief'—that is, the prevention of harmful actions and outcomes.[55] There are arguably two main reasons why Bentham placed prevention at the core of his notion of society. The first relates to his conception of human agency. Since individuals guide their lives through the rational pursuit of happiness, which includes the avoidance of pain, they are characterized as 'worriers and planners'[56] who are constantly occupied with predicting and avoiding situations of risk, and society reflects this tendency in its notion of the common interest. The second, however, arises from Bentham's reformist aims. Instead of basing his theory on a general justification of political power and authority, his main purpose was to improve his own contemporary society, so that the starting point of his theory is that of a civil society already under the government of 'an habitually obeyed sovereign'.[57] In other words, Bentham did not try to establish the foundations of his political society because he believed those foundations were already in place.

This is not to say that Bentham's vision of society did not bring innovations; quite the contrary. His account of criminal law and punishment, in particular, exhibits many notions that were novelties at the time, and his vision's innovative character came to fundamentally shape the subsequent development of both law and policy. Bentham's work can in many ways be seen as one of the main precursors of the 'three basic institutions of criminal justice—the prison, the police, and the criminal code'[58]—as well as many other elements of modern government and social thought more broadly.[59] However, my argument in this section is that while Bentham developed and reformed many elements of modern society, his main purpose in doing so was to secure and perfect an image of civil order which he conceived as fully realizable within his socio-political context. In other words, implicit within Bentham's conception of civil society, there is a firmly grounded conception of the rational state. This concealed assumption in Bentham's work is evidenced by an interesting dialectic in the tension between private and public interest within his account of utility.

The tradition of utilitarian thinking inaugurated by Bentham and further developed by Mill had a significant influence in the development of the criminal law. It inspired the model of rational agency underpinning capacity responsibility and its subjective categories of fault, and it also promoted the idea of a restrained criminal legal system, grounded on notions such as

---

[55] Bentham, *Principles of Morals and Legislation*, 178.
[56] Binder, 'Foundations of the Legislative Panopticon', 82.   [57] Ibid, 80.
[58] Ibid, 81.
[59] A. Ashworth, L. Zedner, *Preventive Justice* (Oxford: Oxford University Press, 2014), 36.

proportionality and fairness.[60] Indeed, many contemporary concepts and categories in criminal law can find their first proper conceptualization in Bentham's work. He conceived of criminal liability as composed primarily of culpable mental states and harmful consequences. Culpability, by its turn, was a matter of cognition, not of desire. Thus intention, for instance, was defined as an awareness that one's actions would bring about certain consequences, and it could be established whether these consequences were directly sought or whether they were obliquely expected. Criminal conduct, in turn, was also divided into actions, circumstances, and consequences. In terms of fairness and proportionality, Bentham is also famous for arguing that punishment was not only addressed at an evil, but was itself evil, because it was a source of pain. Because of that, in order for punishment to be effective, it had to be shown that the pain caused by it was less than the pain avoided through it, otherwise such punishment could not be considered useful. Furthermore, also as a reflection of the need for punishment to be useful in order to be justified, Bentham advocated that there would be many situations in which punishment would not be effective, proportionate or fair, so that these cases would be 'unmeet for punishment'.[61] He discussed excuses from liability such as infancy, insanity, and intoxication, and the possibility of conduct being justified by necessity.[62] From Bentham's discussion of liability, his subject of criminal law was a responsible subject par excellence.

However, Bentham's image of crime changes substantially once the point of perspective shifts from the individual to society. Criminal law and punishment for Bentham have a mainly preventive function in society, which can be examined as occurring on two levels: in terms of the prevention of harm by the criminal more strictly speaking, and in terms of the regulation of conduct more broadly. In terms of harm prevention, it is already clear that the harm in crime is intrinsic to Bentham's whole conceptual framework: offences are defined in terms of harm (either actual or anticipated), and punishment is justified as a response to the harm in crime. However, while the harm in punishment is defined strictly with regards to the individual who is punished, the harm in crime is defined in much broader terms. More specifically, Bentham argued that the harm of a crime should be seen as having primary and secondary consequences, the primary being the direct harm caused to a victim or victims, and the secondary being related to the danger and alarm

---

[60] See N. Lacey, *In Search of Criminal Responsibility: Ideas, Interests and Institutions* (Oxford: Oxford University Press, 2016), 52–3.

[61] Bentham, *Principles of Morals and Legislation*, chapter 13.

[62] Binder, 'Foundations of the Legislative Panopticon', 94.

created by the crime, broadly defined in terms of a loss of security.[63] The secondary consequences of crime have the potential to reach well beyond the primary victim, potentially affecting large portions of society and even society as a whole—especially when, for Bentham, the consequences of crime were understood not only in terms of harm done, but also in terms of anticipated harm. So while the notion of harm is individualized when it comes to punishment, highlighting the individual's responsibility, it is socialized[64] when applied with reference to crime, emphasizing its broader social impact in terms of dangerousness.

Thus Bentham's criminal law already exhibits an ambivalent character in relation to its subject, who is seen as a responsible individual when it comes to her/his agency, and as a social problem when it comes to the consequences of her/his actions. The notion that pain 'irradiates' beyond the victim of crime, over to society, recognizes the complexity of crime, but it also opens up an assessment of the harm of crime that leaves its definition and quantification open to contingency and to interpretation, and which therefore betrays the semblance of rational precision which Bentham aimed to give his system.[65] In this sense, the preventive function of the criminal law can be seen to have a tendency to predominate over concerns with proportionality and individual fairness, since the link between crime, danger, and insecurity means that harm can always outbalance and thus condition other elements of criminal liability. This predominance is further evidenced by the notion that the criminal law not only aims to address a social harm, but it also seeks to produce a social good. And although the deterrence, incapacitation, or rehabilitation of the individual who commits the crime can in itself be seen as a social good, Bentham was clear that for him the main purpose of punishment was to affect other individuals and society in general through the property of 'exemplarity' in punishment.[66] Punishment and criminalization achieve their primary end by being communicated to the public, in order to induce and encourage

---

[63] Bentham, *Principles of Morals and Legislation*, 157–9.

[64] When I say here that the notion of harm is socialized, I mean only that its consequences or impact is seen to extend beyond the direct victims of crime, over to society at large, so that this perspective emphasizes the socially detrimental character of crime. I am not suggesting that what I called the 'social dimension' of crime in earlier chapters refers to a critical awareness about the causes of crime, or about the idea that the concept of crime misinterprets the actual distribution of harm in society. Bentham's notion of harm, just like criminal law's in general, is mostly blind to a broader, more contextual conception of social harm. For such a conception, see D. Dorling, D. Gordon, P. Hillyard, C. Pantazis, S. Pemberton, S. Tombs, *Criminal Obsessions: Why Harm Matters More than Crime* (London: Centre for Crime and Justice Studies, 2008).

[65] See T. Draper, 'An Introduction to Jeremy Bentham's Theory of Punishment' (2002) 5 *Journal of Bentham Studies*, 1–17, 9–12.

[66] Bentham, *Principles of Morals and Legislation*, 193.

law-abiding behaviour. This was achieved by means of general deterrence, that is, by discouraging other individuals from committing crimes, and also by means of reassurance—by '[reassuring] members of the public that their entitlements were secure'.[67] The main means of prevention in Bentham, and the main purpose of his criminal law, was thus the law's reassurance function.

It is worth noting that, from the moment the images of crime and punishment are socialized, we can see a split that was not apparent from the individualized perspective. When looked at from the standpoint of criminal liability, it seems that Bentham's subject of criminal law is homogenous, as it is both the individual criminal who is made responsible and who is punished. However, from the perspective of the social dimension of harm and the social aim of punishment, there is a division: the subject who causes or risks harm is the individual, while the subjects who are the primary recipients of the symbolic message of criminalization and punishment are the general members of society. When punishment is scrutinized from the perspective of civil society as a whole, the dangerousness of crime comes to the fore and the rationality of the criminal dissipates into the background, preserved primarily as a reflection of the social values and expectations which society's civil order has to uphold.

Through this prism, Bentham's conception of civil society appears to have two subjects: one who is at the centre of his 'pannomion'[68] of legal norms, a responsible subject exposed to the rationality of its laws, who receives and appreciates the message of order communicated by the criminal law; and one who is at the periphery of his 'Panopticon',[69] watched and regulated by the omnipresent gaze of the law. Just like in Hegel's work, however, these two subjects can also be interpreted as reflections of the two faces of the state: in opposition to the self-interest of civil society, and in harmony with the public interest of political society. Both of these aspects of the state, its coercive and preventive necessity and its rational justification, are unified in Bentham's work through the notion of public utility, and its purpose 'to rear the fabric of felicity by the hands of reason and of law'.[70] In doing so, Bentham hoped to secure the bases for a modern welfare state, confident that his rational legal system was fully capable of producing social harmony out of individual interest.[71] But the socializing aspect of crime and

---

[67] Binder, 'Foundations of the Legislative Panopticon', 94.

[68] J. Bentham, 'To the President of the United States of America' in P. Schofield, J. Harris (eds), *The Collected Works of Jeremy Bentham: 'Legislator of the World': Writings on Codification, Law, and Education* (Oxford: Oxford University Press, 1998), 7–15.

[69] J. Bentham, *The Panopticon Writings* (London: Verso, 1995).

[70] Bentham, *Principles of Morals and Legislation*, 2.

[71] See A. Norrie, *Crime, Reason and History* (Cambridge: Cambridge University Press, 2014), 22–3.

punishment in his theory betrayed the fact that his harmonious rational state had to be carved out of, and coercively maintained within the conflictive confines of civil society.

CONCLUSION

The theoretical frameworks in Hegel's and Bentham's works theorize and reflect what is arguably the greatest problem in liberal criminal law systems, that of coping with the tension between idealized notions of society and order, in which individuals are conceptualized as responsible subjects invested in the project of political community, and an (also abstract) conception of the actual state of society, in which structural fluidity and individual self-interest are posited as external constraints which need to be regulated by the state. The dichotomic model preserved within liberal political thought justifies the imposition of an ideal model of society over concrete social relations, even by coercive and authoritarian means, whenever the conditions for the actualization of the rational civil order is perceived to be under threat. The theoretical analysis in this chapter has aimed to examine how the main function of the criminal law in such socio-political frameworks is to manage this dichotomy and to repress the ambivalence that stems from it, and how this same dichotomy allows the criminal law to retain its legitimacy in spite of its ambiguities.

Both Hegel's rational state and Bentham's utility are intrinsically linked to the project of civilization which lies at the core of the modern liberal state. Civilization is in itself a dichotomic concept, as it derives its meaning primarily from the distinction between civilization and barbarism, between the civilized citizen and the uncivilized brute.[72] Peace, security, and cooperation are taken to be the hallmarks of civilization, and to exist properly only within its confines. Furthermore, integral to the idea of civilization is the notion of progress; that is, the idea that civilized societies partake in an inexorable march towards greater rationality, peace, and prosperity, and that all that is needed is to protect and preserve the values and conditions of civility—especially individual liberty and the possessive model of society. The main obstacle to this maintenance, however, is seen to be the 'unsocial sociability' of human beings,[73] so that individuals must express and realize the values of rationality, cooperation, and self-control if they wish to fully participate in the project

---

[72] See J.S. Mill, 'Civilization' (1836) 3 *London and Westminster Review*, 1–28.
[73] See Kant, 'Idea for a Universal History with a Cosmopolitan Purpose'.

of citizenship. As one of the main guarantors of civility and guardians of the boundaries between civilization and barbarism, the criminal law appears as an institution at the service of securing civil order and realizing the liberal state, at the same time as it preserves the same conditions that it is supposed to address.

6

Retrieving Subjectivity

Criminal Law, Terrorism, and the Limits of Political Community

> Man is necessarily recognized and necessarily gives recognition. This necessity is his own, not that of our thinking in contrast to the content. As recognizing, man is himself the movement [of recognition], and this movement itself is what negates [*hebt auf*] his natural state: he is recognition.[1]

In light of the investigations so far, there seems to be an essential paradox sustained by the contemporary framework of criminal law, between the way this framework is actualized and the normative images which ground and justify it. The inability on the part of liberal criminal law theory to properly engage with the conflictive and contradictory character of criminal subjectivity arguably owes much to the need and desire to sustain the idea that the criminal law is able to deliver justice to individuals. Criminalization and punishment are such common and pervasive features of modern societies that their legitimacy might easily appear self-evident. As a result, whenever criminal laws and penal measures are judged excessively violent or intrusive, they are naturally considered aberrations, ripples in an otherwise placid lake of order and justice. Thus when preventive criminal offences push against the normatively defined boundaries of the criminal law, there is a tendency in legal scholarship to analyse these instances as exceptions or deviations from the norm, and to scrutinize their causes and address their issues largely in isolation from, or in contrast with, the core framework of criminalization. In the present study, however, I have suggested that the challenges posed by the preventive turn are as much a reflection of elements embedded within the liberal imaginary

---

[1] G.W.F. Hegel, *Hegel and the Human Spirit: A Translation of the Jena Lectures on the Philosophy of Spirit (1805–6) with Commentary* (Detroit: Wayne State University Press, 1983), 111.

The Preventive Turn in Criminal Law. First Edition. Henrique Carvalho. © Henrique Carvalho 2017. Published 2017 by Oxford University Press.

and its conception of criminal law as the result of current circumstances and recent events.

This chapter engages with the question of what the proper place of criminal law within a liberal democratic community is, in order to examine the extent to which the criminal law can concretely realize its values and aspirations in society. Through this question, I hope to address the main issues which lie at the heart of the problems arising from law's abstract individualism, as well as to uncover a theoretical perspective which can point to a possible pathway towards a more dialectically aware, less monovalent,[2] reconceptualization of individual responsibility and subjectivity. The first section explores Antony Duff's account of a normative theory of punishment based on liberal assumptions, but with a particular emphasis on its communicative aspect. By stressing the possibility to 'reconcile punishment with a proper recognition of our fellow citizenship with those whom we punish',[3] this liberal communitarian theory poses punishment as an instrument of recognition. An analysis of Duff's work evidences that the communicative aspect of his account of punishment is a reflection of broader political theoretical assumptions underlying the liberal imaginary and the conception of individual justice sustained by criminal law's morality of form, such as the notion that the criminal law is addressed at responsible citizens. However, such an analysis also suggests that these assumptions are in tension with the actual relation which is established through criminalization and punishment between the individual and the punishing community.

Once the core of this tension is identified as deriving from the notion of recognition underpinning Duff's communicative theory, the second section of this chapter sketches the main elements of a critical theory of recognition, based on a discussion of Hegelian dialectics.[4] This theoretical perspective on recognition is then applied in order to criticize the communicative aspirations in modern criminal law and punishment, elucidating the problems and limitations of the emancipatory promise in liberal legal theory. In order to pursue this aim, I engage with Duff's account of terrorism. The image of the terrorist has particular symbolic importance, for although it still stands as something

---

[2] See R. Bhaskar, *Dialectic: The Pulse of Freedom* (London: Routledge, 2008).

[3] R.A. Duff, 'Notes on Punishment and Terrorism' (2005) 6 *American Behavioral Scientist*, 758–63, 758.

[4] While the previous chapter dealt with the ambivalences in Hegel's broader political theory, the theoretical account of recognition developed in this chapter in relation to criminal law and punishment aims to highlight the more critical aspects of Hegel's work, which stand in contrast with and even contradict his broader socio-political framework. For a more integrated Hegelian perspective on criminal law and punishment, see A. Brudner, *Punishment and Freedom* (Oxford: Oxford University Press, 2009).

of a conceptually open term in legal and social theory, it also represents the most radical example of deviance and dangerousness within the liberal imaginary and its paradigm of criminal law. The terrorist is the dangerous subject par excellence. When liberal law tries to fit a real person into such a complex category, it finds it particularly hard to develop a theoretical justification that still upholds principles of individual responsibility and justice. As Duff himself argues, '[t]errorism poses a significant challenge to a liberal account of punishment that emphasizes its communicative character.'[5] For this reason, a critical discussion of terrorism proves a particularly fertile ground on which to test the limits of liberal law's inclusionary impulse in criminal law.

The chapter concludes by exploring the proposition that the greatest challenge to the communicative aspiration in criminal law is not posed by radical instances of deviance such as terrorism, but by the abstract and unreflective character of the liberal promise of freedom and respect for the individual. A serious examination of the concepts of punishment and responsibility, informed by a critical theory of recognition, can expose their problems and, perhaps, point to a pathway to their solution.

PUNISHMENT, COMMUNICATION, AND RECOGNITION

This section will consider Duff's account of punishment as a communicative endeavour, and relate questions in his notion of communication to the underlying issue of recognition. In his article 'Penance, Punishment and the Limits of Community',[6] Duff advanced an interesting argument regarding how to theorize about punishment; in a nutshell, he stated that 'we should understand criminal punishment as, ideally, a kind of secular penance'.[7] Although this might be a curious claim to pursue in a field which tries to keep away from areas of substantive morality such as religion, and in which categories of fault strive to separate wrongful conduct from inner motives, Duff was in this particular paper addressing a recent surge of theories that aim to produce a thicker account of punishment around 'the idea that punishment should involve such elements as repentance and atonement'.[8] The claims Duff raises in this discussion regarding the nature of punishment highlight important issues around criminal responsibility and subjectivity.

---

[5] Duff, 'Notes on Punishment', 758.
[6] R.A. Duff, 'Penance, Punishment and the Limits of Community' (2003) 5 *Punishment and Society*, 295–312.
[7] Ibid, 300.   [8] Ibid, 298.

The notion of penance constitutes 'something necessarily painful or burdensome that is required of or undertaken by the sinner because of a sin' or, in other words, 'a punishment for that sin'.[9] It has many purposes, among which is the induction of a repentant understanding of the sin and the communication of that repentance to the wronged party, not particularly as a way of evidencing it but more as an essential element of such repentance, that is, 'a way of taking the matter seriously'.[10] 'Penance', says Duff, 'thus looks both backward, to the sin for which it is undertaken, and forward, to the restoration of the sinner's relationships with those whom she wronged.'[11] This goes hand in hand with the common tendency in liberal criminal theory to look for a middle ground between retributivist (backward-looking) and consequentialist (forward-looking) perspectives on punishment.[12] In both instances, Duff claims penance shows itself as intrinsically inclusionary, as it portrays the sinner as a member of a community who violated its values but who, through the act of penance, can repair the relationship with the community that her/his wrongful acts have damaged.[13]

The idea of punishment as secular penance, then, characterizes it as 'a communicative process between the offender and the polity', a way through which 'to make moral reparation for the wrong that was done'.[14] It pursues multiple aims: communicating the deserved censure to the offender; making the offender recognize the wrong for which s/he needs to make moral reparation; bringing her/him to make such reparation, which also constitutes a form of forceful apology; and finally, through this process, reconciling the offender with the community. It is even a reformative enterprise, as in the offender's recognition of her/his wrong, s/he would also 'recognize the need to reform his future conduct'.[15] In a way, then, this notion of punishment can account for all of the main concerns raised by modern theories of punishment focused on individual autonomy.

Although Duff does not go into detail about the communicative character of his theory or about his precise notion of community in the article presently under analysis (such details can mainly be found in his book *Punishment, Communication, and Community*,[16] which is scrutinized below), he engages with a series of criticisms he expects to be directed by liberal scholars against penance playing a proper role in a system of state punishment.

---

[9] Ibid, 299.   [10] Ibid.   [11] Ibid.
[12] For more on this see R.A. Duff, *Punishment, Communication, and Community* (New York: Oxford University Press, 2001); R.A. Duff, D. Garland (eds), *A Reader on Punishment* (Oxford: Oxford University Press, 1994); H.L.A. Hart, *Punishment and Responsibility* (Oxford: Oxford University Press, 2008).
[13] Duff, 'Penance, Punishment', 299.   [14] Ibid, 300.   [15] Ibid, 300–1.
[16] Duff, *Punishment, Communication, and Community*.

This engagement is very illuminating in regard to the particular way in which he envisages that a system of punishment should address its subjects. He anticipates it might be argued that, as previously suggested, penance not only addresses the offender's conduct, but her/his moral attitudes in a deeper sense. Such invasion of the individual sphere can be accepted within a religious community, but not as a general social exigency, for the following reasons: First, members of a religious community are free to leave it if they so choose, whereas citizens cannot actually separate themselves from the state. Second, because the sinner is a voluntary member of the community, s/he has chosen to submit her/himself to its values, whereas a citizen does not have to accept all the values of her/his political community. Third, the confession involved in penance itself is voluntary, whereas punishment cannot be conditional on voluntary confession. And fourth, the sinner is still able to refuse to undertake the penance—at risk of excommunication or other kind of exclusion from the community—whereas punishment is not and could not be optional.[17]

Duff replies to these potential objections in an explanation divided into three parts. First he claims that, whereas punishment 'seeks to engage [the offenders'] moral attitudes and feelings, it does not (it should not) seek to coerce those attitudes and feelings'; instead, 'it aims to persuade, rather than to coerce, their moral understanding'—it is, as he puts it, 'an exercise in forceful moral communication'.[18] Second, 'criminal punishment need not and should not be as ambitious as religious punishment', as the criminal law can rather focus 'on the wrongfulness of the criminal deed, on the wrongful attitudes or concerns directly manifested in that deed'.[19] It does not need to reach as deep as religious punishment, aimed to affect the soul of the offender and thus going over the border set by liberal conceptions of privacy. Third, finally, Duff argues that the expectation that the state 'show its citizens the respect due to them as responsible moral agents' leads to the conclusion that the state 'must address them in the kind of moral language that is central to this account of punishment'.[20] Therefore, the criminal law should be ready to expose the wrongfulness involved in crime, and to censure such wrongfulness in a way that allows citizens to recognize it and repent. More than a practical suggestion, communicative punishment would be a requirement: a 'communicative system of punishment', Duff argues, 'is what we are owed.'[21]

Duff's tripartite defence of his theory of punishment raises concerns that are essential to the justification of punishment in a modern liberal

---

[17] Duff, 'Penance, Punishment', 301–2. [18] Ibid, 302. [19] Ibid, 303.
[20] Ibid. [21] Ibid.

paradigm, but the elements of this theory are not necessarily as harmonious as they seem. To try and understand the tension concealed in Duff's account, we should examine his three claims in the inverse order in which they were presented. To begin, then, within the claim that a communicative system of punishment is owed to citizens lies the assumption that the state ought to respect its citizens as responsible moral agents—as responsible subjects. Particular conceptions of individual freedom and autonomy come thus to the fore, embedded within the liberal imaginary. Duff has long struggled with the attempt to find a compromise between individualist requirements for agency and rationality in the criminal law, and communitarian notions of moral contingency in responsibility, suggesting as previously discussed that such compromise can be found in the idea of the citizen as a moral agent bound by the community of the state.[22] Since Duff's conception of citizenship sees the citizen necessarily as a moral agent, Duff conceives individual autonomy and freedom not only as rational requirements for responsibility, but also as values that are shared and sustained by the political community.[23]

Thus, if punishment seeks to recognize the citizen as a moral agent in order to be consistent with the values of what Duff calls a 'liberal political community',[24] it has to be communicative. In *Punishment, Communication, and Community*, Duff argues against the idea of an 'expressive' purpose in punishment, and in preference of 'its communicative purpose: for communication involves, as expression need not, a reciprocal and rational engagement'.[25] Communication 'aims to engage that person as an active participant in the process who will receive and respond to the communication, and it appeals to the other's reason and understanding'.[26] From what this short description of communication indicates, it seems that Duff's normative conception of punishment contrasts rather significantly with actual penal practices. Nevertheless, as a normative ideal, notions of communication have been used as a critical perspective from which to highlight problems in criminal law and criminal justice.[27]

---

[22] See Duff, *Punishment, Communication, and Community*, chapter 2; R.A. Duff, *Answering for Crime: Responsibility and Liability in Criminal Law* (Portland: Hart Publishing, 2007), chapter 2; A. Norrie, *Punishment, Responsibility, and Justice* (Oxford: Oxford University Press, 2000), chapter 5. See also Chapter 2 of this book.

[23] Duff, *Punishment, Communication, and Community*, 35.   [24] Ibid, 79.

[25] Ibid.   [26] Ibid.

[27] See for instance R.A. Duff, L. Farmer, S. Marshall, V. Tadros (eds), *The Trial on Trial: Volume 1: Truth and Due Process* (Oxford: Hart, 2004); *The Trial on Trial: Volume Two: Judgment and Calling to Account* (Oxford: Hart, 2006); *The Trial on Trial: Volume Three: Towards a Normative Theory of the Criminal Law* (Oxford: Hart, 2007).

Second, the critical perspective enunciated by the first claim is followed by the statement that the criminal law should focus on the 'wrongfulness' of the offender's deed.[28] To think in terms of wrongfulness without deeply qualifying it is, before anything, to imply a specific and previous moral judgment concerning the attitude of the offender, which is here dependent on the shared values implied by a particular conception of community. The way in which the wrongful nature of the conduct is defined carries the weight of Duff's communitarian perspective on punishment, for the criminal law is interested in 'public' wrongs, understood as 'wrongs in which "the public," the community as a whole, is properly interested'.[29] Such public interest would be assessed and reflected by the state, through its democratic structures, and fed into the system of criminal law and punishment. Third, finally, upon determining such wrongfulness and identifying it in the offender's conduct, the legal system would then engage in forceful moral communication. Duff's connotation of this idea is that, although punishment is to be imposed on offenders against their will, it should be aimed at persuading, rather than coercing, their moral understanding. It must provide a clear moral message to the offender, but in Duff's words, '[w]e can try to force them to hear the message that their punishment aims to convey: but we must not try to force them to accept it—or even to listen to it or to take it seriously.'[30]

Despite the image of non authoritarian communication presented in Duff's work, however, there is no doubt that the two poles of the communicative relation are not symmetrical. Furthermore, in *Punishment, Communication, and Community*, Duff claims that one aspect of communication is that it also seeks 'to affect future conduct' by declaring some kinds of conduct as wrong in order 'to persuade citizens (those who need persuading) to refrain from such conduct'.[31] Suddenly, the earlier reciprocal aspect of communication seems to lose focus in favour of a more pragmatic notion of persuasion. Although the idea of persuasion can be nuanced in ethical, practical, and strategic ways, Duff is clear that the law aims at persuading the citizen to refrain from some forms of conduct. The main idea here is thus not to engage with criminals in reciprocal dialogue, but to convince them of the wrongfulness of their actions. Dialogue in this sense has a limited, one-way quality, and the communicative aspect appears to be primarily a means to achieve persuasion. It aims 'to bring citizens to recognize and to accept'[32] the wrongfulness of their conduct, but says nothing of recognizing any of the citizen's claims in

---

[28] Duff, 'Penance, Punishment', 303.
[29] Duff, *Punishment, Communication, and Community*, 61.
[30] Duff, 'Penance, Punishment', 302.
[31] Duff, *Punishment, Communication, and Community*, 80.   [32] Ibid, 81.

return. If the law identifies any 'direct manifestation' of 'attitudes or concerns' that fit pre-established moral considerations, the citizen's position is taken to be 'wrongful'[33] from the outset.

The actual outcome of this framework is that offenders are forcefully exposed to a moral message that they are deemed to be able to understand and to accept—and even though they are not forced to do either, the legal system ignores any argument to the contrary of its predetermined moral judgment. The justification for that is that the wrongfulness is public—that is, it represents the community's (including here the offender's) interests—so that, even if the law is basically saying to the offender 'you are wrong, whether you accept it or not', the process is deemed reciprocal. But such a formal recognition of the autonomy of the offender does not seem to fit into Duff's previously bold and rather substantial enunciation of what communication entails: 'a reciprocal and rational engagement' of the agent 'as an active participant in the process who will receive and respond to the communication'.[34] Rather, it would be better understood as the previously eschewed notion of expressive punishment or, even worse (because it aims to persuade), as forced acceptance or imposition, which is not far short of indoctrination. The offender's options are reduced either to consent with the discourse contained within the criminal law or to remain silent, to submit. The pre-judgment contained in the wrongfulness of her/his actions already predetermines what s/he may be allowed to say, should s/he choose to 'communicate'. Such an authoritative notion of communication can hardly be said to be reciprocal.

If Duff is right that we, as members of the political community, are owed a communicative engagement on the part of the legal system—an assumption that seems to lie not only within Duff's liberal communitarian perspective, but also within general liberal notions of individual autonomy and justice—the core of the matter, then, becomes the question, can such a normative theory of punishment be up to the task of doing justice to the assumptions within its own conception of the moral order underpinning liberal law and society? Moreover, if this claim is to be taken seriously, can any system of punishment achieve this level of communication with the offender? That is, can the state recognize those it seeks to punish as responsible moral agents and engage with them in reciprocal dialogue, instead of merely forcing them to unidirectionally accept the system's norms and rules?

---

[33] Duff, 'Penance, Punishment', 303.
[34] Duff, *Punishment, Communication, and Community*, 79.

Punishment seems to derive its justification from its backward-looking relation to the crime and its forward-looking relation to the preservation of community bonds. Both relationships seem to be dependent on some notion of communication, which is in itself grounded on a conception of political community. The communicative engagement, by its turn, aims at recognizing the subject as a responsible moral agent. If Duff is right that a normative theory of punishment has 'to reconcile punishment with a proper recognition of our fellow citizenship with those whom we punish',[35] such recognition seems to represent the main ground for responsible moral agency, so that it deserves special attention from a critical examination of the normative framework in which criminal law and punishment operate. Recognition is arguably the key to understanding the problematic relationship between criminalization, punishment, and responsibility.

THE PROCESS OF RECOGNITION

If the idea of recognition is to be taken seriously, there is no better way to start than with Hegel, whose work on the topic has retained its significance in contemporary social theory. The quote at the start of this chapter refers to Hegel's *Jena Lectures on the Philosophy of Spirit*,[36] the most comprehensive of his texts on recognition, developed right before his work on the *Phenomenology of Spirit*.[37] Hegel's account of recognition is one of the greatest modern influences on the idea of mutual interdependence in society, and on communitarian challenges to atomistic notions of individuality.[38] From the prefatory quote it is possible to highlight the idea of solidarity in terms of reciprocity, as '[m]an is necessarily recognized and necessarily gives recognition',[39] and the notion that recognition—as a constituent of human agency—is intrinsic to human being and becoming: 'This necessity is his own ... man ... is recognition.'[40] Taking these two initial thoughts into account, this section will first look into a discussion of recognition from Duff's perspective, then move on to consider how recognition is linked with punishment in Hegel's political philosophy, before delving into a deeper reflection on the concept. This will be done in dialogue with Axel Honneth's comment on Hegel's early critique of the social

---

[35] Duff, 'Notes on Punishment', 758.   [36] Hegel, *Hegel and the Human Spirit*.
[37] G.W.F. Hegel, *Phenomenology of Spirit* (Oxford: Oxford University Press, 1977).
[38] See C. Taylor, *Sources of the Self* (Cambridge: Cambridge University Press, 1992).
[39] Hegel, *Hegel and the Human Spirit*, 111.   [40] Ibid.

contract,[41] and with Hegel's account of 'Independence and Dependence of Self-Consciousness: Lordship and Bondage'[42] in the *Phenomenology of Spirit*, along with Alexandre Kojève's own interpretation of it.[43]

In *Punishment, Communication, and Community*, Duff emphasizes how moral agency must involve 'the "recognition" of fellowship ... in a political community',[44] contrasting this idea with the liberal individualist conception of choice, which emphasizes the volitional character of choosing what to believe, what values and principles to accept. Duff sees recognition as 'basic to moral life and thought', because '[w]e must attend to the world and to other people as sources of moral demands on us ... and we must recognize others as our fellows.'[45] At the heart of this perspective is the notion that such bonds, such recognition of fellowship, is 'given in moral experience'.[46] That is, it is something that can be rationally questioned but that cannot be denied or set aside: 'I might not be required by either psychology or logic to accept these bonds ... but I am, morally, stuck with them.'[47] Such understanding resonates with Duff's idea of wrongfulness as a moral demand from the community upon the individual, and it is indeed central to the claim to normative validity embedded within crime and punishment. However, the extent to which the normative demand contained in criminal law and punishment is given in an individual's moral experience is arguably something which demands further investigation. For that, we must examine the place of recognition in Hegel's political theory.

Recognition is at the core of Hegel's idea of right, reflected mainly on the notion of property, where '[t]he embodiment which my willing thereby attains involves its recognisability by others.'[48] In other words, property is only actualized as a right when it is recognized by others. Such recognition is guaranteed by the realization of a contract which represents the common will of the parties. The idea of wrong appears in Hegel as a negation of the common, universal will made by a particular party to the contract.[49] The fundamental aspect of wrongfulness, then, is that it goes against the common will established in the contract. What is important to realize here—something with which Duff would probably agree—is that '[w]rong thus presupposes the establishment and existence of some mutually recognized common will

---

[41] A. Honneth, *The Struggle for Recognition* (Cambridge: Polity Press, 1995).
[42] Hegel, *Phenomenology of Spirit*, 111–19.
[43] A. Kojève, *Introduction to the Reading of Hegel* (New York: Basic Books, 1980), 3–30.
[44] Duff, *Punishment, Communication, and Community*, 53.   [45] Ibid.   [46] Ibid.
[47] Ibid.
[48] G.W.F. Hegel, *Hegel's Philosophy of Right* (Oxford: Oxford University Press, 1967), 45.
[49] Ibid, 64.

that finds expression in contract';[50] that is, without a contract, without some previous agreement or meeting of wills, there is no wrong.

The worst kind of wrong to Hegel is the wrong of transgression, or crime. Crime, as seen earlier, is 'characterised by a criminal's rejection of another will's capacity for rights';[51] in other words, it is an open negation of someone else's rights. Punishment comes thus to the fore as a way of asserting the nullity of crime's negation of rights, as right 'reasserts itself by negating this negation of itself'.[52] Basically, when the criminal betrays the common will, s/he creates a law that can only be good for her/himself, and then punishment returns the criminal's own law back to her/him, thus evidencing the wrongfulness of her/his actions and reaffirming the right manifested in the common will. The most relevant point here to a discussion of recognition is precisely to understand that punishment presupposes a common will, a social contract that is grounded on mutual recognition.

This social contract, in turn, is an essential element of an established political community. As was previously discussed, Hegel did not believe that the establishment of political society constituted an all-new social order that completely contradicted some conception of a pre-political society, or state of nature. Instead, 'Hegel wishes to show that the emergence of the social contract—and, thereby, of legal relations—represents a practical event that necessarily follows from the initial social situation of the state of nature itself.'[53] In the very presupposition of a common agreement organizing individual conduct, 'theoretical attention must be shifted to the intersubjective social relations that always already guarantee a minimal normative consensus in advance'.[54] In other words, the institution of legal relations does not generate, but instead presupposes the existence of mutual recognition. Hegel thus asserts the necessity 'to integrate the obligation of mutual recognition into the state of nature [the pre-political moment] as a social fact',[55] as a necessary condition for the establishment of legal rights and obligations.

Thus instead of individuals simply coming together in order to establish a community which will generate and maintain moral demands towards its members, Hegel's critique of the social contract inserts a dialectical movement in this relation, asserting that fellowship is also what generates and conditions individuality—so that a specific social environment is necessary

[50] R.R. Williams, *Hegel's Ethics of Recognition* (Berkeley: University of California Press, 1997), 152.

[51] T. Brooks, *Hegel's Political Philosophy* (Edinburgh: Edinburgh University Press, 2009), 43.

[52] Hegel, *Philosophy of Right*, 64. For a detailed discussion of Hegel's account of crime and punishment, see Chapter 5 above.

[53] Honneth, *The Struggle for Recognition*, 41.   [54] Ibid, 42.   [55] Ibid, 43.

before certain moral demands can be imposed on individuals. It is worth noting that, in attempting to integrate mutual recognition into the pre-political moment, Hegel is not suggesting that there is no struggle in civil society; quite the contrary. What he is challenging is the character of this conflict. Whereas a classic interpretation of the state of nature would simply maintain that such a state is permeated with 'struggles for self-assertion', a Hegelian reading of the pre-political moment highlights how civil society hosts a process in which 'individuals learn to see themselves as being fitted out with intersubjectively accepted rights', involved in a 'struggle for recognition'.[56] What this means is that the conflicts in civil society are not merely defined by the self-interest of opposing subjects; instead, the struggle itself also shapes and defines these subjects in return. As Honneth points out, it is incorrect to see the antagonists in the pre-political moment as isolated, self-contained beings, since 'the social meaning of the conflict can only be adequately understood by ascribing to both parties knowledge of their dependence on the other'.[57] In other words, conflicts in civil society are not only struggles for competition, but also struggles for cooperation.

It is precisely this interdependence, evident in Hegel's work, which would justify the need to address wrongs in order to preserve the mutual recognition guaranteed by right. The problem that I aim to highlight in this chapter, though, is that the justification for criminalization and punishment has to come from the nature of wrong as a breach of the common will. In this sense, wrong is taken to be a 'wilful disregard for mutual recognition'[58] on the part of a responsible subject voluntarily breaking a previous contract which s/he recognized, and in which s/he was recognized. It is imperative to ask, then, whether this account is or can be made coherent with the way in which individuals are actually recognized in contemporary social conditions. One perspective through which to address this question theoretically can be sought in Hegel's work before the *Philosophy of Right*, especially in his examination of the development of self-consciousness in the *Phenomenology of Spirit*. Though systematic accounts of Hegel's work tend to consider the *Phenomenology* as a preliminary work before his encyclopaedic systematization of themes and concepts,[59] the discussion of self-consciousness not only provides the most elaborate account of recognition as part of the movement of freedom in society, but it also examines the aim of the process of recognition and, of

---

[56] Ibid.   [57] Ibid, 45.   [58] Brooks, *Hegel's Political Philosophy*, 44.
[59] See e.g. Brooks, ibid. Dudley Knowles (*Hegel and the Philosophy of Right*), on the other hand, acknowledges the importance that the development of recognition in the *Phenomenology* has for Hegel's political philosophy, even though he claims that in the end Hegel falls short of his own demands for mutual recognition in the *Philosophy of Right* (ibid, 106). I agree with Knowles on this point, and aim precisely to develop how punishment in particular falls short of such demands.

particular interest to the present study, instances in which the process can deviate from its aim.

Recognition and Self-Consciousness

Alexandre Kojève's work probably constitutes the most sophisticated analysis of Hegel's development of history as a process of recognition, as it brings elements of Hegel's earlier work on recognition together with the account in the *Phenomenology* through the Marxist elements in his interpretation. Kojève's account starts with the idea that 'Man [*sic*] is Self-Consciousness';[60] what constitutes humanity, human subjectivity, is the fact that human being is (or rather has the potential to be) 'conscious of himself, of his human reality and dignity'.[61] This essential subjectivism is implied in the essence of contemporary liberal philosophical conceptions of responsibility and autonomy; what is unique in Hegel, however, is his argument that self-consciousness is underpinned by processes of recognition, so that what first appears as a mainly subjective perspective is in reality inherently intersubjective.

The development of self-consciousness is for Hegel part of a long process of awareness, with alternating moments of integration and differentiation between subject and object. Understanding this genealogy of self-consciousness, the 'origin'[62] of subjectivity and the philosophical conditions for its flourishing, then, provides an intrinsic tool through which to understand human being in itself. The dialectics of self-consciousness, which informs this understanding, is essentially the movement between knowing and being or, in Kojève's account, between knowledge and desire. Desire always presents itself as a lack: man desires what he lacks, what he is not. Thus, by desiring, man acknowledges his own limits, and through these limits he sets up the boundaries of his own being, he defines himself. Whereas knowledge seems to bring forth synthesis and integration, desire initially highlights monadic antagonism and separation.

But '[i]n contrast to the knowledge that keeps man in a passive quietude, desire dis-quiets him and moves him to action';[63] so man is moved to act upon the world and satisfy his desire, to negate his lack. 'Thus, all action is "negating"',[64] is transforming the world in pursuit of the satisfaction of a desire. These mechanics can be seen in simple examples like feeding, in which the lack of sustenance leads to the destruction (transformation, 'real negation'[65]) of food for the satisfaction of hunger. Hegel refers to the developing subject

---

[60] Kojève, *Introduction to the Reading of Hegel*, 3.   [61] Ibid.   [62] Ibid.
[63] Ibid, 4.   [64] Ibid.
[65] See A. Norrie, *Dialectic and Difference* (Oxon: Routledge, 2010), 25.

in this particular moment as 'life', and this desire for survival distinguishes the subject from her/his surroundings through this process of active negation, in which 'Life in the universal fluid medium, a passive separating-out of the shapes becomes, just by so doing, a movement of those shapes or becomes Life as a *process*.'[66] This process is, for Hegel, the 'genus'[67] of consciousness and individuality.

Just as life as a process turns a passive knowledge of one's surroundings into an active participation in the world (moved by the feeling of lack, desire), consciousness reflects upon the contrast between the world and itself. It is only by means of this comparison, through this process, that consciousness is able to know anything about itself; that it is able to become self-consciousness. It is desire—the feeling of absence, of difference—that puts this shifting of knowledge in motion, and it is precisely the action to satisfy a desire that transforms the subject's relations with the world. This whole process of interaction shapes not only the subject's knowledge of the world, but also her/his knowledge of her/himself. Thus it is, for example, the desire for self-preservation and proliferation, and the specific ways in which their satisfaction is possible, that teach the subject about her/his animal nature. The main point about recognition, however, is that to become conscious of their human nature, subjects need something in the world to reflect such humanity back to them; in other words, they need other human beings. Therein lies the limit of desire and the secret of the process of self-consciousness: to know itself, it must have itself as an object. In other words, a subject can only be aware of her/his own individuality if s/he can compare her/himself to another subject. Kojève said that '[h]uman Desire must be directed towards another Desire',[68] toward another desiring subject, following Hegel's claim that '[s]elf-consciousness achieves its satisfaction only in another self-consciousness.'[69]

Thus '[s]elf-consciousness exists in and for itself when, and by the fact that, it so exists for another; that is, it exists only in being acknowledged.'[70] This statement gives the full thrust of Hegel's critique of individualist conceptions of the state of nature, for the subject is only a proper individual through the acknowledgement of kinship with another individual—true individuality exists only within a social reality. Self-consciousness needs to 'come out of itself'[71] and see its own subjectivity reflected in another being. This is what constitutes and initiates what Hegel calls the 'process of Recognition'.[72] There is a necessary reciprocity in this movement, as it only works if one subject can recognize her/himself in the other. 'Action by one side only would be

[66] Hegel, *Phenomenology of Spirit*, 107 (emphasis added).   [67] Ibid, 109.
[68] Kojève, *Introduction to the Reading of Hegel*, 5.
[69] Hegel, *Phenomenology of Spirit*, 110.   [70] Ibid, 111.   [71] Ibid.   [72] Ibid.

useless because what is to happen can only be brought about by both.'[73] The process of self-consciousness must appear as a middle term through which subjects 'recognize themselves as mutually recognizing one another'.[74] The dialectics of subjectivity, according to this particular narrative, lead to the conclusion that the essence of human desire is to place human being as the end of desire itself. This qualitatively distinct human desire for individuality (self-consciousness) can only be properly satisfied through mutual recognition. 'All human Desire is a function of the desire for "recognition".'[75] Since such recognition is necessarily intersubjective, it has to be reciprocal. There thus is a fundamental aspect of solidarity in this process, for in order to be an individual—to be acknowledged and valued as a subject—one needs to belong to a society of individuals. The mutual recognition implied in the social contract is not merely engendered by individuals: it shapes individuality as well.

The Life-and-Death Struggle

There is, however, a problem with recognition. There has to be mutual recognition for subjectivity to be realized. While an individual might be aware of her/his own subjectivity, this awareness is not concrete until this subjectivity is equally recognized by another subject, because 'for an idea to be a truth, it must reveal an objective reality'.[76] Moreover, besides the notion that human individuality can only exist through recognition of the other's equally human desires, there is also the matter of the satisfaction of such desires. The mere acknowledgment of another desiring subject, as might be implied from Hobbes's work,[77] may simply mean that there are two people in the world desiring something that may not be enough for both; the anxiety behind this threat looms ever present in the process of recognition, which as mentioned takes the shape of a struggle. Thus whereas the desire for recognition generates self-consciousness and individuality, the pursuit of this desire leads to conflict.

The ideal outcome of such conflicts is likely one in which human values sustain a mutual understanding of reality, which can therefore be truly understood as a social reality—or, in Duff's terms, a community in which all of its members are properly and equally recognized. But this community, which in the abstract is a presupposition of every social interaction, can only

---

[73] Ibid, 112.   [74] Ibid.   [75] Kojève, *Introduction to the Reading of Hegel*, 7.
[76] Ibid, 11.
[77] T. Hobbes, *Leviathan* (Oxford: Oxford University Press, 1996), 83. See the detailed discussion of Hobbes's work in Chapter 3 above.

be concretely (objectively) realized in the end of a process of awareness and solidarity. However, what instead is seen throughout history is a variety of incomplete, partial, one-sided forms of recognition. The acknowledgment of a mutual desire does not necessarily lead to cooperation towards mutual satisfaction; indeed, history usually tells a story in which the opposite is the rule. As a result, what starts as a 'pure' conception of recognition results in a process in which recognition goes wrong, since it is not (yet) properly grounded in reciprocity. Hegel's account of the mythical first encounter between two subjectivities thus takes the form of a life-and-death struggle resulting from the competitive quality inherent to opposing claims of subjectivity. But the satisfaction of recognition necessitates an objective reality, as said before, and before long 'self-consciousness learns that life is ... essential to it'.[78] When this happens, the struggle becomes one of domination as one subject (the lord, the Master) imposes her/his recognition over another (the bondsman, the Slave)—'one being only recognized, the other only recognizing'.[79] The lord's essential nature is 'to be for itself', to be independent, whereas the bondsman's nature 'is simply to live or to be for another',[80] to live in submission.

The conflictive and often violent character of human relations, especially within a social imaginary that privileges self-interest over mutual cooperation, leads to a condition of unequal, and therefore unfinished, recognition. It may seem at first that this inequality is unsatisfactory because it is unfair that only one side is recognized. Although this is certainly true, the full thrust of Hegel's critique is that, in reality, *neither* of the parties to the conflict is fully recognized, not even the lord, as 'for recognition proper the moment is lacking, that what the lord does to the other he also does to himself, and what the bondsman does to himself he should also do to the other'.[81] In other words, when the lord is recognized by the bondsman, s/he is recognized by someone whose autonomy s/he does not fully recognize, and so the bondsman's recognition of the lord is also imperfect—'For he can be satisfied only by recognition from one whom he recognizes as worthy of recognizing him.'[82] To be properly recognized, one needs to properly recognize: that is the essence of concrete reciprocity.

The mutuality inherent in Hegel's account of recognition provides the basis for a substantially communicative, relational framework. As Honneth pointed out in his argument, a recognitive social theory should undoubtedly be communicative. But what Hegel's and mainly Kojève's[83] dialectics of

---

[78] Hegel, *Phenomenology of Spirit*, 115.   [79] Ibid, 112.   [80] Ibid, 115.
[81] Ibid, 116.   [82] Kojève, *Introduction to the Reading of Hegel*, 19.
[83] As briefly discussed above, Kojève's account of the dialectics of recognition radicalizes Hegel's account with a focus on a material dialectic through the use of a Marxist perspective. See Kojève, ibid, at 3–30.

recognition indicate is that the recognition that underlies communication does not in itself guarantee solidarity, and the process can go wrong. As we saw earlier, punishment requires the pre-existence of a common will, of a community. It is not clear, however, how the process of recognition evolves from the Master–Slave dialectic to a situation of concrete mutual recognition. Hegel does not resolve this problem in the *Phenomenology*, showing instead that this dialectic repeats itself at higher levels of self-consciousness.[84] In his post-phenomenological work he does not address this problem directly, but rather only suggests that political society both requires and generates mutual recognition. However, a critical understanding of the process of recognition can arguably be used to highlight the origins of the challenges and paradoxes surrounding criminalization and punishment in liberal democratic societies.

As discussed in the previous chapter, in the *Philosophy of Right*, Hegel's examination of criminal law and punishment occurs in two moments. From the perspective of abstract right, the definition of right and crime has a predominantly subjective character. The problem of crime is essentially that, by denying someone else's right, the criminal is negating right as such, and thus s/he is attempting against the basis of her/his own rights. At the same time, however, because right at this moment still does not possess an objective reality, 'acts of punishment at the level of abstract right are acts of revenge, as there is no designated penal power'.[85] In other words, although at this moment all individuals have the same basis for their rights, there is still no mutual recognition objectively in place. Hegel states that punishment in the abstract is in fact essentially equated to crime as, without a common will to legitimate it, the right that punishment strives to preserve is as contingent as the right the criminal evokes in her/his actions. In the abstract, both crime and punishment display the same disregard for the other party's claim to right. That is why Hegel stresses that although there are many considerations to be taken in a theory of punishment, the essential point is to keep in mind that 'all these considerations presuppose as their foundation the fact that punishment is inherently and actually just'.[86]

There is a gap between this abstract account of punishment and what systematic readers of the *Philosophy of Right*[87] consider Hegel's concrete account of punishment in the sphere of ethical life. There the focus of punishment changes from a direct relation with the wrongfulness of the criminal's deed to a relation between the state and the condition of civil society, where the stability or sense of security of a society can directly influence

[84] Williams, *Hegel's Ethics of Recognition*, 68.
[85] Brooks, *Hegel's Political Philosophy*, 44.   [86] Hegel, *Philosophy of Right*, 70.
[87] See e.g. Brooks, *Hegel's Political Philosophy*.

how punishments are envisaged.[88] This aspect of Hegel's account represents a significant shift in what is considered to be a mainly retributive theory of punishment.[89] Although it seems that the administration of justice retains a retributive core, it is certain that the 'penal code, then, is primarily the child of its age and the state of civil society at the time'.[90] But what if, as the conflictive relations of civil society suggest, the state of civil society under a modern context of possessive market relations does not give rise to a condition of mutual recognition? If it is acknowledged that structural problems hinder the presumption of a common will, the justification of punishment as a communicative endeavour is not very far from the Master's illusion that the submission of the Slave will grant her/him the recognition s/he desires; it is a situation of false consciousness. Concrete recognition would require the conditions for a mutual satisfaction of human desires, which is not likely to occur unless structural problems of injustice and inequality are resolved or at least substantially addressed. This structural disharmony generates dissonance between the individual's moral experiences and the state's ethical and normative expectations. Recognition, taken seriously as the grounds for genuinely reciprocal communication, raises important questions for thinking about an account of criminal law and punishment as liberal institutions.

THE LIMITS OF COMMUNITY

This chapter has so far considered Duff's account of punishment as communication, noting his underlying commitment to recognition, and examined in some depth a critical perspective on recognition provided by an analysis of Hegel's work. Problems in the process of recognition, in which this process can go wrong and lead to an unequal, and therefore unsatisfactory, condition, were found to be related to questions of social structure and justice. This situation of broken recognition, in turn, seems to compromise

---

[88] Hegel, *Philosophy of Right*, 140.
[89] Other commentators such as Dudley Knowles (*Hegel and the Philosophy of Right*) argue that it is precisely this instance of administration of justice that will give coherence and substance to Hegel's theory of punishment, since it brings together the universal restoration of right and the particular right of the criminal. But the focus in the subjective part still is on the fact 'that the criminal must recognize that his punishment is legitimate *in so far as it procures the restoration of right*' (ibid, 156, emphasis in original). Such restoration is not only dependent on social mechanisms that 'demonstrate to all, honest and criminal citizens alike, the nature of their rights' (ibid, 157), but also on the previously mentioned common will.
[90] Hegel, *Philosophy of Right*, 140.

the liberal democratic justification for criminalization and punishment—which presupposes a situation of fellowship within the political community. Individual autonomy, responsibility, and communication can all be tied together and examined through the perspective of recognition. Duff's claim that we are owed a communicative engagement on the part of the legal system refers to the notion of responsible subjectivity which the liberal civil order strives to uphold, and which aims to reflect the actualization of mutual recognition in society. However, these normative aspirations find themselves in tension with categories and practices which are embedded within the framework of criminal law and punishment. Punishment, even if conceptualized as forceful moral communication, carries within itself an exclusionary logic of violence and domination, as the punisher is always at least partly concerned with communication as a means through which to make the criminal conform to pre-established rules, and as thus cannot fully recognize her/his agency. This same exclusionary logic is manifested in criminalization. There is a paradox within liberal law, between the paradigm it uses to justify its practices and the socio-political function and consequences of the practices themselves. The process of recognition seems to indicate that force goes against reciprocal communication, and there is no criminalization or punishment without force.[91]

A recognitive perspective, on the other hand, indicates that it must be acknowledged that socialization occurs in a complex and multifaceted manner, and that it espouses different levels or dimensions. First, a critical theory of recognition reformulates the nature of the social contract, by placing individuality as interdependent with sociability. Individuals do not gather to form a society, rather individuality and society are both generated through social coexistence. Second, although sociability is inherent to human beings, the clash of competing claims and expectations born of the multitude of desires in society, as well as of structural factors which hinder or complicate social relations, means that the process of recognition is replete with struggles. And third, although the struggle for recognition commonly generates situations of violence, inequality, and domination, the inherent solidarity in human sociability implies that the desire for recognition can only be fully satisfied in a condition of mutual and reciprocal understanding, where subjects are fully recognized by others whom they fully recognize. Thus while it is quite understandable and desirable—indeed necessary—that a liberal legal order would

---

[91] Andrew von Hirsch has a similar critique of Duff's theory in relation to this point, although not from the perspective of recognition. See A. von Hirsch, 'Proportionate Sentences: A Desert Perspective' in A. Von Hirsch, A. Ashworth, J. Roberts (eds), *Principled Sentencing: Readings on Theory and Policy* (Portland: Hart Publishing, 2009), 115–25.

seek to realize mutual recognition, the very social existence of the categories of crime and punishment implies that the struggle for recognition still persists, since the recognition that such categories provide can, at best, be partial and unequal.

The communicative logic in accounts such as Duff's seems to begin from the end. That is, it starts with the assumption that a liberal political community is already providing—or at least can potentially provide—a situation of mutual recognition, and that it is crime that drags individuals from this situation back into the struggle. Likewise, this same logic has been identified at the core of the liberal imaginary and of its civil order. The liberal model of criminal law, in particular, appears to profess that individual autonomy can be fully realized through responsible subjectivity, so that if the criminal law addresses individuals as responsible subjects it is maintaining mutual respect, and is therefore justified. However, in light of the ambivalences within criminal subjectivity, and in light of the structural inequality preserved within the liberal model of society, what rather seems to be the case is that the emancipatory elements of the legal framework embody values and aspirations that are still struggling to be fully recognized in society. In many instances, these aspirations may find themselves in conflict with competing claims brought forth by individuals, and criminalization and punishment may appear as the manifestation of this struggle. But it is worth noting that, as the parable of the Master and the Slave illustrates, forceful communication not only fails to recognize the criminal, but it also does the system (and liberal society) itself a disservice. Although there is certainly an inclusionary impulse behind criminal justice—which is often expressed through the language of freedom and recognition—such impulse necessitates rather than assures mutual respect and solidarity.

Furthermore, the idea that individuality is socially generated—and precisely because of that, it is not generated equally in different circumstances—elucidates that the struggle for recognition occurs between differentiated subjectivities, which due to their distinct social contexts do not necessarily share a common social, political, or legal understanding. The legal framework and its abstract individualism, along with its image of an abstract (concretized) political community, fail to account for this social complexity. The law promotes the idea that every individual is, at least potentially, an integral member of this political community—that is, that the struggle for recognition as a social reality is basically over; from this perspective, which is similar to Hegel's notion of the rational state,[92] punishment does seem to be

---

[92] It is worth noting that some interpretations of Hegelian scholarship suggest that the conception of the rational state is Hegel's description of how the state sees itself rather than a normative

a legitimate endeavour, since it is grounded on a shared notion of the public interest. The only ripple in this otherwise placid lake of theory, however, is that if every individual is fully recognized within a set of values that they fully understand and accept, then they would not desire anything outside of the system, and then punishment would not be necessary—or would be reserved to a select group of unenlightened few. The very fact that punishment exists and that society (even if reluctantly) accepts its categories and practices suggests that the community to which the legal system aspires is not yet fully realized.

Instead, what transpires is that the offender has a desire that the legal system is presently unable or unwilling to recognize. Although it is very likely that the offender's desire is being expressed in an inappropriate way (it is in itself at best an example of forceful moral communication), the punisher's answer seems to suffer from the same vice. The system and the community it represents act as if threatened or harmed, and so it threatens (or retaliates) in return. One way to break out of this vicious circle would be to concretely communicate the recognition of the offender's humanity, of her/his value, and this can arguably only be done through a real dialogue that properly addresses the social context in which the offender's actions are situated.[93] But this seems highly incompatible with the way in which punishment operates. The normative assumption of the criminal's expectations as wrongful is unable to provide a reciprocal engagement, since it represses the existence of the struggle for recognition. This is indeed an issue for how contemporary criminal justice systems are envisioned and theorized: by pre-establishing the wrongfulness of some course of action and only then pursuing the relationality between individual and community, theories of punishment seem to invert the logic of recognition, thus rendering the proposed communication inexistent at worst, insufficient—because it is one-sided—at best.

description of how the state should ideally be seen by individuals in society (see R. Fine, *Political Investigations* (New York: Routledge, 2001)). Interestingly, there is some indication to that effect, in that Hegel sometimes contrasts the political community of the state with problems he identifies in civil society. Endemic poverty, for instance, is a situation which 'immediately takes the form of a wrong done to one class by another' (Hegel, *Philosophy of Right*, 277–8), with the result that 'there is a consequent loss of the sense of right and wrong' (ibid, 150).

[93] Although there are many similarities between what is being proposed and the postulated aims of restorative justice, this is not necessarily what is being advocated here. There are problems and difficulties with how restorative justice is actualized which may severely compromise its validity, but which however are beyond the scope of the present study. For a short discussion of the matter, See A. Ashworth, 'Responsibilities, Rights and Restorative Justice' (2002) 42 *British Journal of Criminology*, 578–95. See also M. Rossner, *Just Emotions: Rituals of Restorative Justice* (Oxford: Oxford University Press, 2013).

This is of course not to say that replacing the categories of criminalization and punishment is something simple or even presently possible; neither is it to say that the notion that categories of punishment contradictorily reflect aspirations for mutual recognition is something only to be regretted. The main point I am raising is that it is necessary to advance the argument that, if a theory of punishment is to be grounded upon notions of responsibility that strive to respect concrete individuality, that theory needs to be aware that communication is a project and a process, and proper recognition still an aspiration. Otherwise, its categories start to challenge and contradict themselves, and the system finds itself working against the same principles it allegedly preserves. The case of the treatment of terrorism by the criminal law provides a particularly vivid and relevant example of this paradox.

The Terrorist Threat

Possibly the most exemplary manifestation of the problems identified with the preventive turn can be found in the ensemble of anti-terrorism legislation, as there is no other area of criminalization where the need to promote security has been as pervasive, or where the dangerousness within criminal subjectivity has been as accentuated. The terrorist is the fundamental folk devil[94] of the twenty-first century. Furthermore, the place of primacy of the terrorist in the contemporary imaginary of insecurity is reflected by the framework of criminal law, in that the gamut of terrorism criminal offences involves nearly all the spectrum of preventive criminalization, from possession and preparation offences, to offences of participation in a criminal organization, over to offences of breach of a preventive measure. In light of this, the suggestion by Manuel Cancio Meliá that '[t]he evolution of criminal law in the twenty-first century is closely intertwined with the way in which it is used to react to terrorism'[95] is no exaggeration.

One of the main reasons behind the exacerbation of the dangerousness inherent to the image of the terrorist lies in the essential link between terrorism and the state. Although the danger inherent to crime stems from the notion that every crime has the potential to threaten or harm society as a whole, terrorism is distinguished from other, 'normal' crimes precisely on the basis that it expresses a clear socio-political motivation. As Clive Walker has identified, legal definitions of terrorism usually focus on three specific aspects: a political purpose; the aim to communicate or to instil terror on the

---

[94] S. Cohen, *Folk Devils and Moral Panics* (London: Routledge, 2002).
[95] M.C. Meliá, 'Terrorism and Criminal Law: The Dream of Prevention, the Nightmare of the Rule of Law' (2011) 14(1) *New Criminal Law Review*, 108–22, 110.

broader population; the use of violence, usually on a mass scale.[96] These aspects are reflected in the definition of terrorism presented in the Terrorism Act 2000.[97] In a sense, then, terrorism is distinguished from other crimes only to the extent that it exposes and magnifies the danger inherent to the idea of crime, by aiming directly to cause what, to most other crimes, is only a secondary consequence of their primary harm—the harm threatened against the community and its conditions. For this reason, there are important insights that can be taken from an analysis of the relation between terrorism and criminal law, regarding the socio-political character of crime and punishment.

The UK provides the paradigmatic criminal justice model of anti-terrorism legislation, due to the country's involvement in counter-terrorism in former colonies, and due especially to the relationship between criminal justice and terrorism with regards to Northern Ireland, going back to the Northern Ireland (Emergency Provisions) Acts 1973–98.[98] This model, which attempts to deal with terrorism primarily through the criminal law (instead of by means of exceptional powers, such as the 'war on terror' conducted by the United States of America after the New York attacks of 11 September 2001), has been generally hailed by legal scholars as the most appropriate way in which to deal with the terrorist threat. This is mainly due to the capacity ascribed to the criminal law, because of its principles and procedural guarantees, to both condemn and prevent wrongdoing and to treat individuals fairly, thus containing the possible excesses of an overzealous state.[99]

However, although the criminal law has been seen as the most appropriate framework through which to deal with terrorists, its ordinary contours have also been considered insufficient for addressing and containing the danger surrounding terrorism. This resulted in the enactment of several acts dedicated to anti-terrorism, which created a series of terrorist criminal offences alongside special preventive measures, police and other investigatory powers, which have been widely deemed to be 'grossly disproportionate'.[100] This expansion of the criminal law was primarily grounded on three levels of justification, according to Clive Walker: firstly, the terrorist threat calls upon the duty and the power of the state to protect itself and its political community, a prerogative which is recognized by the European Convention of

[96] C. Walker, *Blackstone's Guide to Anti-Terrorism Legislation* (Oxford: Oxford University Press, 2009).

[97] Terrorism Act 2000, s. 1.

[98] See C. Walker, 'Terrorism and Criminal Justice: Past, Present and Future' (2004) *Criminal Law Review*, 311–27, 312.

[99] J. Waldron, *Torture, Terror and Trade-Offs* (New York: Oxford University Press, 2010); L. Zedner, 'Terrorizing Criminal Law' (2014) 8(1) *Criminal Law and Philosophy*, 99–121.

[100] Meliá, 'Terrorism and Criminal Law', 110.

Human Rights[101] as possible grounds for the derogation of individual rights. Secondly, repressive measures are justified by 'the illegitimacy of terrorism as a mode of political expression',[102] which incurs a felt need to repress such expression, which is reinforced by the notion that terrorism usually involves the commission of serious and dangerous crimes. And thirdly, the pervasive and invasive nature of anti-terrorism laws is based on the notion 'that terrorism is a specialised form of criminality that presents peculiar difficulties in terms of policing and criminal process',[103] linked to factors such as its organized, ideological, and systemic character.

The result of this justificatory framework is a system of specialized norms which nevertheless have a high degree of pervasiveness, affecting the whole structure of criminal law and criminal justice. What is special about terrorism in relation to the criminal law is not necessarily that terrorism laws defy the logic of criminalization, but rather that they push elements of this logic to their limits. Terrorism, more than other recent substantive changes to the criminal law, exposes ideological aspects of punishment and responsibility which, while not irremediably harming their justificatory framework, do point to limitations in the capacity of liberal law to properly deliver some of its most fundamental promises.

Terrorism and Recognition

Duff concludes his article about punishment as secular penance with a question concerning what he calls 'the limits of community'. He starts by saying that punishment, as an essentially inclusionary activity, 'is supposed to constitute a mode of moral reparation through which [the offender] is to be reconciled with those he has wronged—through which the bonds of political community are to be repaired and strengthened'.[104] This leads to a question of 'whether there are any crimes whose character is such that we need not, or should not, or cannot maintain such community with the offender'[105]—that is, crimes that negate the inclusionary character of punishment but do so in a 'legitimate, appropriate or even necessary'[106] way, since the very nature of the crime denies the possibility of community. Duff presses the issue by suggesting that many kinds of punishment reflect precisely that assumption, such as the death penalty or life imprisonment under a whole life order, since they do not leave open any real possibility of reintegration of the offender with the

---

[101] European Convention of Human Rights, articles 2, 15, and 17.
[102] Walker, 'Terrorism and Criminal Justice', 316.   [103] Ibid.
[104] Duff, 'Penance, Punishment', 305.   [105] Ibid, 305–6.   [106] Ibid, 306.

community. He rejects a general application of such categories of punishment within the remit of his theory, for '[w]ith at least the vast majority of crimes and criminals, we should continue to see and to treat them as fellow members of the normative community who must be punished, but whose moral standing as members is not to be denied or qualified.'[107] But then he raises the possibility of there being exceptions to the rule, in which some extreme forms of wrongful conduct might be enough to give rise to an un-repairable breach of solidarity with the offender.

Duff argues that three particular scenarios are exemplary of the reasoning behind this compromise. The first refers to some crimes being so terrible in themselves that they preclude any possibility of the restoration or continuation of community between criminal and society; the second corresponds to criminal careers, that is, the 'persistent commission of dangerous and violent crimes, which display in the end such an incorrigible rejection of the community's central values' as to lead to the aforementioned breach; and the third case finally relates to terrorist attacks 'such as, most terribly, those committed on New York and Washington in September 2001'.[108] Considering whether or not any of these examples would preclude the possibility of communicative punishment, Duff claims he is fairly confident that the first case should be answered with a negative, as 'no single deed, however terrible, should put a person beyond civic redemption'.[109] He is slightly more hesitant when it comes to the second case, as the insistence on wrongful behaviour could be significantly damaging to the bond between offender and community, and to deny the possibility of measures such as permanent detention in these cases would be 'to believe that the bonds of community, and the status of citizenship, are unconditional and absolute— that nothing, not even a person's own persistent demonstration that he utterly rejects the demands of citizenship and community, can destroy them'.[110] Duff seems to be reluctant to accept this possibility, which he approximates to a religious ideal unsuitable for the modern state. However, from a recognitive perspective, it could be inquired first of all whether the breach of community in question is a consequence of the criminal's actions, or whether it is primarily related to the social context and consequently only interpreted by the law as being a rejection on the part of the criminal.

As regards the matter of the terrorist attack, Duff complicates the problem by introducing a further discussion on law and punishment. He considers the hypothesis of a terrorist attack in which there is a good idea of who the perpetrators are, then asks whether, assuming those probable suspects are actually under pursuit, we should 'treat this as an attempt to arrest suspected

---

[107] Ibid.   [108] Ibid.   [109] Ibid.   [110] Ibid, 307.

criminals ... or as a defensive war to prosecute against an alien enemy'.[111] He reflects that, although moral constraints have to be acknowledged with regard to the treatment of these suspects, 'the aims even of a just war and the moral constraints on its conduct clearly differ from the aims and constraints of a system of communicative punishments. War aims not at reconciliation with the enemy ... but at victory.'[112] He further claims that the terrorists themselves probably see their own activities under the same light, as a war against an enemy regime or a state. But then he asks, 'should we take this view?'[113]

In the article presently under discussion, Duff does not have a clear answer to this problem; instead, he says that 'any normatively plausible account of the situation would need to be much more complex and nuanced than such a simple "either/or" allows.'[114] He further argues that 'we should surely be very reluctant to abandon the moral constraints that belong with the enterprise of criminal justice, in favour of the rather weaker constraints that apply to the conduct of war', and that 'we should also be very reluctant to exclude the perpetrator from any prospect of community with us'.[115] Two years later, however, in his article 'Notes on Punishment and Terrorism',[116] Duff addresses the same problem again and offers a rather different answer. The main theme of this article is the question of whether we should see the terrorist as a criminal (subject to the criminal law of the state), as an enemy combatant (protected by international humanitarian law), or as an 'unlawful combatant'[117] (that is, as someone with 'no such moral claims on our respect or concern and whom we may treat in any way that seems necessary to ensure our own safety and to "defeat terrorism"'[118]). Duff says, first of all, that to see terrorists as criminals 'is to see them as moral agents with whom we must still seek to communicate', and under such view they would be 'entitled to the same protections as any citizen'.[119] 'However,' he continues, 'we might plausibly feel that especially with the more serious kinds of international (as distinct from domestic) terrorism, we are faced by something that is more like war than crime.'[120]

The main argument Duff uses in support of his view[121] is that, given the extreme nature of the wrongfulness involved in certain terrorist activities, the

---

[111] Ibid.   [112] Ibid.   [113] Ibid.   [114] Ibid, 308.   [115] Ibid.
[116] Duff, 'Notes on Punishment'.   [117] Ibid, 758.
[118] Ibid, 760. Duff is here clearly referring to the approach purported by the U.S. government for many years, reflected in regimes of detention without trial such as Guantanamo Bay. The United Kingdom had a similar approach in Belmarsh prison with the Anti-terrorism, Crime and Security Act 2001 until the Prevention of Terrorism Act 2005 repealed the provisions for detention without trial.
[119] Duff, 'Notes on Punishment', 759.   [120] Ibid.
[121] It should be noted that Duff does not assert that he supports the view that the terrorist should be treated as an enemy combatant; instead, his claim is 'that the rules of war mark the minimal constraints that we must respect in our dealings with other human beings, whatever they have done'

interaction between a community and its perpetrators would be better interpreted as a situation of war than one of punishment. And he believes such is an important distinction because '[i]t is true that warfare does not aim—as punishment should aim—at moral communication with the enemy.'[122] What seems to be confusing in this situation is to what conception of communication Duff is referring. If communication would be simply some attempt to reach out to the other in order to convince or persuade them (that is, forceful moral communication), then certainly the terrorist is trying to communicate something—even if it is an extreme and fundamentalist message. Looking at legislation in the United Kingdom, the definition of terrorism in the Terrorist Act 2000 states that it includes an intent 'to influence the government or an international governmental organization or to intimidate the public or a section of the public', and must have 'the purpose of advancing a political, religious, racial or ideological cause',[123] which necessarily implies that there is some message being transmitted through an act of terrorism, related to its political purpose.

Within a normative framework that takes recognition (and communication) seriously, the possibility that the specific attitudes of the terrorist may place her/him outside of any notion of community go against the very principles of responsibility and autonomy upheld by the tenets of liberal law that Duff espouses. This is so not because a sense of community would be taken as absolute, but because the actions of the terrorist should not be interpreted as directed completely against the community, but rather as an expression of the same desire for recognition that is taken as a presupposition of that community. To say that war does not aim at moral communication with the enemy, from the perspective of a liberal normative framework, would be an argument against the legitimacy of war, rather than against the possibility of punishment.[124] Duff's discussion about the limits of community rather hints at situations in which the justificatory logic of punishment exposes its own limitations.

(ibid, 761). But it can be argued that, by saying this, Duff is accepting the possibility of denying a terrorist access to the system of punishment.

[122] Ibid, 759.   [123] Terrorism Act 2000, s. 1(1).

[124] This is particularly relevant if we consider that war is politics by other means, and that politics can also be seen as the continuation of war by other means. See M. Foucault, *Society Must Be Defended: Lectures at the Collège de France 1975-1976* (London: Penguin, 2004). Also, for more on the dichotomy between crime and war, see L. Zedner, 'Securing Liberty in the Face of Terror: Reflections from Criminal Justice' (2005) 32(4) *Journal of Law and Society*, 507–33; N. Feldman, 'Choices of Law, Choices of War' (2002) 25 *Harvard Journal of Law and Public Policy*, 457–85.

The Politics of Responsibility and Community

Terrorism challenges liberal conceptions of punishment precisely because its radical political nature exposes contradictions which are inherent to the justification of punishment and of the criminal law. The book *Philosophy in a Time of Terror*[125] presents interviews with Jürgen Habermas and Jacques Derrida about the attacks of 11 September 2001, shortly after they occurred. There, Habermas provides a compelling explanation of how terrorism in the twenty-first century, inflamed by fundamentalism, can be largely understood as the result of frustrated claims of communities that are not adapted to the modern secular framework of Western society.[126] Furthermore, Western society in itself contains 'a structural violence that, to a certain degree, we have gotten used to, that is, unconscionable social inequality, degrading discrimination, pauperization, and marginalization'.[127] This structural violence is deeply related to a distortion in communication that arises from conflicting expectations, and that if left unchecked, one feeds into the other until communication is no longer possible.[128]

This particular view arguably 'explains why attempts at understanding have a chance only under symmetrical conditions of mutual perspective-taking'[129] where communication would be free from distortion. And although Habermas admits that 'communication is always ambiguous, suspect of latent violence',[130] he advises that seeing communication as embedded purely in violence and letting force respond to force misses the point, 'that the critical power to put a stop to violence, without reproducing it in circles of new violence, can only dwell in the telos of mutual understanding'.[131] This is a call to continued recognition and solidarity in structural conditions where all parties share some responsibility for what occurs; legal categories of guilt and wrongfulness go against this logic of mutual understanding, which is something that liberal theories of punishment seem to ignore.

Activities that are taken to be emblematic of terrorism are never to be endorsed, downplayed, or ignored; rather, it is necessary to address and engage with them. But to properly confront the threat of extreme violence embedded in terrorism in a way that seriously considers the value of human dignity and individual autonomy, legal systems must do better than to neglect the social context in which such violence occurs. Otherwise, the law's pretensions of seeking communication and recognition will remain largely ideological, and will continue to obscure the other dimensions of punishment and

---

[125] G. Borradori, *Philosophy in a Time of Terror* (Chicago: University of Chicago Press, 2003).
[126] J. Habermas in Borradori, ibid, 30–3.   [127] Ibid, 35.   [128] Ibid.
[129] Ibid, 37.   [130] Ibid, 38.   [131] Ibid.

criminalization which continue to drive them. Instead, we should arguably seek, as Derrida says, to 'condemn [terrorist extreme violence] unconditionally ... without having to ignore the real or alleged conditions that made it possible'.[132] A critical account of September 11 is an example of how it is possible to try and understand terrorism from beyond this 'lexicon of violence' that is 'legitimated by the prevailing system'.[133] In a sense, international terrorism[134] seems to follow a rather similar logic to the one displayed by punishment, prevention, and criminalization, as 'all terrorism presents itself as a response in a situation that continues to escalate'.[135] And in this globalized situation of violence, 'dialogue (at once verbal and peaceful) is not taking place. Recourse to the worst violence is thus often presented as the only "response" to a "deaf ear".'[136] This seems to be the expressed justification given by terrorists for their actions; surely a legal system normatively committed to communication and mutual recognition should do better.

Even if terrorists are subjectively claiming to act against the political community, they are objectively acting in community, against (aspects of) a community that frustrates recognition. The means they choose to reclaim recognition are surely mistaken and lead to terrible consequences, and something indeed ought to be done about it. But the same fundamental problem could be attributed to an overzealous imposition of a normative judgment (any forceful moral communication or, even worse, a refusal to communicate) in response to their activities. The same observations could be directed at less radical forms of criminalization which are the bread and butter of criminal law. Ultimately, an engagement with the context of crime and punishment highlights that both of these notions are essentially political, in that they can be interpreted as reflections of struggles for recognition arising from the pursuit of the project of political community within conditions of structural violence. As Garland has suggested,

[Penality] communicates meaning not just about crime and punishment but also about power, authority, legitimacy, normality, morality, personhood, social relations, and a host of other tangential matters. Penal signs and symbols are one part of an authoritative, institutional discourse which seeks to organise our moral and political understanding and to educate our sentiments and sensibilities.[137]

---

[132] Jacques Derrida in Borradori, ibid, 107.   [133] Ibid, 93.

[134] Although a similar critique could be elaborated in regard to all actions associated with terrorism, this specific critique focuses on the notion of international terrorism endemic to the twenty-first century. For more on that, See B. Hoffman, *Inside Terrorism* (New York: Columbia University Press, 2006).

[135] Derrida, *Philosophy in a Time of Terror*, 107.   [136] Ibid, 122–3.

[137] D. Garland, *Punishment and Modern Society: A Study in Social Theory* (Oxford: Oxford University Press, 1990), 252–3.

This basic element of the environment of criminalization and punishment, and its relation to social conflict, is neglected and repressed by the law's attempt to preserve a civil order grounded on a monovalent assumption of mutual respect and formal equality in civil society. This repression, in turn, is probably the most significant obstacle preventing liberal democratic societies from moving towards actualizing the recognition which their social imaginary ideologically assumes. The way out of such an orientation can only be sought from a much broader perspective than that of the law, as it is a problem related to our contemporary socio-political experience. But if heed is to be paid to a serious account of the values behind ideas such as individual freedom and solidarity, it should at the very least be required that the law acknowledge its limitations.

CONCLUSION

This chapter has aimed to illustrate and examine problems in values and aspirations embedded within liberal justifications for punishment, that arise from the tension between the law's justificatory and normative framework, and the socio-political context in which such aspirations need to be actualized. It did so in order to suggest that although it may be true that criminalization and punishment have a place and a function in society, this function should not be confused with a normative justification that implies that violence and coercion can preserve or promote a framework of reciprocal communication and recognition. Duff's contribution, of engaging with difficult challenges and pushing forward the need to think normatively about punishment, is welcome and necessary, but perhaps there it is necessary to acknowledge that the normative aspirations within such accounts depend on broader projects of social change, which punishment in itself is not only unable to address, but also likely to harm.

Criminalization is one of the most important debates occurring in criminal law and punishment scholarship, and such debate relies heavily on an examination of what the criminal law and its subject should be, in order to determine what should or should not be criminalized. This chapter embraced an examination of the law's normative limits, hopefully offering a reflection on what it means to punish, and what may be one of the forces behind this need. Such reflection invites the view that a shift in perspective—from punishment to recognition—is necessary if harmful conflicts in society are to be properly identified and concretely dealt with. Then, maybe a properly communicative conception of responsibility and subjectivity can begin to unfurl within the legal framework, and problems such as terrorism and other categories of otherness can be better understood by the criminal law.

Moreover, the theory of recognition sketched in this chapter was aimed at suggesting that the image of community ideally expressed by legal principles relies on the existence and development of mutual understanding, and curtailing or neglecting such understanding constitutes an affront to the very concepts that ground and justify the legal order in the first place. This tension between mutual recognition and one-sided communication poses a paradox for the legal system, and any normative theory of punishment or criminal law aimed at advocating a need for recognition and respect for the individual has in the very least to acknowledge this paradox, and ideally to engage with it. Only then can the possibility of dealing with the real problems found in seeking justice through punishment come to the fore.

7

The Preventive Turn

An Ambivalent Law in an Insecure World

> While we think of ourselves as a society of equal opportunities and social inclusion, our criminal justice system serves to legitimise the impact of structural inequalities based on social cleavages, such as race, by labelling manifestations of allegedly dangerous difference as criminal.[1]

After uncovering the conceptual foundations of the ambivalence at the core of criminal subjectivity, and examining the limitations to the emancipatory project within criminal law, which are linked to this ambivalence, this final chapter turns from political theory back into political sociology in order to trace the dynamics of criminal subjectivity throughout the modern history of criminal law and punishment. It does so by interacting with the relation, established in recent scholarship in criminal law and criminology, between the modern development of criminal law and punishment, and the unfolding of democratic citizenship in English society. The nexus between changes and transformations in the liberal civil order and shifting notions of criminal subjectivity provided by the political sociology of citizenship is that of political belonging, that is, of citizenship as representative of an individual's status as a member of a specific political community. Examined from this prism, criminal subjectivity is defined precisely through the interaction between individual autonomy and political authority, and as such it says something not only about those who come to be subjected to the authority of the criminal law, but also about the general relation between state, individuals, and society. In this sense, the main argument of this chapter is that a critical engagement with the current state of the criminal law can offer broader insights and lessons with regards to the problematic condition of law within liberal societies.

---

[1] N. Lacey, *In Search of Criminal Responsibility: Ideas, Interests and Institutions* (Oxford: Oxford University Press, 2016), 172.

The first section of this chapter establishes the link between criminal subjectivity and the modern development of citizenship in English society, paying particular attention to the connection between the rise of subjective responsibility in criminal law and the inclusionary impulse of citizenship in modernity. However, a deeper engagement with the political sociology of citizenship, specifically through the work of T.H. Marshall, reveals that what might appear as a linear progression towards inclusivity, in reality conceals an inherent tension between these emancipatory aspirations and the preservation of an unequal and in many ways exclusionary model of society, which is manifested through ambivalences in the structures of criminalization and punishment. This remains the case even in the highest point of modern democratic citizenship, the welfare state of the mid-twentieth century.

The second section delves further into the conditionality of the universalizing aspirations of citizenship, by examining the state of criminal subjectivity in the preventive turn. This state is characterized as one of radical ambivalence, in the sense that the dynamics of criminal subjectivity, under conditions of social unravelling and insecurity, lead to both responsibility and dangerousness being intermeshed and over-emphasized, so that the criminal law needs to pursue radical forms of criminalization, such as preventive criminal offences, in order to deploy its reassurance function. The third section then explores the consequences of this radical ambivalence to the liberal project of criminal law.

THE CONDITIONALITY
OF DEMOCRATIC CITIZENSHIP

As previously discussed, there are good reasons to believe that the normative notions of individual autonomy and responsibility which lie at the core of the criminal law are best understood if contextualized within a liberal democratic polity, and within the environment of the rights and duties of citizenship. However, in order to properly engage with the perplexities within criminal subjectivity, it is necessary to recognize that citizenship in itself is an open concept which allows for different and complex interpretations of what it entails. For instance, conceptions of citizenship can tend towards universalism, 'seeking ultimately to include all people in citizenship', or they can be primarily exclusive, limiting membership of the community only to particular groups of individuals.[2] Furthermore, the axiomatic character of the notion

---

[2] R. Reiner, 'Citizenship, Crime, Criminalization: Marshalling a Social Democratic Perspective' (2010) 13(2) *New Criminal Law Review*, 241–61, 243.

of citizenship means that it reflects a normative aspiration as well as a set of structural elements. Just like the idea of the state in Hegel's work, citizenship figures in the liberal imaginary both as the purpose of civil society and as a condition for it. The aim of this section is to examine to what extent the liberal conception of criminal subjectivity is tied to a specific image of political community—which is in turn primarily expressed by a particular conception of citizenship—and to what degree transformations in the environment of citizenship can affect criminal subjectivity as well as political community. A theoretical examination of the relation between citizenship, criminal law, and punishment can arguably expose the tensions in the framework of criminal subjectivity and liability, as well as the conditions which allowed for the rise of preventive criminal offences.

Recent scholarship in criminal law and criminal justice have consistently relied on the tripartite conception of social democratic citizenship enunciated by T.H. Marshall in his seminal 1949 lecture, 'Citizenship and Social Class',[3] as a lens through which to analyse the context of modern and contemporary criminalization and punishment. Marshall's lecture constitutes the 'locus classicus for much debate about citizenship in the last half-century',[4] having presented a notion of citizenship that 'embodied a universalistic and inclusive ideal' and promoted 'a process of inclusion of all people in a common status ... by virtue of their humanity'.[5] For Marshall, citizenship represented 'full membership of the community'[6] in which an individual participates, and was constituted of three essential elements or dimensions: civil ('composed of the rights necessary for individual freedom',[7] most importantly property rights), political ('the right to participate in the exercise of political power'[8]), and social ('the whole range from the right to a modicum of economic welfare and security to the right to share to the full in the social heritage and to live the life of a civilized being according to the standards prevailing in the society'[9]) citizenship. These dimensions of citizenship also indicated for Marshall steps or generations in a gradual progression towards a fuller conception of political belonging in modern English society. This progression started with the establishment of civil citizenship in the eighteenth century, followed by the development of political citizenship throughout the nineteenth and twentieth centuries, and then by the emergence of social citizenship from the late nineteenth century onwards.[10] Marshall's analysis culminated in the coming

[3] T.H. Marshall, *Citizenship and Social Class* (London: Pluto Press, 1992).
[4] Reiner, 'Citizenship, Crime, Criminalization', 244.   [5] Ibid.
[6] Marshall, *Citizenship and Social Class*, 18.   [7] Ibid, 8.   [8] Ibid.   [9] Ibid.
[10] Ibid, 10–13.

together of all three forms in the environment of the rights and duties of citizenship in the democratic welfare state.

The elements of democratic citizenship theorized by Marshall, together with their historical development and the 'flow and ebb' between these elements, arguably provide 'the vital context' in which to analyse shifts and developments in criminal law and justice, as well as to explore 'the trajectory of criminal behaviour' and subjectivity.[11] Marshall's political sociology highlights how the modern project of citizenship has an intrinsic inclusionary impulse, as the development of the forms of citizenship tends towards a broadening and thickening of the notion of membership in a political community. On the other hand, however, his perspective also emphasizes how the structure of modern democratic citizenship is 'a dynamic, contingent affair',[12] and how it represents 'the achievement of a particular historical experience in which antithetical principles are only reconciled for a time, for as long as specific conditions hold'.[13] The tension between these two elements of citizenship, its inclusionary aspiration and its socio-historical contingency, can be linked to the inherent ambivalence within its sociopolitical environment.

One of Marshall's main concerns in *Citizenship and Social Class* was to understand the proper relation between the substantive equality propagated by democratic citizenship on the one hand, and the structural violence inherent to modern liberal societies on the other. For him, the greatest perplexity in the institutional framework of citizenship was that its growth and development in England coincided with that of the 'system of ... inequality' of capitalist market relations.[14] Marshall saw this relation as a conflict between 'opposing principles', a fundamental war fought between capitalism and social justice in English society, which '[sprung] from the very roots' of its socio-historical context.[15] The consequence of this conflict was that even the thick environment of social democratic citizenship constituted a compromise between egalitarian principles and an 'inegalitarian' social order which was 'not dictated by logic', and thus unlikely to continue indefinitely.[16] These dialectics inherently condition the environment of citizenship, and this conditionality is primarily expressed through the existence of 'degrees of participation'[17] in the political community. There is thus a fundamental inequality

---

[11] Reiner, 'Citizenship, Crime, Criminalization', 250.

[12] B. Vaughan, 'Punishment and Conditional Citizenship' (2000) 2(1) *Punishment and Society*, 23–39, 25.

[13] P. Ramsay, 'The Responsible Subject as Citizen: Criminal Law, Democracy and the Welfare State' (2006) 69(1) *Modern Law Review*, 31, 56.

[14] Marshall, *Citizenship and Social Class*, 18.   [15] Ibid.   [16] Ibid.

[17] D. Held, 'Between State and Civil Society: Citizenship' in G. Andrews (ed), *Citizenship* (London: Lawrence & Wishart, 1991), 19–25, 20.

of access to citizenship, which is limited by the structural violence existent in modern liberal societies and managed by institutional mechanisms that espouse an exclusionary aspect which is necessary to restrain and counterbalance the inclusivity of citizenship in order to maintain civil order. One such mechanism is engendered by processes of criminalization.

The exclusionary aspect of criminalization is primarily linked to the stigmatizing and coercive character of the penal system, which has traditionally been geared at 'identify[ing] those prospective citizens who seem to be unable to fulfil the demands of citizenship'.[18] The more political participation expanded in modern society, the more those individuals who were identified as potential deviants found themselves forced to either 'become responsible, conforming subjects, whose regularity, political stability and industrious performance deems them capable of entering into institutions of representative democracy', or to be 'supervised and segregated from the normal social realm in a manner that minimises (and individualises) any "damage" they can do'.[19] Criminalization exposes the conditionality of citizenship by illustrating how 'citizenship is granted only if one abides by an accepted standard of behaviour', and how even acquired rights in society can be restrained or taken away through the imposition of punishment.[20] In light of this analysis, Barry Vaughan suggests that there is a 'reciprocal relationship between citizenship and punishment: the cultural conditions of citizenship direct how people will be punished and punishment reinforces notions about who is thought worthy of citizenship'.[21] As a result, those who undergo punishment find themselves in 'the purgatory' of being considered conditional citizens.[22]

Criminal subjectivity can be seen to represent the gateway and point of intersection in this reciprocal relationship, where the ambivalence of conditional citizenship is even more accentuated due to its liminal character. While punishment focuses on what should be done to the criminal, on the limits of state coercion and exclusion, criminalization involves the broader and more complex task of thinking about 'what and who should be treated as criminal under the law and the ways it can be justified'.[23] The subject of criminal law is thus in an even more uncertain state with regards to her/his political status than the subject of punishment, occupying a twilight zone in which s/he appears both as a citizen and as a potential threat

---

[18] Vaughan, 'Punishment and Conditional Citizenship', 24.
[19] D. Garland, *Punishment and Welfare: A History of Penal Strategies* (Aldershot: Gower, 1985), 249.
[20] Vaughan, 'Punishment and Conditional Citizenship', 26.   [21] Ibid, 28.
[22] Ibid, 26.
[23] L. Farmer, *Making the Modern Criminal Law: Criminalization and Civil Order* (Oxford: Oxford University Press, 2016), 1.

to the political community. However, this ambivalence is not openly rec-ognized in the framework of criminal law. Instead, what appears is that the law attempts to construct a clear message about who the subjects of criminal law are and why they are being criminalized, a message which is essential to the deployment of its reassurance function. However, since this function is tied to the state of civil society, the criminal law's capacity to contain the ambivalence within criminal subjectivity is limited and con-tingent, and affected by changes in the socio-political environment. These dynamics, which are reflected in criminal subjectivity by shifts in the bal-ance between responsibility and dangerousness, can be observed through a relation between transformations in the framework of criminalization and punishment, and developments in the architecture of citizenship in modern society.

Criminal Subjectivity and the Inclusionary Impulse in Modernity

By tracing the accounts presented by criminal law scholars on the historical development of conceptions of criminal responsibility alongside Marshall's theorization of the development of the forms of citizenship in modernity, it is possible to suggest that the modern institution of the criminal law pos-sesses an intrinsic relation with civil rights. The idea of individual rights is the main legal and political manifestation of the notions of individual autonomy and freedom that are embedded within the liberal imaginary. Civil rights are thus at the core of the civil order which the criminal law is supposed to secure. In addition, these rights are directly linked to the transformation of socio-economic relations after the industrial revolution, which encour-aged the reinforcement of notions of self-control, etiquette, and politeness in society.[24] The first generation of citizenship is therefore directly connected to the gradual emergence in modernity of the rational, responsible, self-regulat-ing individual as the image of the ideal member of civil society. Under this perspective, the beginnings of modern criminal law can be taken to largely coincide with the rise of civil citizenship in the eighteenth century. At that time, the main function of the criminal law was to define 'an outer limit of civil rights' by rendering the breach of civil duties 'liable to punishment'.[25] This way, the distribution of civil rights and duties could be presented as formally universal and substantively neutral, and limited primarily by the boundaries of acceptable, law-abiding behaviour.

[24] See N. Elias, *The Civilizing Process* (Oxford: Blackwell, 1994).
[25] Ramsay, 'The Responsible Subject as Citizen', 41.

However, the impulse towards formal equality embedded in civil rights was betrayed by the explicit political and material inequality prevalent in English society at the time. Consequently, while civil citizenship fed into the notion of individual justice, the criminal law of the eighteenth century primarily reflected the fragmentation and inequality of its socio-political environment, characterized by 'a non-democratic political system, a society structured by status hierarchy, and a decentralized social order'.[26] Criminal responsibility in this period was thus primarily tied to conceptions of 'bad character' and disposition,[27] engendering an 'explicit moral evaluation of the defendant's conduct'.[28] In addition, the exclusionary character of political participation expressed itself in the structure of criminal law through a strong bias embedded in the idea of crime, which was largely interpreted as a threat posed against respectable society by the 'dangerous classes', who were 'virtually outlawed' by their own agency.[29] The eighteenth century also saw the 'birth of the prison'[30] as an alternative to capital punishment, through which 'the burgeoning middle class tried to impose their own standards of behaviour upon those who were thought to be worthy of inclusion within society but not yet able to take their place voluntarily'.[31] Ideas of subjective responsibility existed mostly in the form of a presumption of capacity,[32] while in practice the criminal trial was essentially an exculpatory process,[33] operating under a practical 'presumption of guilt'.[34] Although there were already arguments in favour of a more substantial role for individual justice in criminal law, they were resisted by the judiciary, which experienced no 'compelling practical grounds for change'.[35]

[26] Lacey, *In Search of Criminal Responsibility*, 136.   [27] Ibid.

[28] Ramsay, 'The Responsible Subject as Citizen', 44. For more on the concept of responsibility in the eighteenth and nineteenth centuries, see N. Lacey, 'Responsibility and Modernity in Criminal Law' (2001) 9(3) *Journal of Political Philosophy*, 249–76.

[29] B. Bosanquet, *The Philosophical Theory of the State* (London: MacMillan, 1965), ix. See also J. Pratt, 'Dangerousness and Modern Society' in M. Brown, J. Pratt (eds), *Dangerous Offenders: Punishment and Social Order* (London: Routledge, 2000), 35–48.

[30] See M. Foucault, *Discipline and Punish* (London: Penguin, 1979).

[31] Vaughan, 'Punishment and Conditional Citizenship', 28.

[32] Lacey, *In Search of Criminal Responsibility*, 136.

[33] N. Lacey, 'In Search of the Responsible Subject: History, Philosophy and Social Sciences in Criminal Law Theory' (2001) 64(3) *Modern Law Review*, 350–71, 361.

[34] L. Farmer, *Criminal Law, Tradition and Legal Order* (Cambridge: Cambridge University Press, 1997), 182; N. Lacey, 'Character, Capacity, Outcome: Toward a Framework for Assessing the Shifting Pattern of Criminal Responsibility in Modern English Law' in M.D. Dubber, L. Farmer (eds), *Modern Histories of Crime and Punishment* (Stanford: Stanford University Press, 2007), 14–41, 21.

[35] K.J.M. Smith, *Lawyers, Legislators and Theorists: Developments in English Criminal Jurisprudence 1800-1957* (1998), 370, cited in Ramsay, 'The Responsible Subject as Citizen', 43.

In terms of criminal subjectivity, therefore, this period was characterized as one in which the subject of criminal law had a predominant semblance of dangerousness, and in which the nascent civil order was highly dependent on the reassurance function of the criminal law. Since the idea of citizenship was tied to the civil dimension of rights, it was mostly individualized, so that those who had their civil rights restricted or removed by the criminal law were effectively no longer characterized as citizens—and criminals in general were not deemed worthy of citizenship. In this period, then, the ambivalence of criminal subjectivity was managed by containing dangerousness within the boundaries of the criminal law, and keeping responsibility mostly apart from it, as it was symbolically attached to a notion of citizenship that was not available to most individuals who were criminalized.

The formal equality and the ideas of rational agency embedded in civil citizenship only slowly begin to creep further into the framework of criminal subjectivity with the furtherance of political rights, particularly after the establishment of universal suffrage in Britain, when the state effectively makes a formal commitment to social neutrality and thus 'acquires authority on the grounds of its universality'.[36] This development reinforced and formalized the repression of the political conflict in the liberal civil order, as the state, by positing political equality, promoted the image that individuals were formally equal in spite of being substantively unequal. Once citizenship acquires a political dimension in addition to the civil, the criminal law can no longer provide its reassurance function by merely distinguishing responsible from dangerous subjects, as the contrast between 'the spread of egalitarian sentiments' and the 'inegalitarian impact of criminalization' accentuated 'the problem of political legitimation'.[37] For it to appear as part of the project of political inclusion, the criminal law had to start to promote and preserve the normality of responsibility and the exceptionality of dangerousness.

Thus from the mid-nineteenth century until the end of the twentieth century, the balance between responsibility and dangerousness within criminal subjectivity slowly shifts towards responsibility. This is manifested by means of the eclipsing of character responsibility and the 'gradual realization' of capacity responsibility alongside an expansion of the terrain of regulatory offences.[38] Responsible subjectivity comes forward in criminal law to embrace and legitimize the commitment towards political citizenship, '[representing] punishment as a vindication of the offender's own status as a citizen, of her formal equality with all other citizens'.[39] Arguably then, '[d]emocracy necessitated the adoption of the responsible subject of criminal law as orthodoxy',[40]

---

[36] Ramsay, 'The Responsible Subject as Citizen', 44.
[37] Lacey, *In Search of Criminal Responsibility*, 140.   [38] Ibid, 138.
[39] Ramsay, 'The Responsible Subject as Citizen', 44–5.   [40] Ibid, 46.

as the project of civil order required the criminal law to promote the univer-sality of responsible agency and the normative position of trust in society. In other words, once political equality advances the idea that every member of society is a citizen with equal rights, the criminal law can no longer reas-sure responsible subjectivity by directly denying it to its subjects. Instead, the criminal law must reaffirm the equal status of those who come before it, and it must symbolically maintain the conditions for political citizenship, by asserting that most individuals are capable of responsible agency, and that those who do not can be appropriately identified and dealt with by the state.

However, it is important not to overstress the inclusionary impulse of political rights, and thus not to lose sight of the contradictions embedded in the environment of citizenship. The ascension of the responsible subject to prominence in the imaginary of criminal law not only generated 'new legiti-mation problems as well as new challenges of coordination',[41] but it also had to be forcefully distinguished from notions of dangerousness within crim-inal subjectivity. Furthermore, while the general idea of the criminal law was becoming that of a largely rational affair increasingly concerned with indi-vidual justice, punishment was still predominantly severe and exclusionary. Although punishment was progressively acquiring a civilized aspect and was increasingly supposed to have a civilizing effect upon society, this 'did not necessarily mean the suppression of violence but its transfer away from a public space into institutional confines'.[42] The need to remove the violence of punishment from the public sphere coincided with the emergence of the prison as a pervasive form of punishment and a totalizing institution of social control at the service of the civilizing process.[43] The more ideas of responsible subjectivity spread throughout society, the more social order, welfare, and security were established as pervasive institutional concerns, so that the pre-vention of threats to the civil order became 'a central motivating force of early nineteenth-century state-building'.[44] The abstract and ideological character of political citizenship meant that the formal equality propagated by political rights required a reinforced system of social regulation, which was manifested not only through the suppression of dangerousness by punishment, but also by means of the proliferation of regulatory offences and the general policing of behaviour, particularly that of the poorer parts of the population.

It is worth noting that the shift in balance from dangerousness to respon-sibility in the normative framework of criminal law, albeit necessitated by

---

[41] Lacey, *In Search of Criminal Responsibility*, 141.

[42] Vaughan, 'Punishment and Conditional Citizenship', 30.

[43] See Foucault, *Discipline and Punish*; J. Pratt, *Punishment and Civilization: Penal Tolerance and Intolerance in Modern Society* (London: Sage, 2002).

[44] A. Ashworth, L. Zedner, *Preventive Justice* (Oxford: Oxford University Press, 2014), 37.

the thickening of the conception of citizenship, effectively heightened the ambivalence of criminal subjectivity, since the morality of form increasingly propagated by the criminal law conflicted with the exclusionary character of punishment (even if progressively hidden from view) and with the inherent inequality of criminalization—which reflected the substantive inequality present in society. The expansion of the regulatory framework of criminal justice can in this sense be seen as a reflection of the need to socialize the burden for certain risks and harms, and therefore to contribute 'to the equalisation of the basic conditions on which people live'.[45] The spread and practical predominance of regulatory offences from the late nineteenth century onwards can thus be related to the development of social rights and their focus on the socialization of responsibility.[46] From this prism, the regulation of health and safety, work conditions, socio-economic relations, and others by the criminal law was part of efforts to ensure the preservation of the 'single civilization promoted by social citizenship',[47] by maintaining the structural violence inherent to liberal societies within limits that a democratic polity could tolerate.

Dangerousness, Welfare, and the Liberal Model of Criminal Law

Both the rise of subjective responsibility and the spread of regulatory laws can therefore be linked to 'the underlying context [of] the gradual incorporation of the mass of the population into social as well as civil and political citizenship—what David Garland has called the "solidarity project" '.[48] This project emerged together with a new liberal ideology which 'promoted the idea that active government was a better guardian of liberty and that collectivist provision was a better guarantee of welfare' than the minimal state of classical liberalism,[49] and which led to the development of social security and culminated in the environment of democratic citizenship of the welfare state. Just as the individualism of civil rights and the socializing character of social rights came together under democratic citizenship, within criminal law, a complex tapestry of conceptions of responsibility and subjectivity was tentatively conjoined and reconciled. During the period of the welfare state, the criminal law espoused both a strong conception of responsible subjectivity,

---

[45] Ramsay, 'The Responsible Subject as Citizen', 49.

[46] See Farmer, *Criminal Law, Tradition and Legal Order*, 140.

[47] Ramsay, 'The Responsible Subject as Citizen', 49–50.

[48] Reiner, 'Citizenship, Crime, Criminalization', 252. See also D. Garland, *The Culture of Control: Crime and Social Order in Contemporary Society* (Chicago: The University of Chicago Press, 2001), 199.

[49] Ashworth, Zedner, *Preventive Justice*, 47.

manifested through capacity responsibility and its subjective categories of fault, and a pervasive regulatory function expressed by strict liability offences and their underlying conception of outcome responsibility, while character responsibility and its underlying aspect of dangerousness were relegated to a status of exceptionality.[50] Given this configuration, the condition of citizenship of the welfare state can be considered the environment which provided the optimum context for the liberal model of criminal law, when this model acquired normative primacy.

Even in the sphere of punishment it was possible to see in this period a reflection of the sense of trustworthiness given to criminal subjectivity, in that the penal system was infused with a belief in its ability to rehabilitate offenders and reintegrate them within society. However, at the same time as dangerousness saw its normative value with regards to reassurance weakened in this period, it remained an important element of the substantial technocratic apparatus of risk management of the welfare state, which continued to rely heavily on the criminal justice system.[51] On the one hand, dangerousness was heavily 'pathologised', reinterpreted as the expression of a lack of capacity in certain individuals to exercise 'the essentials of citizenship'.[52] Nevertheless, the practical result of this evaluation of conduct was the enactment of 'special regulatory regimes' for categories of individuals such as 'the feeble-minded, the inebriate, the vagrant, and the fallen woman'.[53] The rehabilitative ideal in punishment also had its dangerous side, the primary illustration of which was the extensive use of indeterminate sentencing targeted at groups such as juvenile offenders[54] and, in essence if not in form, at those labelled as insane.[55] In addition, in the framework of criminal liability, although the notion of dangerousness was weakened by the decline of character, the rise of the importance of outcomes as a source of responsibility inevitably highlighted the possibility of crime generating dangerous consequences. Individuals were thus still being recognized as dangerous, and even if this label was given different connotations, most of them were equally stigmatizing. Therefore, dangerousness was not necessarily weakened during this period, but mainly reshaped and displaced.

---

[50] See Lacey, *In Search of Criminal Responsibility*, 145–7.

[51] See P. O'Malley, 'Risk Societies and the Government of Crime' in M. Brown, J. Pratt (eds), *Dangerous Offenders: Punishment and Social Order* (London: Routledge, 2000), 17–34.

[52] L. Zedner, 'Fixing the Future? The Pre-emptive Turn in Criminal Justice' in B. McSherry, A. Norrie, S. Bronitt (eds), *Regulating Deviance* (Portland: Hart, 2009), 37–9. See also A. Loughnan, *Manifest Madness: Mental Incapacity in Criminal Law* (Oxford: Oxford University Press, 2012).

[53] Lacey, *In Search of Criminal Responsibility*, 146.

[54] See Vaughan, 'Punishment and Conditional Citizenship', 34.

[55] See Loughnan, *Manifest Madness: Mental Incapacity in Criminal Law*.

SOCIAL UNRAVELLING, INSECURITY, AND THE RADICAL AMBIVALENCE OF PREVENTION

If the rise of individual responsibility to the centre stage of the normative framework of criminal law can be related to the coming together of the three forms of citizenship in the context of the welfare state, it is only expected that the resurgence of dangerousness in the preventive turn can be somehow linked to a process of friction and fission among these elements.[56] While the environment of democratic citizenship of the welfare state allowed for the conception of freedom promoted by liberal society to present 'an inescapably "social form"',[57] towards the end of the twentieth century, this conception becomes largely contested. Social integration gives way to a process of social unravelling,[58] as society 'dissociates into a variety of ethical and cultural communities with incompatible allegiances and incommensurable obligations'.[59] The erosion of the social basis for mutual benefit generated by the structure of trust of the post-war period results in a 'more general [feeling of] insecurity— deriving from tenuous employment and fragile social relations'[60]—which finds no counter-balance in the emphasis on civil duties and active citizenship advanced by the rising neo-liberal social order. Amidst these shifts in the liberal imaginary, the solidarity project of the post-war period acquires the semblance of a failure.

The changes in socio-political conditions thus resulted in an erosion of the confidence on the capacity of the welfare state to properly address the problem of crime, which quickly resonated with the criminal justice system through a growing distrust on ideas of rehabilitation,[61] and a shift towards a law and order stance as part of 'a rhetoric of reassurance'[62] in public discourse, meant to address feelings of insecurity about crime. This insecurity became even more pervasive in the twenty-first century, a century so far characterized by a

---

[56] See A. Norrie, 'Citizenship, Authoritarianism and the Changing Shape of the Criminal Law' in B. McSherry, A. Norrie, S. Bronitt (eds), *Regulating Deviance* (Portland: Hart Publishing, 2009), 13–34.

[57] N. Rose, *Powers of Freedom: Reframing Political Thought* (Cambridge: Cambridge University Press, 1999), 83.

[58] R. Ericson, *Crime in an Insecure World* (Cambridge: Polity Press, 2007), 213.

[59] Rose, *Powers of Freedom*, 136.

[60] D. Garland, 'The Limits of the Sovereign State: Strategies of Crime Control in Contemporary Society' (1996) 36(4) *British Journal of Criminology*, 445–71, 460.

[61] R. Martinson, 'What Works?—Questions and Answers about Prison Reform' (1974) 35 *The Public Interest*, 22–54.

[62] Ericson, *Crime in an Insecure World*, 14.

series of economic and geo-political crises, the perceived rise of global terrorism, and the raising awareness of global environmental issues. In addition, and
perhaps most importantly, the last few decades have seen an unprecedented
rise in levels of inequality in Western liberal countries,[63] which has significantly affected the experience of socio-political belonging in these societies.[64]
The resurgence of dangerousness as a primary concept guiding developments
in criminalization, reflected in the framework of criminal responsibility by
a predominance of character and risk responsibility,[65] can thus be seen to
be directly connected to 'a crisis of security' in which the perceived danger
in crime has been heightened by a general sense of insecurity, so that the
criminal law finds itself under political pressure to '[reach] for definitions
and mechanisms which can reassure an anxious public that their concerns are
being taken seriously—and that "the criminal threat" can be contained'.[66] In
a sense, then, the preventive turn is the consequence of criminal law finding
itself in an insecure world.

From this perspective, the authoritarian excesses of the preventive state can
be seen as 'peculiarly modern phenomenon in that it is a response, despite its
archaic vestiges, to its failings to make good the promise of social rights'.[67] But
while the ebb and flow of democratic citizenship provides a useful explana-
tory tool to examine and identify the dynamics of criminal subjectivity in
different moments of modernity, such realization should not undermine the
persistent aspects of this relation. In this sense, it is important to remember
that the progress of democratic citizenship in itself also contains a persistent
tension between the inclusionary impulse of citizenship and the exclusionary social structure of possessive market relations. Likewise, although the
configuration of responsibility and dangerousness in the framework of criminal law has changed over time, these movements were manifestations of the
enduring tension between these two dimensions of criminal subjectivity. It
is precisely the dynamicity and malleability of the dialectic relation between
responsibility and dangerousness which grounds the ideological efficiency
of the reassurance function of the criminal law. Furthermore, this dynamic
relationship is also inherently complex, so that rather than expecting to find

---

[63] See T. Picketty, A. Goldhammer, *Capital in the Twenty-First Century* (Cambridge: Harvard
University Press, 2014).

[64] See K. Pickett, R. Wilkinson, *The Spirit Level: Why Equality is Better for Everyone*
(London: Penguin Books, 2010).

[65] See Lacey, *In Search of Criminal Responsibility*, 147–8.

[66] N. Lacey, 'The Resurgence of Character: Responsibility in the Context of Criminalization' in
R.A. Duff, S.P. Green (eds), *Philosophical Foundations of Criminal Law* (Oxford: Oxford University
Press, 2011), 151–78, 161–5, 173.

[67] Vaughan, 'Punishment and Conditional Citizenship', 35.

either dangerousness or responsibility as the guiding factor behind a specific form of criminal liability, we should seek to understand how the interplay between these two categories shapes and conditions the environment of criminalization.

Once our perspective shifts from a focus on either responsibility or dangerousness to an awareness of the complex and dynamic composition of criminal subjectivity, it is possible to unlock a different level of analysis of forms and rules of criminal liability. Elements of the law on intoxication can provide a good illustration of this. The practical equation between recklessness and voluntary intoxication put forward by *Majewski*,[68] in which intoxication provides no defence to crimes of basic intent even when it can be shown to have prevented the defendant from forming the necessary *mens rea*, conjoins a concern with recognizing the defendant as a responsible subject, with a clear preoccupation with public order related to the dangerous link between intoxication and crime.[69] The same applies with even more clarity to the maxim that a drunken intent is still an intent.[70] Another, already mentioned example which reproduces a similar logic is the 'special verdict' of not guilty by reason of insanity,[71] negating criminal liability as an expression of respect for the individual's lack of responsibility at the same time as it allows for potentially severe restrictions to the individual's liberty on the grounds of the danger the individual may pose.[72] It should thus not be assumed that, just because dangerousness represents a polar opposite concept to responsibility, this means that criminal offences concerned with identifying and managing dangerousness tend to downplay the importance of subjective forms of *mens rea*. This might be the case with regulatory offences and with the many instances of constructive liability,[73] but the opposite conclusion can be reached with regards to inchoate offences, such as attempts and conspiracies, where their preventive aspect is directly linked to a presumed dangerousness in the intent required for these crimes. A perhaps safer assumption in terms of the configuration of the element of criminal liability would be that a greater influence of dangerousness in a particular criminal offence tends to destabilize the 'harm-plus-culpability' model in one way or another.

It is thus important to bear in mind that, although the preventive turn can be interpreted as expressing a resurgence of dangerousness within the

---

[68] *DPP v Majewski* [1977] AC 443.

[69] See C. Wells, O. Quick, *Lacey, Wells and Quick: Reconstructing Criminal Law: Texts and Materials* (Cambridge: Cambridge University Press, 2010), 268–91.

[70] *R v Kingston* [1994] 3 WLR 519.   [71] Trial of Lunatics Act 1883, s. 2.

[72] Criminal Procedure (Insanity) Act 1964, s. 5.

[73] Examples include s. 20 and s. 47 of the Offences Against the Person Act 1861, and dangerous and unlawful act manslaughter.

framework of criminal responsibility, the current process of 'dangerization'[74] of criminal subjectivity is different from the prevalence of dangerousness in the eighteenth and nineteenth centuries, when individual responsibility figured mainly as a regulative idea. The universalization of the demand for individual responsibility and autonomy is one of the core aspects of the liberal moral order, so that once it is embedded within the normative framework of criminal law, it cannot simply be removed or even fully displaced. Instead, the defining and most perplexing feature of criminal subjectivity in the preventive turn is precisely that it espouses a conceptual framework in which both responsibility and dangerousness are emphasized—one might say over-emphasized. The demise of the premises of the welfare state have generated an alignment between liberty and insecurity, which engendered 'a novel way of framing the relations between freedom, security and government, in which freedom, understood in the sense of the autonomization and responsibilization of actors, was to become the governing principle which had to be aligned in new "post-social" ways with the imperatives of security'.[75] This new configuration has significant implications to the reassurance function of the criminal law.

To a large extent, civil and social rights represent opposite forces in the liberal civil order, the first having a primarily individualizing tendency, and the second an emphasis on solidarity and reciprocity. They, in many ways, represent the two poles of the conflict identified by Marshall between capitalism and citizenship. Likewise, in terms of criminal subjectivity, the individualizing character of civil citizenship tends to highlight the dangerousness of crime as a threat to the enjoyment of individual rights, while social citizenship tends to promote the need to universalize the conditions for responsible subjectivity, and to share the burden of their unequal distribution. For most of the twentieth century, this universalizing aspect of citizenship was supported by a strong structure of trust in society, so that it had a generally positive influence on the criminal law, where the rise of subjective responsibility symbolized an effort to treat the subjects of criminal law in a fair and respectful manner. When this structure starts to falter towards the end of the twentieth century, however, the emphasis of the universalism promoted by citizenship shifts from social security to social insecurity, and the criminal law reacts accordingly.

---

[74] See M. Lianos, M. Douglas, 'Dangerization and the End of Deviance: the Institutional Environment' in D. Garland, R. Sparks (eds), *Criminology and Social Theory* (New York: Oxford University Press, 2000), 103–26.

[75] F. Lentzos, N. Rose, 'Governing Insecurity: Contingency Planning, Protection, Resilience' (2009) 38(2) *Economy and Society*, 230–54, 234.

Thus, what seemed to be an emancipatory development in the criminal law, an effort to treat individuals as responsible subjects, is transformed into a problematic practice of responsibilization after the preventive turn.[76] This practice effectively re-conceptualizes responsible subjectivity as a duty instead of a right, in the sense that it places a burden on individuals to constantly and actively behave responsibly—which effectively means that the burden of social insecurity is taken from society and placed in the hands of individuals. 'Removing the contextualising manifold of principles of social citizenship, welfare and justice places renewed emphasis on individual responsibility as a primary legitimating and dominatory ideological device.'[77] This perspective on responsibility places responsible subjectivity much closer to dangerousness, as the need to actively demand individuals to demonstrate their responsibility implies that they carry within themselves the potential of being or becoming dangerous, which needs to be constantly surveyed and regulated. This link is also reflected by the renewed link between responsibility and retribution which, especially with regards to serious or dangerous offences, results in an increased punitiveness in criminal law and criminal justice.[78]

The other side of this tendency towards responsibilization is that dangerousness is reconfigured in criminal law from a pathological to a political character. Responsibility and dangerousness are effectively enmeshed in the preventive turn, as dangerous crimes are seen not as the consequence of an incapacity to act responsibly, but as the result of an abuse of capacity—a voluntary commitment towards wrongful and harmful behaviour. Here, the anxiety behind responsibilization is taken to its ultimate consequences, as responsible subjects are taken to have the capacity to seriously endanger the integrity of the political community by means of their agency. This image fuels a tendency towards prevention, as any individual who is identified as potentially dangerous has to be contained before s/he can put the community at risk. This heightened ambivalence within criminal subjectivity is clearly expressed in the framework of preventive criminal offences. On the one hand, one of the main rationales behind these offences relates to an effort to re-establish and reinforce categories of dangerousness within criminal law, in order to distinguish the responsible subject of the liberal model from the dangerous other of the preventive turn—categories such as 'the anti-social

---

[76] See Norrie, 'Citizenship, Authoritarianism and the Changing Shape of the Criminal Law', 15.
[77] Ibid, 30.
[78] See A. Ashworth, L. Zedner, 'Just Prevention: Preventive Rationales and the Limits of the Criminal Law' in R.A. Duff, S.P. Green (eds), *Philosophical Foundations of Criminal Law* (Oxford: Oxford University Press, 2011), 279–303.

youth, the sex offender, the migrant, and, above all, the terrorist', which are 'appropriate symbols of "otherness" relative to contemporary anxieties and technologies'.[79] On the other hand, these categories of otherness are often defined in abstract form, linking liability for preventive criminal offences to the offender's state of mind or to an established or potential link between the offender's conduct and the prohibited risk or harm. Only exceptionally are these offences defined by direct reference to the offender's status.

The insertion of responsible subjectivity into the framework of criminal law makes it difficult for the law to legitimately maintain a conceptual distinction between responsible and dangerous subjects, so that the substantive developments which are put in place in order to deal with dangerousness have to be wide in scope and reach—they have to be applicable at any time and place, even though in practice they are employed through techniques which ensure their unequal and localized application, such as profiling. As a result, preventive criminal offences and measures tend to be both broadly conceptualized and narrowly deployed.[80] Thus, even though preventive laws have the purpose of distinguishing between responsible and dangerous subjectivity, they have to do so whilst still upholding the premise that this distinction is grounded on assessments of risk based on individual agency, and not on any political prejudice towards any specific population,[81] so that these laws can potentially apply to any and every citizen.[82] This same anxious attitude towards the need to preserve the conditions for responsible subjectivity in a context of insecurity also generates consequences in the framework of regulatory laws, which becomes excessive and hyperactive in an attempt to compensate for the unravelling of social security.

The modern trajectory of the criminal law can thus be interpreted as largely influenced by the struggle to contain the inherent ambivalence of criminal subjectivity, which is itself a manifestation of the conflict, within liberal society, between its emancipatory aspirations and its structural violence. With regards to the development of the conception of citizenship, the ambivalence of criminal subjectivity can also be seen to have three distinct moments. The first is one in which the criminal law attempted to suppress the ambivalence

---

[79] Lacey, 'The Resurgence of Character', 173.

[80] See Zedner, 'Fixing the Future?', 35–58.

[81] Even though this prejudice may substantially influence how the law is applied in practice.

[82] Terrorist offences are particularly emblematic of this concerning tendency. See J. Hodgson, V. Tadros, 'How to Make a Terrorist Out of Nothing' (2009) 72(6) *Modern Law Review*, 984–98; R.A. Duff, 'Perversions and Subversions of Criminal Law' in R.A. Duff, L. Farmer, S.E. Marshall, M. Renzo, V. Tadros (eds), *The Boundaries of the Criminal Law* (Oxford: Oxford University Press, 2010).

of criminal subjectivity by linking it primarily with dangerousness, reassuring responsible subjectivity by keeping it apart from insecurity, which it ascribed to crime. The second moment inverts this logic, and attempts to manage insecurity by positing the normative prevalence of responsible subjectivity even within the criminal law, subsiding dangerousness into a status of exceptionality, made possible and necessary by the structure of trust provided by the environment of democratic citizenship. Finally, the third moment can be conceptualized as one in which both responsibility and dangerousness share the normative position in the criminal law. Instead of being suppressed, the preventive turn manifests the ambivalence of criminal subjectivity, intermeshing practices of responsibilization and dangerization within a framework of expanded liability and pervasive criminalization.

THE PERPLEXITIES OF CRIMINAL LAW

The persistent ambivalence of criminal subjectivity thus provides a lens through which to critically examine the conditions which led to the contemporary setting of criminal law and criminalization. This perspective also allows us to engage with what Farmer has called the 'paradox of the modern criminal law', namely, 'that despite being shaped by a liberal sensibility that state power should be limited and the desire to respect individual rights and liberties, it has expanded in scope, more or less continually, since the late eighteenth century'.[83] A focus only on responsible subjectivity is unable to explain why, throughout modernity, the impulse to treat individuals as responsible has controversially made them increasingly responsible for more,[84] and thus restricted as much as it enabled their freedom.

This paradox is arguably a direct consequence of the abstract character of the liberal conception of individual autonomy and liberty. The idea of responsibility at the core of the liberal model is seen as a condition for individual justice, but its emancipatory potential is inextricably dependent on socio-political conditions, which themselves conceal an element of structural violence which compromises this very potential. Once this conception loses its structural grounding, its latent ambivalence comes to the fore, manifesting the same exclusionary and authoritarian aspects of punishment and state power that the liberal model hoped to restrain and dispel. The subject of preventive criminal law is therefore the result of 'the need to govern security *through* insecurity, by using and indeed intensifying subjective states of

---

[83] Farmer, *Making the Modern Criminal Law*, 298.   [84] See ibid, 192.

doubt, anxiety, apprehension and the like, with the aim of making individuals responsible for key aspects of security'.[85] Under these conditions, the criminal law finds itself incapable of either upholding the emancipatory potential of responsible subjectivity, or completely circumventing it in the name of prevention and of the reassurance of the civil order. Rather, the resurgence of dangerousness expressed by preventive criminal offences reveals both the limitations of the liberal model and the problematic, exclusionary character of contemporary criminal law.

Furthermore, the perspective developed in this book can help understand the difficulties of liberal criminal law in addressing the challenges posed by the preventive turn. As previously discussed, the rise of the liberal model of criminal law is deeply connected with the rise of a specific notion of civil order, grounded on a rich and inclusionary idea of citizenship. When this idea reaches its contemporary apex with the welfare state, liberal models of responsibility and punishment partake of this hegemonic moment and appear fully actualizable—indeed, for some they might have appeared fully actualized. Especially in criminal law, a very strong conviction was generated that the liberal model was capable of sustaining a legal system that could appropriately treat the subject of criminal law as a responsible legal subject. Using Hegel's jargon, the rise of the liberal model to doctrine and orthodoxy was taken by many criminal law theorists to represent the actualization of the concrete liberal state, so that freedom acquired within this system an appearance of objective reality. The liberal model's structural conditions, by their turn, were largely neglected, overshadowed by the model's rational appeal, so that instead of socio-political conditions giving rise to a subjective idea of criminal responsibility, it was subjective responsibility which was taken to allow the criminal law to respect individuals as citizens and responsible subjects. The contingent nature of this subjectivity was mostly ignored.

What is thus significant and particularly modern about the preventive turn in criminal law and criminal justice is that the collapse of the structural conditions for trust occurs just after the erection of an ideological structure which was deemed to be capable of fully eliminating, or at least aptly managing, the insecurity and ambivalence contained within ideas of punishment and responsibility. The result of the current historical moment is a crisis: the backlash of dangerousness within criminal law and criminal justice coexists and conflicts with an ideal, 'neo-classical'[86] model of criminal law which cannot

---

[85] Lentzos, Rose, 'Governing Insecurity', 235. See also J. Simon, *Governing Through Crime: How the War on Crime Transformed American Democracy and Created a Culture of Fear* (New York: Oxford University Press, 2007).

[86] See Farmer, *Making the Modern Criminal Law*, 103.

be reconciled with its own contingency. On the one hand, the current state of insecurity is a direct consequence of 'the failure of the nation-state to secure participation within society for all those who reside within its boundaries'.[87] On the other hand, however, this failure is precisely what the liberal state cannot recognize, for it is a persistent aspect of the socio-political structure of liberal societies. To recognize it would thus be to compromise the very normative assumptions on which the liberal model of criminal law is grounded: the inclusionary nature of liberal society.

Therefore, the same radical ambivalence identified in preventive criminal offences can also be related to the current condition of liberal law. Essentially, the liberal state cannot possibly provide the reassurance which is required of it with regards to the expectations generated by a liberal democratic model of society; but neither can it embrace its failures and posit the need for comprehensive social reform. Instead, the state is required to sustain and protect its normative ideological basis within a context of socio-political insecurity. Under such conditions, the state portrays a rather contradictory character, as it is forced to heavily intervene in civil society in order to 'discharge the reassurance function'[88] at the same time as it must somehow maintain that such intervention is necessitated by problems which are not internal to liberal society, but instead due to 'external' circumstances—migration, terrorism, and the dangerousness inherent to some offenders are just a few examples. In other words, the preventive liberal state is required to both embrace and deny its own insecurity. This generates a particular challenge for the much needed reassuring function of the criminal law. The desire to preserve the normative ideal of liberal society's assimilation into the liberal state, amidst the erosion of the structural conditions which made this hegemonic moment possible, heightens and radicalizes the paradox within criminal law and punishment. Here is where security as the main premise of state intervention comes in: the discourse on security is the predominant ideological device used in order for the state to manage and suppress the insecurity of its current socio-political conditions. Through this discourse, liberal society's problems are reinterpreted as problems of security—the social unravelling of late modernity is perceived under this prism as an erosion of the barriers and protections which kept liberal society safe in place, and which are now in dire need of protection from the state.

[87] Vaughan, 'Punishment and Conditional Citizenship', 36.
[88] B. Ackerman, 'The Emergency Constitution' (2004) 113 *Yale Law Journal*, 1029–91, 1037.

The preventive turn can therefore be conceptualized as the state's attempt to manage the ambivalence within liberal law (and society) and to preserve the normative premises of liberal society—all the assumptions, conditions, and promises of the democratic liberal state—by constituting these premises as vulnerable, in need of protection from external threats, that is, from threats that are external to the liberal model of society. Due to the contemporary pervasiveness of the concern with security, without engaging with it, 'scholarship which decries the expanding criminal law is at even greater risk than normal of being dismissed as irrelevant'.[89] However, in order to be effective, this engagement with the importance of security cannot fall back into the dichotomy between liberty and security, which either contrasts or balances one value against the other. As long as this dichotomic model is maintained, the paradoxes and ambivalences within the liberal imaginary will only be preserved, even if eventually suppressed.

CONCLUSION

This chapter has placed the conceptual analysis endeavoured in previous chapters within the socio-political context of the modern development of citizenship in order to grasp the full scope and dynamics of the ideological construction of criminal subjectivity. In pursuing a political sociology of the relationship between criminal subjectivity and citizenship in the modern development of English civil society, I have highlighted 'the implication of liberal law in the evolution of authoritarianism within criminal justice'.[90] From this perspective, the preventive turn is ultimately the consequence of enduring problems in the constitution of modern criminal law, which in turn are derived from tensions and contradictions which are inherent to the ways in which liberal societies are imagined and socio-politically structured. If this understanding is correct, and if criminal law scholarship hopes to overcome the contemporary challenges to the project of a liberal law which can recognize all its subjects as equals and treat them with respect, legal theory ought to acknowledge the extent to which the criminal law is a gateway to its own insecurity.

[89] V. Tadros, 'Crimes and Security' (2008) 71(6) *Modern Law Review*, 940–70, 941.
[90] A. Norrie, 'Historical Differentiation, Moral Judgment and the Modern Criminal Law' (2007) 1(3) *Criminal Law and Philosophy*, 251–7, 257.

Epilogue
Criminal Law, Prevention, and the Promise of Politics

> But where danger threatens
> That which saves from it also grows.[1]

The problem of preventive criminal offences is inherently related to issues contained within the liberal model of criminal law itself; that is, to the boundaries of liberal law's conception of individualism. The tension between individual freedom and political authority experienced in contemporary criminal law is not simply the consequence of the preventive turn, but also, and to a significant extent, the reflection of an intrinsic aspect of how the legal order is imagined within contemporary liberal societies. Legal individualism permanently espouses a political conflict between responsibility and dangerousness, between individual freedom and the insecurity which is linked to this freedom, as a mechanism through which the state manages and represses a deeper socio-political conflict between an idealistic moral order and unequal and violent structural conditions which prevent its concrete realization. Therefore, the liberal model of criminal law cannot fully provide for the rational resolution of tensions that arise from an intrinsic contradiction within the liberal state.

This realization, however, should not be seen as a call to abandon the aspirations contained within the liberal model of criminal law; nor is it an attempt to downplay the threat against these aspirations represented by the state of insecurity of the preventive turn by giving it a semblance of inevitability. Rather, the critical analysis in this book was an effort to stress that there are intrinsic problems within the project of liberal law which, if left unexamined, threaten to erode and undo all the important accomplishments achieved by liberal society. The preventive turn in this sense does not merely represent another expression of this order, but rather is the result of the unreflexive reproduction of its problematic aspects, which are not addressed as long as liberal society's structural violence continues to be both repressed and

---

[1] F. Hölderlin, *Selected Poems and Fragments* (London: Penguin Books, 1994), 231.

The Preventive Turn in Criminal Law. First Edition. Henrique Carvalho. © Henrique Carvalho 2017. Published 2017 by Oxford University Press.

preserved. As long as the law uncritically replicates its ideological individualism and the structural conditions which preserve and demand it, it will remain a gateway to its own insecurity, one of the conditions for its own unravelling. If we hope to resist this 'autoimmunitary'[2] impulse, criminal law theory needs to continue to strive to be reflexive,[3] and thus sensitive to its social, political, and historical context.

The most significant implication of the theoretical perspective developed throughout this work is the need to re-conceptualize subjectivity in ways which can avoid essentializing the notions of human agency which come out of it, so that it can allow for a richer and more substantive conception of individual freedom in the law. The present study suggested that the most appropriate pathway to such a re-conceptualization is through a phenomenological perspective on responsibility and subjectivity, one which can highlight and uphold the intrinsic reciprocity and interdependence of the human condition. When applied directly to the framework of criminal law, such a perspective most prominently portrayed the political nature of juridical relations, political in the sense that they are a reflection of human relations in an inherently conflictive social environment, in which individual demands are not just claimed and addressed, but negotiated in a much more fluid and complex way than that recognized by legal categories.

The criminal law's efforts to manage, protect, and (to a limited extent) respect social relations is to some degree an acknowledgement of this political aspect of responsibility, but to a great extent it is also a denial of it, in that the criminal law attempts to coercively reduce the complexity of social relations through its normative categories of crime and punishment. For Hannah Arendt, one of the 'reasons why philosophy has never found a place where politics can take shape' lay in its commonly held 'assumption that there is something political in man [*sic*] that belongs to his essence'.[4] For her, however, this was simply not true, because '[p]olitics arises between [human beings] and is established as relationships'.[5] The ambivalent relation between criminal law and its subject is arguably one of the most significant and remarkable expressions of this paradox. Through its categories, the criminal law seems to assume that freedom lies within individuals, in a way that is to a large extent isolated from society. From this perspective, subjective agency becomes something at the same time sacred and mysterious, a source of both respect and insecurity. However, in this book I have argued that the

---

[2] J. Derrida in G. Borradori, *Philosophy in a Time of Terror: Dialogues with Jürgen Habermas and Jacques Derrida* (Chicago: University of Chicago Press, 2003), 95.

[3] See P. Bourdieu, L. Wacquant, *An Invitation to Reflexive Sociology* (Cambridge: Polity Press, 1992).

[4] H. Arendt, *The Promise of Politics* (New York: Random House, 2005), 95.   [5] Ibid.

problems of contemporary criminal law can only be comprehensively under-stood through the relations that tie individual autonomy, political author-ity, and liberal society together. From this perspective, freedom cannot be found within individuals, but rather 'only in the unique intermediary space of politics'.[6] Therefore, the fundamental question of how to achieve justice for individuals is one that criminal law scholarship can only address through a critical engagement with political theory.

While political theory predominantly strives to find an ethical and effi-cient solution to the problem of conflict in society, its conceptual foundations cannot help being fundamentally constituted by the very conflict which its proposed solutions seek to manage and eliminate. This book aimed to tap into this conflictive essence of political society in order to engage with the dialectical nature of criminal subjectivity, so as to denounce and examine the abstract and ideological aspects of liberal society and liberal law. Arguably, such engagement is in particular demand due to the crisis of normativity and legitimacy which is apparent to the contemporary framework of criminal law and criminal justice. As liberal law battles with the insecurity born of its own normative foundations, the climate of authoritarianism and individual and social injustice prevalent in criminal law in the twenty-first century, terrible though it is, provides legal theory with an unrivalled opportunity to rethink its premises and, perhaps, re vindicate its promises.

---

[6] Ibid.

Bibliography

Ackerman, B. 'The Emergency Constitution' (2004) 113 *Yale Law Journal*, 1029–91

Anderson, J., Honneth, A. 'Autonomy, Vulnerability, Recognition, and Justice' in J. Christman, J. Anderson (eds), *Autonomy and the Challenges to Liberalism: New Essays* (Cambridge: Cambridge University Press, 2005), 127–49

Arendt, H. *The Promise of Politics* (New York: Random House, 2005)

Ashworth, A. 'Is the Criminal Law a Lost Cause?' (2000) 116 *Law Quarterly Review*, 225–56

Ashworth, A. 'Responsibilities, Rights and Restorative Justice' (2002) 42 *British Journal of Criminology*, 578–95

Ashworth, A. 'Conceptions of Overcriminalization' (2008) 5 *Ohio State Journal of Criminal Law*, 407–25

Ashworth, A., Horder, J. *Principles of Criminal Law*, 7th ed. (Oxford: Oxford University Press, 2013)

Ashworth, A., Zedner, L. 'Defending the Criminal Law: Reflections on the Changing Character of Crime, Procedure, and Sanctions' (2008) 2 *Criminal Law and Philosophy*, 21–51

Ashworth, A., Zedner, L. 'Just Prevention: Preventive Rationales and the Limits of the Criminal Law' in R.A. Duff, S.P. Green (eds), *Philosophical Foundations of Criminal Law* (Oxford: Oxford University Press, 2011), 279–303

Ashworth, A., Zedner, L. *Preventive Justice* (Oxford: Oxford University Press, 2014)

Ashworth, A., Zedner, L., Tomlin, P. (eds), *Prevention and the Limits of the Criminal Law* (Oxford: Oxford University Press, 2013)

Bartky, S.L. *Femininity and Domination: Studies in the Phenomenology of Oppression* (New York: Routledge, 1990)

Bauman, Z. *Modernity and Ambivalence* (Cambridge: Polity Press, 1991)

Bauman, Z., May, T. *Thinking Sociologically* (Oxford: Blackwell Publishing, 1990)

Bayles, M. 'Character, Purpose, and Criminal Responsibility' (1982) 1 *Law and Philosophy*, 5–20

Beccaria, C. *On Crimes and Punishments and Other Writings* (Cambridge: Cambridge University Press, 1995)

Beck, U. *Risk Society: Towards a New Modernity* (London: Sage, 1992)

Bentham, J. *The Principles of Morals and Legislation* (Amherst: Prometheus Books, 1988)

Bentham, J. *The Panopticon Writings* (London: Verso, 1995)

Bentham, J. 'To the President of the United States of America' in P. Schofield, J. Harris (eds), *The Collected Works of Jeremy Bentham: 'Legislator of the World': Writings on Codification, Law, and Education* (Oxford: Oxford University Press, 1998), 7–15

Bhaskar, R. *Dialectic: The Pulse of Freedom* (London: Routledge, 2008)

Binder, G. 'Foundations of the Legislative Panopticon: Bentham's *Principles of Morals and Legislation*' in M.D. Dubber (ed), *Foundational Texts in Modern Criminal Law* (Oxford: Oxford University Press, 2014), 79–99

Bobbio, B. 'Gramsci and the Conception of Civil Society' in C. Mouffe (ed), *Gramsci and Marxist Theory* (New York: Routledge, 1979), 21–47

Borradori, G. *Philosophy in a Time of Terror* (Chicago: University of Chicago Press, 2003)

Bosanquet, B. *The Philosophical Theory of the State* (London: MacMillan, 1965)

Bourdieu, P., Wacquant, L. *An Invitation to Reflexive Sociology* (Cambridge: Polity Press, 1992)

Brooks, T. *Hegel's Political Philosophy* (Edinburgh: Edinburgh University Press, 2009)

Brown, M., Pratt, J. (eds), *Dangerous Offenders: Punishment and Social Order* (London: Routledge, 2000)

Brudner, A. *Punishment and Freedom* (Oxford: Oxford University Press, 2009)

Carvalho, H. 'Terrorism, Punishment, and Recognition' (2012) 15(3) *New Criminal Law Review*, 345–74

Carvalho, H. 'Liberty and Insecurity in the Criminal Law: Lessons from Thomas Hobbes' (2015) *Criminal Law and Philosophy* (Online First), 1–23

Carvalho, H., Chamberlen, A. 'Punishment, Justice, and Emotions' (2016) *Oxford Handbooks Online* (criminology and criminal justice; punishment theory)

Chamberlen, A. *Embodying Punishment: Emotions, Identities, and Lived Experiences in Women's Prisons* (Oxford: Oxford University Press, forthcoming)

Cohen, S. *Visions of Social Control* (Cambridge: Polity Press, 1985)

Cohen, S. *Folk Devils and Moral Panics* (London: Routledge, 2002)

Cotterrell, R. *Law's Community* (Oxford: Oxford University Press, 1995)

Crawford, A. (ed), *Crime Prevention Policies in Comparative Perspective* (Cullompton: Willan Publishing, 2009)

Curran, E. 'An Immodest Proposal: Hobbes Rather than Locke Provides a Forerunner for Modern Rights Theory' (2013) 32 *Law and Philosophy*, 515–38

Dennis, I. 'The Critical Condition of Criminal Law' (1997) 50 *Current Legal Problems*, 213–49

Dorling, D., Gordon, D., Hillyard, P., Pantazis, C., Pemberton, S., Tombs, S. *Criminal Obsessions: Why Harm Matters More than Crime* (London: Centre for Crime and Justice Studies, 2008)

Douglas, M. *Purity and Danger* (London: Routledge, 1966)

Draper, T. 'An Introduction to Jeremy Bentham's Theory of Punishment' (2002) 5 *Journal of Bentham Studies*, 1–17

Dubber, M.D. *The Police Power: Patriarchy and the Foundations of American Government* (New York: Columbia University Press, 2005)

Dubber, M.D. 'Citizenship and Penal Law' (2010) 13(2) *New Criminal Law Review*, 190–215

Dubber, M.D., Farmer, L. (eds), *Modern Histories of Crime and Punishment* (Stanford: Stanford University Press, 2007)

Duff, R.A. *Intention, Agency and Criminal Liability* (Oxford: Wiley-Blackwell, 1990)

Duff, R.A. 'Choice, Character, and Criminal Liability' (1993) 12(4) *Law and Philosophy*, 345–83

Duff, R.A. *Punishment, Communication, and Community* (New York: Oxford University Press, 2001)

Duff, R.A. 'Penance, Punishment and the Limits of Community' (2003) 5 *Punishment and Society*, 295–312

Duff, R.A. 'Notes on Punishment and Terrorism' (2005) 6 *American Behavioral Scientist*, 758–63

Duff, R.A. 'Criminalising Endangerment' in R.A. Duff, S.P. Green (eds), *Defining Crimes: Essays on the Special Part of the Criminal Law* (Oxford: Oxford University Press, 2005), 43–64

Duff, R.A. *Answering for Crime: Responsibility and Liability in Criminal Law* (Portland: Hart Publishing, 2007)

Duff, R.A. 'Perversions and Subversions of Criminal Law' in R.A. Duff, L. Farmer, S.E. Marshall, M. Renzo, V. Tadros (eds), *The Boundaries of the Criminal Law* (New York: Oxford University Press, 2010), 88–112

Duff, R.A. 'Responsibility, Citizenship and Criminal Law' in R.A. Duff, S.P. Green (eds), *Philosophical Foundations of Criminal Law* (Oxford: Oxford University Press, 2011), 125–49

Duff, R.A. 'Pre-Trial Detention and the Presumption of Innocence' in A. Ashworth, L. Zedner, P. Tomlin (eds), *Prevention and the Limits of the Criminal Law* (Oxford: Oxford University Press, 2012), 115–32

Duff, R.A., Farmer, L., Marshall, S.E., Renzo, M., Tadros, V. (eds), *The Boundaries of the Criminal Law* (New York: Oxford University Press, 2010)

Duff, R.A., Farmer, L., Marshall, S.E., Renzo, M., Tadros, V. (eds), *The Structures of the Criminal Law* (New York: Oxford University Press, 2011)

Duff, R.A., Farmer, L., Marshall, S.E., Renzo, M., Tadros, V. (eds), *The Constitution of the Criminal Law* (New York: Oxford University Press, 2013)

Duff, R.A., Farmer, L., Marshall, S.E., Renzo, M., Tadros, V. (eds), *Criminalization: The Political Morality of the Criminal Law* (New York: Oxford University Press, 2014)

Duff, R.A., Farmer, L., Marshall, S., Tadros, V. (eds), *The Trial on Trial: Volume 1: Truth and Due Process* (Oxford: Hart, 2004)

Duff, R.A., Farmer, L., Marshall, S., Tadros, V. (eds), *The Trial on Trial: Volume Two: Judgment and Calling to Account* (Oxford: Hart, 2006)

Duff, R.A., Farmer, L., Marshall, S., Tadros, V. (eds), *The Trial on Trial: Volume Three: Towards a Normative Theory of the Criminal Law* (Oxford: Hart, 2007)

Duff, R.A., Garland, D. (eds), *A Reader on Punishment* (Oxford: Oxford University Press, 1994)

Duff, R.A., Green, S.P. (eds), *Philosophical Foundations of Criminal Law* (Oxford: Oxford University Press, 2011)

Dyzenhaus, D. 'How Hobbes Met the "Hobbes Challenge"' (2009) 72(3) *Modern Law Review*, 488–506

Dyzenhaus, D., Poole, T. (eds), *Hobbes and the Law* (Cambridge: Cambridge University Press, 2012)

Elias, N. *The Society of Individuals* (New York: Continuum, 1991)

Elias, N. *The Civilizing Process* (Oxford: Blackwell, 1994)

Ericson, R. *Crime in an Insecure World* (Cambridge: Polity Press, 2007)

Farmer, L. 'The Obsession with Definition: The Nature of Crime and Critical Legal Theory' (1996) 5 *Social and Legal Studies*, 57–73

Farmer, L. *Criminal Law, Tradition and Legal Order* (Cambridge: Cambridge University Press, 1997)

Farmer, L. 'Reconstructing the English Codification Debate: The Criminal Law Commissioners, 1833–45' (2000) 18 *Law & History Review*, 397–426

Farmer, L. *Making the Modern Criminal Law: Criminalization and Civil Order* (Oxford: Oxford University Press, 2016)

Farmer, P. 'An Anthropology of Structural Violence' (2004) 45(3) *Current Anthropology*, 305–25

Feinberg, J. *Harm to Others, 1 The Moral Limits of the Criminal Law* (Oxford: Oxford University Press, 1984)

Feldman, N. 'Choices of Law, Choices of War' (2002) 25 *Harvard Journal of Law and Public Policy*, 457–85

Fine, R. *Political Investigations* (New York: Routledge, 2001)

Fletcher, G.P. *Rethinking Criminal Law* (Oxford: Oxford University Press, 1978)

Fletcher, G.P. *Basic Concepts of Criminal Law* (New York: Oxford University Press, 1998)

Foucault, M. *Discipline and Punish* (London: Penguin, 1979)

Foucault, M. 'The Subject and Power' (1982) 8(4) *Critical Inquiry*, 777–95

Foucault, M. *Society Must Be Defended: Lectures at the Collège de France 1975–1976* (London: Penguin, 2004)

Foucault, M. *Security, Territory, Population: Lectures at the Collège de France 1977–1978* (Hampshire: Palgrave Macmillan, 2007)

Freud, S. *Civilization and its Discontents* (Mansfield: Martino Publishing, 2010)

Galtung, J. 'Violence, Peace, and Peace Research' (1969) 6(3) *Journal of Peace Research*, 167–91

Gardner, J. 'On the General Part of Criminal Law' in R.A. Duff (ed), *Philosophy and the Criminal Law: Principle and Critique* (Cambridge: Cambridge University Press, 1998), 205–56

Garland, D. *Punishment and Welfare: A History of Penal Strategies* (Aldershot: Gower, 1985)

Garland, D. *Punishment and Modern Society: A Study in Social Theory* (Oxford: Oxford University Press, 1990)

Garland, D. 'The Limits of the Sovereign State: Strategies of Crime Control in Contemporary Society' (1996) 36(4) *British Journal of Criminology*, 445–71

Garland, D. *The Culture of Control: Crime and Social Order in Contemporary Society* (Oxford: Oxford University Press, 2002)

Gauthier, D. 'The Social Contract as Ideology' (1977) 6 *Philosophy and Public Affairs*, 130–64

Gauthier, D. 'Taming Leviathan' (1987) 16 (3) *Philosophy & Public Affairs*, 280–98

Gearty, C. 'Escaping Hobbes: Liberty and Security for our Democratic (Not Anti-Terrorist) Age' in E.D. Reed, M. Dumper (eds), *Civil Liberties, National Security and Prospects for Consensus* (Cambridge: Cambridge University Press, 2012), 35–61

Gearty, C. *Liberty and Security* (Cambridge: Polity Press, 2013)

Giddens, A. *Modernity and Self-Identity: Self and Society in the Late Modern Age* (Cambridge: Polity Press, 1991)

Green, T.H. *Lectures on the Principles of Political Obligation* (London: Longmans and Green, 1901)

Habermas, J. 'Fundamentalism and Terror: a Dialogue with Jürgen Habermas' in G. Borradori (ed), *Philosophy in a Time of Terror* (Chicago: University of Chicago Press, 2003), 25–44

Hallsworth, S. 'Rethinking the Punitive Turn: Economies of Excess and the Criminology of the Other' (2000) 2(2) *Punishment & Society*, 145–60

Hallsworth, S., Lea, J. 'Reconstructing Leviathan: Emerging Contours of the Security State' (2011) 15(2) *Theoretical Criminology*, 141–57

Hampton, J. *Hobbes and the Social Contract Tradition* (Cambridge: Cambridge University Press, 1986)

Harrison, R. *Hobbes, Locke, and Confusion's Masterpiece: An Examination of Seventeenth-Century Political Philosophy* (Cambridge: Cambridge University Press, 2003)

Hart, H.L.A. *Punishment and Responsibility* (Oxford: Oxford University Press, 2008)

Hegel, G.W.F. *Hegel's Philosophy of Right* (Oxford: Oxford University Press, 1967)

Hegel, G.W.F. *Phenomenology of Spirit* (Oxford: Oxford University Press, 1977)

Hegel, G.W.F. *Hegel and the Human Spirit: A Translation of the Jena Lectures on the Philosophy of Spirit (1805–6) with Commentary* (Detroit: Wayne State University Press, 1983)

Held, D. 'Between State and Civil Society: Citizenship' in G. Andrews (ed), *Citizenship* (London: Lawrence & Wishart, 1991), 19–25

Hildebrand, M. 'Proactive Forensic Profiling: Proactive Criminalization?' in R.A. Duff, L. Farmer, S.E. Marshall, M. Renzo, V. Tadros (eds), *The Boundaries of the Criminal Law* (New York: Oxford University Press, 2010), 113–37

von Hirsch, A. 'Proportionate Sentences: A Desert Perspective' in A. Ashworth, A. Von Hirsch, J. Roberts (eds), *Principled Sentencing: Readings on Theory and Policy* (Portland: Hart Publishing, 2009), 115–25

Hobbes, T. *A Dialogue Between a Philosopher and a Student of the Common Laws of England* (Chicago: University of Chicago Press, 1972)

Hobbes, T. *Man and Citizen* (Indianapolis: Hackett Publishing, 1991)

Hobbes, T. *Human Nature and De Corpore Politico* (Oxford: Oxford University Press, 1994)

Hobbes, T. *Leviathan* (Oxford: Oxford University Press, 1996)

Hodgson, J., Tadros, V. 'How to Make a Terrorist Out of Nothing' (2009) 72(6) *Modern Law Review*, 984–98

Hoffman, B. *Inside Terrorism* (New York: Columbia University Press, 2006)

Hölderlin, F. *Selected Poems and Fragments* (London: Penguin Books, 1994)

Honneth, A. *The Struggle for Recognition* (Cambridge: Polity Press, 1995)

Honoré, T. 'Responsibility and Luck: The Moral Basis of Strict Liability' (1988) 104 *Law Quarterly Review*, 530–53

Horder, J. 'Criminal Culpability: The Possibility of a General Theory' (1993) 12 *Law and Philosophy*, 193–215

Horder, J. 'Harmless Wrongdoing and the Anticipatory Perspective on Criminalisation' in R. Sullivan, I. Dennis (eds), *Seeking Security* (Oxford: Hart Publishing, 2012), 79–102

Hughes, G. *Understanding Crime Prevention: Social Control, Risk and Late Modernity* (Maidenhead: Open University Press, 2000)

Husak, D. 'The Criminal Law as a Last Resort' (2004) 24(2) *Oxford Journal of Legal Studies*, 207–35

Husak, D. *Overcriminalization* (Oxford: Oxford University Press, 2008)

Jaume, L. 'Hobbes and the Philosophical Sources of Liberalism' in P. Springbord (ed), *The Cambridge Companion to Hobbes's Leviathan* (Cambridge: Cambridge University Press, 2007), 199–216

Kant, I. *The Metaphysical Elements of Justice* (Indianapolis: Bobbs-Merrill, 1965)

Kant, I. 'Idea for a Universal History with a Cosmopolitan Purpose' in I. Kant, *Political Writings* (Cambridge: Cambridge University Press, 1991), 41–53

Kant, I. 'On the Common Saying: "This May Be True in Theory, But It Does Not Apply in Practice"' in I. Kant, *Political Writings* (Cambridge: Cambridge University Press, 1991), 61–92

Kant, I. *Political Writings* (Cambridge: Cambridge University Press, 1991)

Kant, I. *Metaphysics of Morals: Metaphysical Elements of Justice Pt.1* (Indianapolis: Hackett Publishing, 1999)

Karstedt, S. 'Handle with Care: Emotions, Crime and Justice' in S. Karstedt, I. Loader, H. Strang (eds), *Emotions, Crime and Justice* (Oxford: Hart Publishing, 2011), 1–22

Knowles, D. *Hegel and the Philosophy of Right* (London: Routledge, 2002)

Kojève, A. *Introduction to the Reading of Hegel* (New York: Basic Books, 1980)

Lacey, N. *State Punishment* (New York: Routledge, 1988)

Lacey, N. 'In Search of the Responsible Subject: History, Philosophy and Social Sciences in Criminal Law Theory' (2001) 64(3) *Modern Law Review*, 350–71

Lacey, N. 'Responsibility and Modernity in Criminal Law' (2001) 9(3) *Journal of Political Philosophy*, 249–76

Lacey, N. 'Character, Capacity, Outcome: Toward a Framework for Assessing the Shifting Pattern of Criminal Responsibility in Modern English Law' in M.D. Dubber, L. Farmer (eds), *Modern Histories of Crime and Punishment* (Stanford: Stanford University Press, 2007), 14–41

Lacey, N. 'Space, Time and Function: Intersecting Principles of Responsibility Across the Terrain of Criminal Justice' (2007) 1 *Criminal Law and Philosophy*, 233–50

Lacey, N. *The Prisoners' Dilemma: Political Economy and Punishment in Contemporary Democracies* (Cambridge: Cambridge University Press, 2008)

Lacey, N. 'The Resurgence of Character: Responsibility in the Context of Criminalization' in R.A. Duff, S.P. Green (eds), *Philosophical Foundations of Criminal Law* (Oxford: Oxford University Press, 2011), 151–78

Lacey, N. *In Search of Criminal Responsibility: Ideas, Interests and Institutions* (Oxford: Oxford University Press, 2016)

Lacey, N., Wells, C., Quick, O. *Reconstructing Criminal Law: Texts and Materials* (Cambridge: Cambridge University Press, 2010)

Lentzos, F., Rose, N. 'Governing Insecurity: Contingency Planning, Protection, Resilience' (2009) 38(2) *Economy and Society*, 230–54

Lianos, M., Douglas, M. 'Dangerization and the End of Deviance: the Institutional Environment' in D. Garland, R. Sparks (eds), *Criminology and Social Theory* (New York: Oxford University Press, 2000), 103–26

Loader, I., Walker, N. *Civilizing Security* (Cambridge: Cambridge University Press, 2007)

Locke, J. *Two Treatises of Government* (Cambridge: Cambridge University Press, 2010)

Loughnan, A. *Manifest Madness: Mental Incapacity in Criminal Law* (Oxford: Oxford University Press, 2012)

MacPherson, C.B. *The Political Theory of Possessive Individualism: Hobbes to Locke* (Ontario: Oxford University Press, 2011)

Marshall, T.H. *Citizenship and Social Class* (London: Pluto Press, 1992)

Martinson, R. 'What Works?—Questions and Answers about Prison Reform' (1974) 35 *The Public Interest*, 22–54

Mathiesen, T. *Prison on Trial* (Winchester: Waterside, 2003)

McSherry, B., Norrie, A., Bronitt, S. (eds), *Regulating Deviance* (Portland: Hart Publishing, 2009)

Meliá, M.C. 'Terrorism and Criminal Law: The Dream of Prevention, the Nightmare of the Rule of Law' (2011) 14(1) *New Criminal Law Review*, 108–22

Mill, J.S. 'Civilization' (1836) 3 *London and Westminster Review*, 1–28

Mill, J.S. *On Liberty and Other Writings* (Cambridge: Cambridge University Press, 1989)

Moore, M. *Placing Blame* (Oxford: Oxford University Press, 1997)

Muncie, J., McLaughlin, E. (eds), *The Problem of Crime* (London: Sage, 2001)

Neocleous, M. *Critique of Security* (Edinburgh: Edinburgh University Press, 2008)

Neumann, F. 'The Concept of Political Freedom' in W. Scheuerman (ed), *The Rule of Law Under Siege: Selected Essays of Franz Neumann and Otto Kircheimer* (University of California Press, 1996), 195–230

Norrie, A. 'Thomas Hobbes and the Philosophy of Punishment' (1984) 3 *Law and Philosophy*, 299–320

Norrie, A. *Law, Ideology and Punishment* (Dordrecht: Kluwer Academic Publishers, 1990)

Norrie, A. 'Subjectivity, Morality and Criminal Law' (1999) 3 *Edinburgh Law Review*, 359–67

Norrie, A. *Punishment, Responsibility, and Justice* (Oxford: Oxford University Press, 2000)

Norrie, A. *Law and the Beautiful Soul* (London: GlassHouse Press, 2005)

Norrie, A. 'Historical Differentiation, Moral Judgment and the Modern Criminal Law' (2007) 1(3) *Criminal Law and Philosophy*, 251–7

Norrie, A. 'Citizenship, Authoritarianism and the Changing Shape of the Criminal Law' in B. McSherry, A. Norrie, S. Bronitt (eds), *Regulating Deviance* (Portland: Hart Publishing, 2009), 13–34

Norrie, A. *Dialectic and Difference* (Oxon: Routledge, 2010)

Norrie, A. *Crime, Reason and History* (Cambridge: Cambridge University Press, 2014)

Norrie, A. *Justice and the Slaughter-Bench: Essays on Law's Broken Dialectic* (Oxon: Routledge, 2017)

Oakeshott, M. *Hobbes on Civil Association* (Indianapolis: Liberty Fund, 1975)

Oakeshott, M. 'Introduction to Leviathan' in *Hobbes on Civil Association* (Indianapolis: Liberty Fund, 1975), 1–79

O'Malley, P. 'Risk Societies and the Government of Crime' in M. Brown and J. Pratt (eds), *Dangerous Offenders: Punishment and Social Order* (London: Routledge, 2000), 17–34

Pantazis, C., Pemberton, S. 'From the "Old" to the "New" Suspect Community: Examining the Impacts of Recent UK Counter-Terrorism Legislation' (2009) 49 *British Journal of Criminology*, 646–66

Pettit, P. 'Liberty and Leviathan' (2005) 4 *Politics, Philosophy & Economics*, 131–51

Pickett, K., Wilkinson, R. *The Spirit Level: Why Equality is Better for Everyone* (London: Penguin Books, 2010)

Picketty, T., Goldhammer, A. *Capital in the Twenty-First Century* (Cambridge: Harvard University Press, 2014)

Poole, T. 'Hobbes on Law and Prerogative' in D. Dyzenhaus, T. Poole (eds), *Hobbes and the Law* (Cambridge: Cambridge University Press, 2012), 68–96

Pratt, J. *Governing the Dangerous* (Sydney: The Federation Press, 1997)

Pratt, J. 'Dangerousness and Modern Society' in M. Brown, J. Pratt (eds), *Dangerous Offenders: Punishment and Social Order* (London: Routledge, 2000), 35–48

Pratt, J. *Punishment and Civilization: Penal Tolerance and Intolerance in Modern Society* (London: Sage, 2002)

Pratt, J. 'Norbert Elias, the Civilizing Process, and Punishment' (2016) *Oxford Handbooks Online*, 1–28

Pratt, J., Brown, D., Brown, M., Hallsworth, S. (eds), *The New Punitiveness* (Abingdon: Routledge, 2011)

Ramsay, P. 'The Responsible Subject as Citizen: Criminal Law, Democracy and the Welfare State' (2006) 69(1) *Modern Law Review*, 31

Ramsay, P. 'The Theory of Vulnerable Autonomy and the Legitimacy of Civil Preventative Orders' in B. McSherry, A. Norrie, S. Bronitt (eds), *Regulating Deviance* (Portland: Hart Publishing, 2009), 109–40

Ramsay, P. 'Preparation Offences, Security Interests, Political Freedom' in R.A. Duff, L. Farmer, S.E. Marshall, M. Renzo, V. Tadros (eds), *The Structures of the Criminal Law* (New York: Oxford University Press, 2011), 203–28

Ramsay, P. *The Insecurity State: Vulnerable Autonomy and the Right to Security in the Criminal Law* (Oxford: Oxford University Press, 2012)

Ramsay, P. 'Democratic Limits to Preventive Criminal Law' in A. Ashworth, L. Zedner, P. Tomlin (eds), *Prevention and the Limits of the Criminal Law* (Oxford: Oxford University Press, 2013), 214–34

Reiner, R. 'Citizenship, Crime, Criminalization: Marshalling a Social Democratic Perspective' (2010) 13(2) *New Criminal Law Review*, 241–61

Ripstein, A. 'Justice and Responsibility' (2004) 17 *Canadian Journal of Law & Jurisprudence*, 361–2

Ristroph, A. 'Respect and Resistance in Punishment Theory' (2009) 97 *California Law Review*, 601–32

Ristroph, A. 'Criminal Law for Humans' in D. Dyzenhaus, T. Poole (eds), *Hobbes and the Law* (Cambridge: Cambridge University Press, 2012), 97–117

Ristroph, A. 'Hobbes on "Diffidence" and the Criminal Law' in M.D. Dubber (ed), *Foundational Texts in Modern Criminal Law* (Oxford: Oxford University Press, 2014), 23–38

Rose, N. *Powers of Freedom: Reframing Political Thought* (Cambridge: Cambridge University Press, 1999)

Rossner, M. *Just Emotions: Rituals of Restorative Justice* (Oxford: Oxford University Press, 2013)

Shiner, R. 'Hart and Hobbes' (1980) 22(2) *William and Mary Law Review*, 201–25

Simon, J. *Governing Through Crime: How the War on Crime Transformed American Democracy and Created a Culture of Fear* (New York: Oxford University Press, 2007)

Smith, K.J.M. *Lawyers, Legislators and Theorists: Developments in English Criminal Jurisprudence 1800–1957* (Oxford: Oxford University Press, 1998)

Stewart, H. 'The Limits of the Harm Principle' (2010) 4(1) *Criminal Law and Philosophy*, 17–35

Strauss, L. *What is Political Philosophy?* (Chicago: University of Chicago Press, 1959)

Sullivan, R., Dennis, I. (eds), *Seeking Security* (Oxford: Hart Publishing, 2012)

Tadros, V. *Criminal Responsibility* (Oxford: Oxford University Press, 2005)

Tadros, V. 'Crimes and Security' (2008) 71(6) *Modern Law Review*, 940–70

Taylor, C. *Sources of the Self* (Cambridge: Cambridge University Press, 1992)

Taylor, C. *Modern Social Imaginaries* (Durham: Duke University Press, 2004)

Tierney, B. 'Historical Roots of Modern Rights: Before Locke and After' (2005) 3(1) *Ave Maria Law Review*, 23–43

Tully, J. *An Approach to Political Philosophy: Locke in Contexts* (Cambridge: Cambridge University Press, 1993)

Vaughan, B. 'Punishment and Conditional Citizenship' (2000) 2(1) *Punishment and Society*, 23–39

Wacquant, L. *Punishing the Poor: The Neoliberal Government of Social Insecurity* (London: Duke University Press, 2009)

Wacquant, L. 'Crafting the Neoliberal State: Workfare, Prisonfare, and Social Insecurity' (2010) 25(2) *Sociological Forum*, 197–220

Waldron, J. (ed), *Liberal Rights: Collected Papers 1981–1991* (Cambridge: Cambridge University Press, 1993)

Waldron, J. 'Security and Liberty: The Image of Balance' (2003) 11(2) *Journal of Political Philosophy*, 191–210

Waldron, J. *Torture, Terror and Trade-Offs* (Oxford: Oxford University Press, 2010)

Walker, C. 'Terrorism and Criminal Justice: Past, Present and Future' (2004) *Criminal Law Review*, 311–27

Walker, C. *Blackstone's Guide to Anti-Terrorism Legislation* (Oxford: Oxford University Press, 2009)

Williams, G. 'The Definition of Crime' (1955) *Current Legal Problems*, 107–30

Williams, G. *Criminal Law. The General Part* (London: Stevens and Sons, 1961)

Williams, R.R. *Hegel's Ethics of Recognition* (Berkeley: University of California Press, 1997)

Woodward, K. *Identity and Difference* (Milton Keynes: Open University, 1997)

Wright Mills, C. *The Sociological Imagination* (New York: Oxford University Press, 1959)

Zedner, L. 'Securing Liberty in the Face of Terror: Reflections from Criminal Justice' (2005) 32(4) *Journal of Law and Society*, 507–33

Zedner, L. 'Fixing the Future? The Pre-emptive Turn in Criminal Justice' in B. McSherry, A. Norrie, S. Bronitt (eds), *Regulating Deviance* (Portland: Hart Publishing, 2009), 35–58

Zedner, L. *Security* (Oxon: Routledge, 2009)

Zedner, L. 'Security, the State, and the Citizen: the Changing Architecture of Crime Control' (2010) 13(2) *New Criminal Law Review*, 379–403

Zedner, L. 'Terrorizing Criminal Law' (2014) 8(1) *Criminal Law and Philosophy*, 99–121

Index